The Letters of

SACCO AND VANZETTI

The Letters of
SACCO AND VANZETTI

Edited by

MARION DENMAN FRANKFURTER
AND GARDNER JACKSON

Citadel Press   *Secaucus, N.J.*

"If it had not been for these thing, I might have live out my life talking at street corners to scorning men. I might have die, unmarked, unknown, a failure. Now we are not a failure. This is our career and our triumph. Never in our full life could we hope to do such work for tolerance, for joostice, for man's onderstanding of man as now we do by accident. Our words—our lives—our pains—nothing! The taking of our lives—lives of a good shoemaker and a poor fish-peddler—all! That last moment belongs to us—that agony is our triumph."

FROM A STATEMENT MADE BY VANZETTI
AFTER RECEIVING SENTENCE, APRIL 9, 1927.

PREFACE

THE letters contained in this volume were written by Sacco and Vanzetti during the seven years they spent in prison. At the time of their arrest in 1920, they spoke and understood English with difficulty. Sacco could read but could not write the language, and for some time after his imprisonment showed no interest in learning. It was not until the summer of 1922 that he asked for an English dictionary and wrote his first English letter. The following winter Mrs. Cerise Jack, a member of the New England Civil Liberties Committee, who had attended the trial, began to give Sacco English lessons, which continued for six months or a year. Though he learned to spell and write well enough to make himself understood, his sentence structure remained substantially the same. He used to say that he could never learn English in prison, but if he were free, he would learn in a week.

Vanzetti, on the other hand, applied himself to the study of English as soon as he was confined. He attended evening classes in Charlestown prison, and when he felt that he had learned as much as he could in this way, began to take a correspondence course with Mrs. Virginia MacMechan, who, like Mrs. Jack, had become interested in the two men during the trial. Vanzetti became a prolific correspondent, writing every night in his cell until the lights were extinguished. His prison tasks he completed with all possible speed, so that there might be more time for writing and reading. The lives of the two men in prison were unlike in other ways. Vanzetti, it must be remembered, was convicted of an attempted hold-up before their joint trial on May 31, 1921, and was serving a sentence for that crime. [1] He was therefore employed in the prison industries in Charlestown like any other convicted prisoner. Sacco, throughout the seven years of his confinement, was awaiting the final disposition of his case. He had been convicted but not sentenced, and according to the practise in Massachusetts in such cases, was unemployed during most of those seven years. At one time, a friend arranged to have lessons given him in some form of handicraft, but after quickly mastering the technique, he no longer found the work interesting and flung it aside. He wanted to work in the engine room and the kitchen, where he could learn English from the other prisoners, but this was not allowed.

In the course of seven years, hundreds of letters were written by the men. In addition to those in English, there were many in Italian, addressed to family and friends abroad. The letters in this volume

[1] In this attempted hold-up at Bridgewater the police at first sought to implicate both men, after their joint arrest on May 5, 1920. But Sacco was able to prove an invincible alibi, and the charge was therefore dropped against him. Vanzetti was a fish peddler and hence had only his customers as alibi witnesses. While Sacco was held in Dedham Jail awaiting trial with Vanzetti on the South Braintree murder charge, the Bridgewater charge against Vanzetti was tried at Plymouth, Mass., in June-July, 1920, before Judge Thayer.

are a portion of the English letters only. With one or two exceptions they were written to friends who became so after the arrest and trial of the men, and as a result of the interest evoked by their efforts to free themselves of the charge of murder. The Sacco-Vanzetti Defense Committee, which assisted them in those efforts, collected and assembled the letters, turning them over to the editors to prepare for publication.

Some of the letters received by the Defense Committee were copies of the originals. Undoubtedly errors have thus crept into the text, partly because the handwriting was in some cases illegible. A few of the Vanzetti letters have been published previously and the originals lost, so that only the printed copy was available. But the editors feel sure that such slight changes in the text as have occurred in transcribing leave the authentic character of the letters unimpaired.

The reasons for the omission of material are several. Personal references, allusions to incidents of interest only to the particular correspondent, repetition of matter in other letters, passages whose meaning is entirely obscure, or lengthy recitals of fact relating to political movements in other countries, have all been omitted for the sake of brevity and a greater degree of unity. A minimum number of textual changes has been made, chiefly where comparison with other parts of the text has revealed mistakes in spelling due to carelessness or stress.

Readers of these letters of Sacco and Vanzetti will be struck by the depth of their reliance on the doctrines of anarchy, and the consistency of their belief that what happened to them in those fatal seven years happened because they were anarchists. It explained to them the relentless failure of every effort to secure justice through the courts, and in the extremity of their suffering became their pride and solace. Who can say they were mistaken? Certainly no one who knew the passionate hatred of them and of their views which dominated opinion in Massachusetts during all those years. At the end, as doubt of their guilt grew, the desire to see them dead and forgotten increased in intensity, and it was said openly that "they ought to hang anyway," because they were bad men and dangerous to society.

This, Sacco had always maintained, was the true explanation of their plight. In the record which Mr. William G. Thompson made of his last interview with the men the night they died, occurs this passage:

"It was magnanimous in him [Sacco] not to refer more specifically to our previous differences of opinion, because at the root of it all lay his conviction, often expressed to me, that all efforts on his behalf, either in court or with public authorities, would be useless, because no capitalistic society could afford to accord him justice. I had taken the contrary view; but at this last meeting he did not suggest that the result seemed to justify his view and not mine."

To their friends, the calm with which they accepted the failure of their long struggle for freedom was a manifestation of their innocence and a confirmation of their true character. To the rest of the world, their character can only be revealed by these letters, written for their own and others' comfort during the years of waiting, and by the simple courage with which they met their death.

Sacco, who was executed first, walked firmly into the death chamber and, at a motion from the guard, took his seat in the electric chair. As he did so, he shouted in Italian, "Long live anarchy!" He then paused, growing calmer, and said, in broken English: "Farewell, my wife, and child, and all my friends." Then, glancing around the room which he seemed to see for the first time, he said to the assembled witnesses, "Good-evening, gentlemen." And as the hood was being slipped over his head, he murmured in Italian, "Farewell, Mother."

Vanzetti was brought in a few moments later. He was calm and alert. Advancing steadily into the room, he shook hands with the warden of the prison and three of the guards whom he knew. He sat down in the electric chair and before any move was made to strap him into it, he began, in a low voice, to speak to those present. "I wish to tell you," he said slowly, "that I am an innocent man. I never committed any crime, but sometimes some sin." Turning to the warden he continued: "Thank you for everything you have done for me. I am innocent of all crime—not only this one, but all crime. I am an innocent man." Another pause, and then, with the explicitness which was so characteristic of him, Vanzetti spoke his last words: "I wish to forgive *some* people for what they are now doing to me."

September, 1928

CONTENTS

Part One

NICOLA SACCO

CHAPTER I

NICOLA SACCO was twenty-nine years old when with Vanzetti he was arrested on a street car in Brockton, Massachusetts, on May 5, 1920. Neither he nor Vanzetti had been arrested before. His preceding twelve years in America had been spent mainly as a shoeworker in the manufacturing towns surrounding Boston, where he landed from Italy. His first job was that of water-carrier for a road-construction gang in Milford, Massachusetts. After a period in the foundry room of the machine shops at Hopedale, Massachusetts, he secured employment in a shoe factory at Webster and then in the factory of the Milford Shoe Company at Milford. He worked there steadily from 1909 to 1917, setting aside in the bank regular weekly savings. There he learned the skilled trade of edger.

In 1917 Sacco went to Mexico to avoid the draft. Returning after the war, he was employed at the Three K Shoe Company factory in Stoughton, Massachusetts, by Michael J. Kelley, the owner, at whose school for shoeworkers in Milford he had previously learned his trade in "off" hours. He was working for Mr. Kelley at the time of his arrest and occupied a house on Mr. Kelley's land immediately adjoining the latter's home. In addition to working as an edger, Sacco was employed as watchman of the factory. Mr. Kelley also turned over to Sacco a large section of his property to work as a vegetable and flower garden.

Sacco came to this country from the village of Torremaggiore, province of Foggia, in the extreme south of Italy. His father, Michele, owned substantial olive orchards and vineyards there. Roaming these vineyards and orchards, and sharing their care and supervision, Sacco grew up passionately fond of nature and the out-of-doors. He had no formal schooling, but studied under the devoted eye of Catholic parents and an elder brother who was his constant companion.

He was markedly vigorous and muscular in body and possessed a warm, buoyant personality. To all outward appearances his chief preoccupations were with the things he could see or touch—his tools, the vegetables and flowers which grew in his garden, the trees and the sky.

He was an Italian Republican when he arrived on American shores, but soon changed to socialism and later to anarchism. Pursuing his inquiries and activities as an anarchist, he became a follower of Galleani, an intellectual anarchist, who was living in Massachusetts at the time.

Sacco took part in a number of strikes during this transitional period from republicanism to anarchism. He is described by co-workers in these strikes as having been conscientious to a fault—saying little, but picketing longer hours than anyone else and always willing to run errands or do anything to help the cause.

In 1912 he married a handsome, Titian-haired Italian

woman named Rosa whom he met in Milford. Together they gave plays in the Italian districts to raise funds for strike relief. A son, Dante, was born two years after their marriage, and a daughter, Ines, several months after Sacco's arrest. Sacco was deeply devoted to this family.

The letters written by Sacco from Dedham Jail during the first six years of imprisonment show his struggle to adjust himself to his environment. Denied the usual privilege of physical labor because of a technical rule governing the handling of unsentenced prisoners charged with murder, Sacco discovered that daily exercises in his small cell were a poor substitute.

The rebellion of his body and his spirit found expression in a month's hunger strike in 1923 and in various letters, the one to Fred H. Moore, his first counsel, being a typical example. He abhorred "speculation" on the case and resented the interest of "philanthropist friends." Yet he cherished no grudge against those whom he attacked, no matter how violently. He had satisfied the demands of his integrity. Thereafter he regarded the occurrence simply as a difference of opinion and did not let it interrupt his cheerful conversation on other subjects.

Sacco was not of studious bent. He was not given to reading, nor had he written many letters before his imprisonment. In these prison letters of the first six years is disclosed his effort to overcome this inexperience and to voice the reaction of his vibrantly responsive senses to their environment.

November 30, 1921. *Dedham Jail*

DEAR BARTOLO:[1]

Saturday the 26th my Rosie and the children came to visit me, and this was the first time I seen the children[2] since the time you left Dedham. You can imagine how happy I felt to see them so joyful and so gay and in the best of health, if only you could see little Ines. She got so fat, she is really a dolly, Dante also looks very good. He writes to me every week. Rosa[3] also looks very good after the operation she is gaining daily. I feel very good and I don't do nothing but exercise, read and write. I am very sorry that no one comes and see you, no one comes to see me neither, but Rosie. . . .

[1] Bartolomeo Vanzetti. After their joint arrest, Vanzetti was sent to Plymouth, and Sacco to Dedham Jail. Following his conviction for the Bridgewater hold-up, Vanzetti was committed to Charlestown Prison. Sacco remained at Dedham, save for the time spent in Bridgewater Hospital, until July 1, 1927, when he was removed to Charlestown State Prison. In the spring of 1923, following a 31-day hunger strike, he was taken to the Boston Psychopathic Hospital for observation and thereafter committed to the Bridgewater State Hospital for the Criminal Insane, where he spent several months.

The two men were therefore separated during most of their seven years' imprisonment. They saw each other daily during the trial, May 31 to July 14, 1921, and during the four brief periods when arguments were heard on motions for a new trial. At such times Vanzetti was transferred from Charlestown to Dedham. After sentence was pronounced, April 9, 1927, they were together until the end—in Dedham until July 1, 1927 and in Charlestown thereafter till their execution a few minutes after midnight of August 22, 1927.

[2] Dante, Sacco's son, was seven years old at the time of Sacco's arrest. Ines, his daughter, was born four months thereafter.

[3] He called his wife variously, Rose, Rosina, Rosie, Rosa and Rosetta. This letter was dictated to her.

Do you still exercise? I do every morning. I will close now with best regards.

Your faithful comrade,

NICK SACCO

October 23, 1922. Dedham Jail

MY DEAR MRS. C. CERISE JACK:[1]

After all I have idea to write my salf in Englesh so then I will be sure you will receive my letter, and same time you weell excuse me for my poor Englesh. Before in othor I weell thank you for you modest and noble sentiment you have towards humanity oppressed. So you con imagine ou glad I was to see you, and more because you was look in best health.

Rosy was hea the other dey whit my dear little Ines and I found her moch better from two weeks ago. Rosy from when she went to live in farms shi bin look very fine. So I to feeling weell my self, from the dey I beginning to work; yes because I am joy whin I am work.

P.S. I hope my dey in court bi well and I weell come see you whith my dear Rosy in this beautiful farms.

October, 1923. County Jail, Dedham

DEAR MRS. EVANS:[2]

You never can imagine how much it was great the

---

[1] Mrs. Cerise Jack of Sharon, Mass., who, as a member of the New England Civil Liberties Committee, had attended the trial and visited the men in jail. During the winter of 1923-24 she gave Sacco English lessons.

[2] Mrs. Elizabeth Glendower Evans of Brookline, who became interested in the men during the trial and remained throughout a firm believer in their innocence.

joy of the recluse when I see in that court room all
the noble legion of our friends and comrades, which
they are work hard for forty-one month for the triumph of that consecration and inviolable of the human
justicy and for the liberty of Sacco and Vanzetti.

By the way, my dear mother, you believe we will
have a new trial? I am tol you the truth Mrs. Evans,
I did like very much the way Mr. Thompson and Mr.
Hill [1] they did present the new evidence, and for some
moment they did relief the soul of the sad recluse.
If you happen to see Mr. Thompson and Mr. Hill
give for me my dear and best rigard and for the splen-
dour defence they have made. So I will hope they will
finish this long and dolorus calvary.

Meanwhile salute fraternally all our friends and
comrades, and you dear mother of the human oppressed have one of my warm affectionate embrace
from your now and for ever friend and comrade,
Nicola Sacco.

October 13, 1923. *Dedham Jail*

DEAR MRS. EVANS:

Just a few line to say that afte all your flower I

---

1 Mr. William G. Thompson and Mr. Arthur D. Hill of the
Boston bar became counsel for Sacco and Vanzetti on March 8,
1923, for the limited purpose of arguing motions for a new trial
based upon disclosures which came to light after the verdict,
affecting the misconduct of some of the jurors. Later, when the
case reached the Supreme Court of Massachusetts, Mr. Thompson took charge of the defense and continued in this capacity
until the Governor decided to allow the men to be executed.

Mr. Thompson associated with himself a younger member of
the Boston bar, Mr. Herbert B. Ehrmann. Following Mr.
Thompson's retirement, a series of legal efforts on behalf of
the men was undertaken by Mr. Arthur D. Hill both before the
Massachusetts and the Federal Courts.

been ricieved and with the other several boxs of sea flowers you been sent to me through the last of month, one of the better flower that the perfume will never fail. . . . Monday it was hi my comrade Rosina with my little dear Ines and I did show to her your photograph, and after word she said it is wonderful picture. I wish I could have hi my dear and poor mother photograph where I could put her picture on right sid of yours. Yes, because like you she was good and generous, like you she used to love affectionately all the legion of the human oppressed. Poor mother! All of those noble heart they ought not to die. By thes time I think you no that Monday we must go to the court,[1] so I will hope to see you there. . . .

November 3, 1923. *Dedham Jail*

DEAR MRS. JACK:

Just a fiu line for sey that behind theso dark shadow the beautiful of that light it is begin to come upon, and will be light more light always more brite. Believe me Mrs. Jack that theso today Mr. Tompson was in court he did relief the soul of thes sad reclus. . . .

November 23, 1923. *Dedham Jail*

DEAR MRS. EVANS:

Of course, I will try to read aloud for your sake, and for my own. Of course, I will try to satisfy as best I can that generous mother who for three years has done everything she could for my soul and the

[1] Hearing of arguments for a new trial based on the testimony of gun experts.

soul of my poor family. I begin to read aloud from the day you and Mrs. William James came to see me. I don't read very loud, so as not to disturb anybody. So you see I always try to do the best I could.

Yesterday all the prisoners went out in the yard for two hours because of Thanksgiving Day, and when I come in I feel a little hunger, but when I don't have much air I don't feel hunger at all. So I need air,— air, just as much air as I can have.

I always remember when my brother Sabino and me were on ship board on the way to this free country,[1] the country that was always in my dreams. I was very sick of the seas and one morning my brother conducted me to the Doct and he order for me a good purge and for my brother that felt fine he ordered a good soup. . . .

So that is just the same here. The prisoner who don't like to work, they send him to work, and who really feels like work and need to have air, air, just as much air as he can, they keep him in a cell all day long.

November 24, 1923. *Dedham Jail*

MY DEAR MRS. JACK:

A few line Mrs. Jack to say that does not make any difference if wi dont have any more the opportunity to see out every morning and to could show one to the other that sincere affection and that smile blessed;

[1] Sacco landed with his brother in Boston from Italy in April, 1908. He was seventeen the twenty-second of that month.

but in my mind, in my heart, in my faith they are always the noble ligion of friens and comrades.

Monday I did wrote a letter to our dear Mrs. Evans, and in that letter I was say to Mrs. Evans, that was really a crime and injustice and inhuman to keep in back these terrible bar a hondred and hondred victims among the young people—guilty just because they been oppressed and love the liberty of the human oppressed. It is shame for the humanity and for the good citizen of thes country who are believe in good faith the freedom of thes country. I know it is not for me to say that, but believe me Mrs. Jack that sometime you connot help to put in the truth. . . .

P.S. Give my dear regard to Mrs. M—— and tell her that if my face shows some smile yet after all . . . it is my nature, because I remember my dear and poor mother when she use say that not matter if you work hard the smile shining always on your face.

December 6, 1923. Dedham Jail

MY DEAR MRS. JACK:

I can not the scritto in my poor English the joyful that is manifest in a soul of the reclus when he receivid a visit from e friend who he believe in her or in him to find the sincere brotherly affection. To say Mrs. Jack that I was very how glad to see you last night.

Dante, Mrs. Jack, hi is always in my heart and hi always my dear and lovely boy; many a time I did believe that hi will ben promising boy yes because hi alwas was my dear comradship and I could read in is brite eyes and tru of his little intelligent head the better day. I remember when wi youst live in South Stoughton Mass in our little sweet home and frequently in evening Rosina, Dante and I, we youst go see a frend about a fifteen minute wolk from my house and bey away going to the my friend house hi always surpriset me bey aske me a such heard question that some time it was impesseble for me to explain. So wi youst remain there a few hour and when was about nine ten oclock we youst going back home and Dante in that time of hour hi was always sleeping, so I youst bring him always in my arm away to home; some time Rosina she youst halp me to carry him and in that same time she youst get Dante in her arm both us we youst give him a warm kisses on is rosy face. Those day Mrs. Jack they was a some happy day. . . .

December 14, 1923. *Dedham Jail*

My dear Mrs. Jack:

In the book I have read with you at Tuesday night if you remember when I have read the word *gorgette*, you asked me if I know what gorgette was, and I said, yes Mrs. Jack I know what gorgette is, because I used to buy for wife; and I after say that is not the only gorgette waist I used buy for my comradeship, but almost everything; and another word she wont not go buy anything with out me. I remember Mrs. Jack a years go on our love day when I bouth the first an lovely blu suit for my dear Rosina and the dear remembrance is still rimane in my heart.

That was the first May nineteen twelve in Milford Mass.[1] the celebration day of the five martyrs of Chicago, that in the mind of humanity oppressed it never will be forgot. So in morning May first nineteen twelve I dress up with my new blu suit on and I went over to see my dear Rosina and when I was there I asked her farther if he wont let Rosina came with me in city town to buy something and he said yes. So in after, about one o'clock we both us went in city town, and we went in a big stor and we bouth a broun hat a white underdress a blu suit one pair broun stocking one pair broun shoes and after she was all dress up Mrs. Jack I wish you could see Rosina how nise she was look, while now the sufferance of today had make her look like a old woman.

But Mrs. Jack I never was ambitious to buy her a diomonds and so-so but I always bouth everything could be natural and useful. . . .

February 12, 1924. Dedham Jail

MY DEAR FRIEND MRS. JACK:

. . . . I was so glad to hear from you that after our lesson you went back home happy and cheerful, and so I Mrs. Jack! And I think that you should not bother yourself to buy a dram play because it will be really a drama play right here every once a week! So lat me say right now that every time you are out here I feel that same feeling like when I am near to

[1] Sacco was at this time working in the factory of the Milford Shoe Company. He worked there from 1909 to 1917.

my dear family, and I could hear the sound of your voice full of sincere gratitude that I have heard many time from the lips of my little Rosina and from the goot friends who have loved in good faith the cause of the humanity oppressed.

To day it is Abraham Lincoln birthday and I think that the citizens of this country they should be proud of thier own President, and in my little force of intellectual I always thought that Abraham Lincoln was one of the most respectable and humanity President that ever thought. Of course I have not read much history of this country but I have read little of George Washington and Jefferson and all thi history of Abraham Lincoln. The history of those three great President strike the feeling of the humble reclus. . . .

February 26, 1924. *Dedham Jail*

MY DEAR FRIEND MRS. JACK:

. . . . Every night when the light goes out I take a long walk and really I do not know how long I walk, because the most of the time I forget myself to go to sleep, and so I continue to walk and I count, one, two, three, four steps and turn backward and continue to count, one, two, three four and so on. But between all this time my mind it is always so full of ideas that one gos and one comes. . . . I find one of my mostly beautiful remembrance while I am thinking and walking, frequently I stop to my window cell and through those sad bars I stop and look at the nature into crepuscular of night, and the stars in the beauti blue sky. So last night the stars they was moor bright and the sky it was moor blue than I did ever seen; while I was looking it appear in my mind the idea to think of something of my youth and write the idea to my good friend Mrs. Jack first thing in morning. So here where I am right with you, and always I will try to be, yes, because I am study to understand your beautiful language and I know I will love it. And I will hope that one day I could surprise the feel of my gratitude towards all this fierce legion of friends and comrades.

The flowers you send to me last week it renew in my mind the remembrance of my youth. It complete sixteen years ago this past autumn that I left my father vineyards. Every year in autumn right after the collection I usd take care my father vineyard and sometime I usd keep watch, because near our vineyard they was a few big farmer and surronder our vineyard they was vast extension of prairie and hundreds animal they used pasturage day and night on those vast prairie. So the most of night I remane there to sleep to watch the animal to not let coming near our vineyard. The little town of Torremaggiore it is not very far from our vineyard, only twenty minete of walk and I used go back and forth in morning an night and I usd bring to my dear an poor mother two big basket full of vegetables and fruits and big bounch flowers. The place where I used to sleep it was a big large hayrick that my good father and my brothers and I build. The hayrick it was set in one corner near the well in the middle of our vineyard, and surronde this sweet hayrick they was many plants and flowers except the red rose, because they was pretty hard to find the good red rose and I did love them so much that I was always hunting for find one plant of those good—red rose!

About sixty step from our vineyard we have a large piece of land full of any quantity of vegetables that my brothers and I we used cultivate them. So every morning before the sun shining used comes up and at night after the sun goes out I used put one quart of water on every plant of flowers and vegetables and the smal fruit trees. While I was finishing my work the sun shining was just coming up and I used always jump upon well wall and look at the beauty sun shining and I do not know how long I usd remane there look at that enchanted scene of beautiful. If I was a poet probably I could discribe the red rays of the loving sun shining and the bright blue sky and the perfume of my garden and flowers, the smell of the violet that was comes from the vast verdant prairie, and the singing of the birds, that was almost the joy of deliriany. So after all this enjoyment I used come back to my work singing one of my favourite song an on way singing I used full the bascket of fruit and vegetables and bunch of flowers that I used make a lovely bouquet. And in the middle the longuest flowers I used always put one of lovely red rose and I used walk one mile a way from our place to get one of them good red rose that I always hunting and love to find, the good red rose. . . .

P.S. How you find the day of our dear Mrs. Evans

birthday? I have here very beauti bag to suprise her. If you hap to see her give my warm regard.

April 9, 1924. *Dedham Jail*

MY DEAR FRIEND MRS. JACK:

Yesterday I said to you that when a man remains all day long back of these sad bars you feel your mind sometime very tired and exhausted of ideas, but when we see a friend and especially a friend that we feel to be bound together in one faith and in one fraternal affection many ideas coming back again. It is sweet to see a friend after a little period of time. I remember another day that I had past like yesterday it was right after when I came back from Mexico sometime into the middle of September nineteen seventeen, and at that time I was unoccupied.

So in one lovely morning of September when the rays of sunshine are still warm in the soul of oppressed humanity, I was looking for a job around the city of Boston and away I was going towards South Boston, I met one of my most dear comrades, and just as soon as we saw each other we ran one into the embrace of the other and we kissed each other on both sides of the cheeks. And yet it was not a very long time since we had seen each other, because a few weeks before we were in Mexico together; but this spontaneous affection it shows at all times in the heart of one who has reciprocal love and sublime faith and such a remembrance it will never disappear in the heart of the proletarian.

So your surprise visit Mrs. Jack it was a great relieve for the reclus, and I was enjoy to see you back
again in good health and always in that good old
spirit. . . .

March 15, 1924. *Dedham Jail*

MY DEAR FRIEND MRS. JACK:

It has been past a few day now that I had in my
mind to write you a letter and I always try to find
some good idea, but it was hard because the sky it
has been covered for several day now with full of
cloud; and you know that my most beauty idea I find
by looking at the clear and blue sky. . . .

So Wednesday night I went to sleep with idea to
write you at first thing in morning but when I was into
bed I begen to turn this way an the other way and I
was try my best to sleep. So after while I fall sleep,
enddid I do not know how long I been sleep when I was
up again with a terrible dream . . . terrible I said yes,
but beauty at same time, and here way it is. The
dream it was develope in one place in mine camp of
Pennsylvania state, and here it was a big large number
of laborers in strike for better wages and the masses
of workers they was impatient tired of long waiting,
because the bos who own the col mine there threw out
of the house a big number people, of poor mother
and child and for the moment they were living under
the tent in one concentration camp. But here the poor
mother they was not pacific yet, because they know
that they would soon send the soldiers to chase the
mother out of the camp.

And so the big masse of the workers they was in complete revolt from the cruelty the bos of the mine. In this camp they were two or three speakers and every one of them they was used a kind and warm word for the freedom of the peeple. While the immensity of the work masses they were applauding the speakers, the soldiers comes with bayonet gun for chase the crowd, but after word they find out they was wrong because every one of the strikers they stand still like one man. And so the fight it was beginning, and while the fight was begin I jump upon a little hill in meddle of the crowd and I begin to say, Friend and comrade and brotherhood, not one of us is going to move a step, and who will try to move it will be vile and coward, here the fight is to go to finish. So I turn over towards the soldiers and I said, Brothers you will not fire on your own brothers just because they tell you to fire, no brothers, remember that everyone of us we have mother and child, and you know that we fight for freedom which is your freedom. We want one fatherland, one sole, one house, and better bread. So while I was finish to say that last word one of the soldiers fire towards me and the ball past through my heart, and while I was fall on ground with my right hand close to my heart I awake up with sweet dream! So when I was awake I had my right hand still tightly upon my heart like if it was hold back the speed of the beating of my heart. I turn over towards my window cell and through the shade of night I was looking at sky, and while look the stars it bright my face and the shadow soon disapear. Soon the idea it comes in my mind to write my dream to my dear teacher and for moment I thought that Fairhope, Alabama was to far away but the spirit, the voice the lesson of my dear and good friend and teacher Mrs. Jack it is remained in my heart and blessed my soul. . . .

May 21, 1924. *Dedham Jail*

MY DEAR FRIEND, MRS. JACK:

. . . . I want that you would believe me in good faith that if I didnt write a letter to you in those few weeks it is not mean that I do not study my English lesson, no, no, nothing like that, because you know that I do like to learn this beautiful English language, and I do love to know it so some day I will be able to express my gratitude to all my friends and comrades. So you can be sure about that because even when I am feel depressing I use always try to find a few hours to study my English lesson. . . .

I was very sorry when I here from you that you was very sick, and I had in my mind to write you a letter right way but I was so *sad* that day that I could not write you any more. So today I thought to not wait any more long and sent you my most love and warm regard with hope you are feeling well.

In your last letter you asked me to tell you about the books that I am reading now. . . . I have read Gandhi Mahatma and Eugene V. Debs, and in both books I enjoyed the read, and I am glad to have read the history of life of those two human and great men in the history of the world. I am enjoy also reading the book that you brought to me several weeks ago *Why Men Fight*, by B. Russell. It is a very good book and I find it little hard for me, but I will read it over again. . . .

August 18, 1924. *Dedham Jail*

FRED H. MOORE: [1]

SIR:—Saturday I received your letter with enclose the post card that Mrs. M—— R—— sent to me— and the little pamphlet that you use to send to me it just to insult my soul. Yes, it is true, because you would not forget when you came here two or three times between last month with a groups people—that you know that I did not like to see them any more; but you brought them just seem to make my soul keep just sad as it could be. And I can see how clever and cynic you are, because after all my protest, after I have been chase you and all your philanthropists friends, you are still continue the infamous speculation on the shoulder of Sacco-Vanzetti case. So this morning before these things going any more long, I thought to send you these few lines to advise you and all your philanthropist friends of the "New Trail League Committee" [2] to not print any more these lettters with my picture and name on, and to be sure to take my name out if they should print any more of these little pam-

---

[1] Counsel for Sacco and Vanzetti at the Dedham trial.

[2] A group formed after the original Sacco-Vanzetti Defense Committee had disagreed with Mr. Moore so that they could no longer work together. The new group disbanded a few months after forming, and several of its members joined the Defense Committee.

phlets, because you and your philanthropists has been
use it from last three years like a instrument of infamous speculation.   It is something to carry any man
insane or tuberculosis when I think that after all my
protest to have my case finish you and all your legione
of friends still play the infame game.   But, I would
like to know if yours all are the boss of my life!   I
would like to know who his this men that ar abuse to
take all the authority to do everything that he does
feel like without my responsibility, and carry my case
always more long, against all my wish.   I would like
to know who his this—generous—ma!!!   Mr.—
Moore—!   I am telling you that you goin to stop this
dirty game!   You hear me?   I mean every them word
I said here, because I do not want have anything to do
any more with "New Trail League Committee," because it does repugnant my coscience.

Many time you have been deluder and abuse on
weakness of my comrades good faith, but I want you
to stop now and if you please get out of my case, because you know that you are the obstacle of the case;
and say! I been told you that from last May 25th—
that was the last time you came to see me, and with
you came the comrade Felicani and the Profess Guadagni.[1]   Do you remember?   Well, from that day I
told you to get out of my case, and you promised me
that you was goin to get out, but my—dear—Mr.
Moore!   I see that you are still here in my case, and

---

[3] Aldino Felicani, a printer and friend of both men, who founded
the Defense Committee; Felice Guadagni, a radical professor,
one of his early helpers.

you are still continued to play your famous gam. Of
course it is pretty hard to refuse a such sweet pay that
has been come to you right long—in—this big—game.
It is no true what I said? If it is not the truth, why
did you not finish my case then? Another word, if
this was not the truth you would quit this job for long
time. It has been past one year last June when you and
Mr. Grella from New York came to see me into
Bridgewater Hospital [1] and that day between you and
I we had another fight—and you will remember when
I told this Mr. Moore! I want you to finish my case
and I do not want to have anything to do with this
politics in my case because it does repugnant my coscience—and your answer to me was this: Nick, if
you don't want, Vanzetti does want! Do you remember when you said that? Well, do you think I believe
you when you said that to me? No, because I know
that you are the one that brings always in these mud
in Sacco-Vanzetti case. Otherwise, how I could believe you when you been deluder me many times with
your false promise? Well—! anyhow, wherever you
do if you do not intent to get out of my case, remember
this, that per September I want my case finish. But
remember that we are right near September now and
I don't see anything and any move yet. So tell me
please, why you waiting now for? Do you wait till I

[1] Sacco was committed for observation to the Boston Psychopathic Hospital on March 17, 1923, at the end of a 31-day
hunger strike. On April 20, an order was issued for his com-
mitment to the Bridgewater State Hospital for the Criminal Insane. He remained in Bridgewater till early fall and was then
returned to the Dedham Jail.

hang myself? That's what you wish? Let me tell you right now don't be illuse yourself because I would not be surprise if somebody will find you some morning hang on lamp-post.

Your implacable enemy, now and forever,

NICK SACCO

P.S. Enclose in this letter you find the letter and the pamphlet that you sent to me and I return to you, so if your philanthropist friends of the "New Trail League Committee" should print some more these or any kind these letters and pamphlets, you can show them just the way to print next time. So you be advised now, that if any other my post card or letter should come to you address, please sent to me just my own, and not . . . these.

December 28, 1924. *Dedham Jail*

MY DEAR BARTOLO:

This morning only I have received your dear kind letter that you sent to me in Nov. 26, and you can imagine how glad I was to get it. Yes, it is great for me to get once in a while one of your letter, because they are always full of thought and faithful. Well, I have here a mount of things to tell you but however that would be too long, and so I will only say that I hope that we will see each other soon.

You are quite right when you say—that after all we are still on our feet—of course, because we are always keep in our soul the hope and faithful in our innocent; and I am sure that we will keep this hope and faithful till the bright day of our triumph.

Yes Bartolo, it is very croock means, but the comrades and the proletariat of the world they are always with us, indeed much more today than ever was. Therefore, you will let me say to you courage my dear friend, because this fight we are going to win, because I am faithful to this new legion of our dear comrades.

I will close now to say that I was glad to hear from you that you are feeling good and so am I. Meanwhile have my warm embrace with my most brotherly affection.

Your faithful comrade now and forever,

FERDINANDO [1] SACCO

May 23, 1925. Dedham Jail

MY DEAR BARTOLOMEO:

The day before yesterday our dear comrade Fabbri [2] were out here to see me, and he give to me your letter of April 24th. I was so glad to get your welcome letter, and I was glad also to hear that you are feeling well.

In your letter you say that meanwhile you thought to write me,—well, my dear comrade, it was very kind idea when you thought of it, and you can so well

---

[1] A family name often used by Sacco instead of Nicola or Nick. He was christened "Ferdinando," but adopted his elder brother's name, Nicola, when that brother died.

[2] Amleto Fabbri, Italian shoe-worker, secretary of the Defense Committee from 1924 to 1926.

imagine how joyful I felt when I received it. And if you please let me explain to you that, I also did myself wrote you a letter, right after they did brought you back to Charlestown prison. And so, I thought to do better by give it to my dear wife, because I was pretty sure that she would come down to see you soon, because I know that many times she did express to me the wish to see you. So, you see that it is not my fault if you didn't get my letter before. I said before, yes, because Fabbri told me that Rosina was out here to see you with my little beauty Ines, and certainly she brought to you my letter.

Yes Bartolomeo, I will send your regards in everyone of my letters, that I do send to the friends and comrades. I do forget sometimes, but I always did send your regards. Meantime I will hope that you are in the best of health with surely to hear from you soon.

With all my warm and brotherly embrace,
Your faithful comrade,
FERDINANDO

June 6, 1925. Dedham Jail

DEAR MRS. SHURTLEFF:[1]

June the 4th, our dear friend Mrs. Evans was out here to see me, and she brought me the little small elegant sweater which you send it for my little dear Ines, and I thank you ever so much for it and for the

[1] Mrs. Arthur A. Shurtleff of Boston.

kind and excellent thought that you had towards my little beauty Ines.

I was so glad to get it because I know that it will prepare a great suprise to my little Ines. She is so dear to me that I cannot express myself how I do love her. Everytime that she does come see me, she always hug me, kiss me and kept on asking me if I have something for her, because she know that I do always prepare for her some little thing which my friends they bring to me. One of this most active friend which does always bring to me little of something or other for my little Ines, it is our dear friend Mrs. Jack. But, it is for few times now that she didn't feel cheerfuly that she used to, of course, poor little dear!—she didn't feel good, specially last time that she was out here to see me with her dear mother, she felt so badly that her mother she had to bring her at home right way. And the mother! she was also look so depressed that I don't remember to have see her so badly. . . . Poor little dear mother! If they do not finish this iniquitous case sooner, I am afraid, that they will kill her before long. It is . . . to much sufferince all together insed and outsede the prison. . . .

June 18, 1925. *Dedham Jail*

My dear Comrade Vanzetti:

This morning right after I was waken my first thought it was to write you these few lines, and send you my most kind and warm wish for your birthday, with hope that it will be the last of yours and mine birthdays that we spend in this terrible and iniquitous bastile, of the land of the free . . . country!

The last time that my comrade Rosina was out here to see me, she told me that she was out here to see you with my little Ines, and you can so well imagine how glad I was when I heard it. Afterwards I asked her why she didn't bring Dante too, and she said that he had to go to school, but she will bring him to see you just as soon she will have the chance. And therefore, I suppose that they will be over to see you pretty soon because June 21 Dante will have the school vacation, and I know just how much anxious my boy is to coming over to see you yes, because he told me so. . . .

Well, my dear comrade, it seems to me that this old degenerate world has not shown any better day for us yet, but we will always hope that someday the sunshine will bright our souls again. Meanwhile, I will close to say, that in spite of all I do feel pretty good, and I hope to hear from you the same. . . .

August 2, 1925. *Dedham Jail*

DEAR MRS. EVANS:

I have received your welcome card the other day, and I was glad to hear from you that you are feeling good and enjoy the vacation.

In your card you ask me to know how goes the life with me. Well, my dear Mrs. Evans, I think I did told you once that since I was a little boy and in all my life of adolescent, it was pretty hard work for my family to know from me something about the pain of my ill, but only my poor old dear mother she used succeed to know from me once in a while, the pain that I was suffering when I used be sik. And that is why I am telling you sincere from the deep of my heart, because since the day that I have meet you, you been occupied in my heart my mother her place, and so I been respect you and I been loved you, that this terrible life it is insupportable, and I feel so nervous and tired of this miserably life that I hate to see my own shade. . . . And therefore, you can so well realise how hard it is after I been shut up for five long dolorous years in this terrible hole, away from the warming kisses of my dear companion and children, and from all what's nice and beauty, and from the joy of the liberty.

I understood from your card that you will be out here to see me sometime this month, and without doubt you will be always the dear welcome for me. . . .

August 18, 1925. *Dedham Jail*

MY DEAR COMRADE BARTOLO:

I have your both welcome letters—one of May 30th and the other of June 21st, which our dear comrade Fabbri brought to me Thursday night of August 13th, and you can so well imagine how glad I felt to get them. It is so pleasure to hear your voice once in a while for the reciprocal fraternal warm words that they use bring to us. Yes, Vanzetti, Ines she is a dear little child and I knew that you have enjoyed very much seeing her, and really I felt very sorry when I heard from my dear companionship that she brought with her to see you only Ines. I knew that Dante will bring you a great surprise; he is quite a boy now, almost big as his mother, and he seemed to me that he does love his mother very much and certain it does bring a relief to me. I love him so much and without doubt I do love also my little dear Ines, and I wish you could see us out here when they came to see me how happy and joyful we feel nearest one another. Yes, I am happy of them, and I love them so much that I couldn't describe you how much I do love them. Hence, I will write my companionship right away and I will tell her that you like to see Dante, and I will tell her also to not forget to bring him over to see you before they will open the school. . . .

Thank you comrade, ever so much for the congratulation that you have sent to me for my progress English language. Yes, Bartolo, I do study all the time with very care to get near always nearest to definite and perfection this beautiful English language, but woe is me! it is very hard for me to reach into definitely perfection and final pronounciation of Shakespeare language.

It is very true indeed, what you saying—that we can never be good and well again for the future—as we want to be. No, I guess not: we can never get back that old young energy again, because of these dolorous long years confinement waiting for the new trial today and tomorrow. . . .

September 13, 1925. *Dedham Jail*

DEAR COMRADE DONOVAN: [1]

Your welcome visit with our dear Comrade Fabbri was a very surprised visit for me, while I was thinking that you were in the great city of London at the time. . . .

We had discussed a whole lot of things, but one thing which I was very anxious to tell you I did forget. And so this morning I thought to write to you about what I promised to tell you. If I am not mistaken, one week or so after you went to Europe, my dearest family came to see me, and just as soon as they came, I gave to my dear little Ines the beautiful dolly that you sent to me by our dear Comrade Fabbri, and I wish you could have been here to see how happy and joyful my little Ines was. She jumped on my neck, hugged me and kissed me, and smiled at me with that smile of joy. Oh, she is a bright little dear child, and I do love her so much, that I could not describe to you how much I do love her. . . .

September 16, 1925. *Dedham Jail*

DEAR MRS. EVANS:

I just finished to write my dearest companionship a letter and I felt that I could not go without write you an letter; no, I couldnt, you are the next to my companionship. Yes, because you being occupied in my

---

[1] Mary Donovan, who became recording secretary of the Defense Committee in 1924.

heart the place of my good and poor old dear mother that I have been love her so much.

Your surprised visit certainly it were dear and welcome to me because . . . your motion, your act, the way you describe your young thought, your ineffable smile that I have read in your noble soul in all this time of these dolorous long years of my struggle fight, it is more sincere and dear to me than that I have seeing on your face. And that is exactly why I have being told my dear Rosetta and also my dear comrade Fabbri, that you wish with us to see to finish these sad and long angry way. . . .

P.S. Thank you mother, for the nice things you have brought to me.

September 25, 1925. *Dedham Jail*

DEAR MRS. EVANS:

I know it is very hard to make understanding on a dumbling like me and I can't help it, but I understood very plainly that you wish just as much as we wish to finish this struggle fight; and that is all the end.

About the old time then, I should say that the old law they was much less cruil when they used hang a man after few weeks, and not the civilisation . . . law of today, that they do kill a man too hundred thousand time before they hang. . . .

June 18, 1926. *Dedham Jail*

DEAR MRS. EVANS:

It was an earely bright morning when the harmony
of the nature were resting upon the soil of the mother
nature, while I were looking through the iron bars and
contemplate the little sweet space of the nature, a
noble old image in mine eyes appear—while she were
coming toward me, a little gay breezes blow from the
azure river seaside moving her lovely gray hair. Then,
sudden after I wake from this bliss sweet vision I could
see that were none other than the idea that I had since
several day before . . . to write you to-day. . . .
Therefore, this morning—in spite of all, I could not
go any longer without write you these few lines, I
stood so long without write you a single word, but
after your last welcome visit you give to me I could
never rest without sent you—that through all the struggle long year have been kind to me as an dear mother
can be—my warm heart greeting.

Yes, your last grateful visit were a good relief for
me because, after you had read to me your truly and
good faithful article that you wrote for our freedom,
I felt such commotion that remind me of the same
commotion that I felt in my sweet youth in the embrace
of my poor dear good mother, for I have find in you
that same sincere and faithful that my dear mother she
always had toward me. Therefore, let me tell you
right now that if the puritan of Massachusetts they

have lost all the sense of the human feeling, your image should live forever as example of noble tradition of English woman, while surely if you should die you will leave the proselytes among your friends that I know and unknowing that I love. . . .

October 19, 1926. *Dedham Jail*

DEAR MRS. EVANS:

I have just finished to read a comment article about your dear friend LaFollette into *The Christian Science Monitor* of Oct. 16th. Therefore, I thought to cut it and sent it to you at once because I know that it will please your noble heart a great deal. It seems that the hope and the fate is with Bob LaFollette for the next re-election of 1926.

Here mother, the days are increasing always more rigid and sad and I do feel always more thoroughly loneliness away from those image whom are dearest to me. Have you know any news yet? Oh, how impatient I am to hear this answer. . . .

October 24, 1926. *Dedham Jail*

DEAR ABBOTT: [1]

I have your welcome letter of Oct. 20th, and I was going to answer you right away, if it weren't that I had some other hurry duty that was calling me. But this morning, my first idea went toward you, and so I thought to send you these few lines to tell you that you didn't trouble me at all, but that I was pleased to send you the book.

[1] Leonard Abbott of New York, an anarchist friend.

Yes, the great noble soul of Eugene Debs has gone forever! And with him disappears one of the most model and sincere faithfulness to the class workers of the American socialist movement, but the example of his noble faith has remained with us to continue the struggle fight into the bright road for the conquest, the joy of liberty and the happiness of all. I do not remember to have met Debs personally in the past years, and I am very sorry to not to have seen him the last time he was out here, but I think I have heard him speak and I have read lots about him and loved him. . . .

November 12, 1926. *Dedham Jail*

DEAR FRIEND MRS. JACK:

I have not forgot you and not your dear household no, I haven't, and I want you to know that on the contrary often I were thinking of you, even in the sad days your image appear to my vision always with more vividly remembrance. . . . I could see your dear household, the green grass, the beautiful flowers and the lovely fruit trees that only Mr. Jack can take care.

For also, you will excuse my poor Shakespear English: poor, yes, because I have not get yet all the song and the harmony of this beautiful language, as I have promise you that some day I would have surprise you with one of my good English letter. But, I want you to believe me sincerely, my dear teacher, that if it didnt succeed at my promise it is not my fault. No, it isn't, because I have tryed with all my passion for the success of this beautiful language, not only for the sake

of my family and for the promise I have made to you
—but for my own individual satisfaction, to know and
to be able to read and write correct English.   But woe
is me! It wasn't so; no, because the sadness of these
close and cold walls, the idea to be away from my
dear family, for all the beauty and the joy of liberty—
had more than once exhaust my passion.

And then, you be surprise that after all these cruel
and long sagragation years, they still have courage to
bring me an English teacher—while they keeping my
family away from me that I long so much to see them
at least once a week.   It is a real shame.   Poor humanity! . . .

November 21, 1926. *Dedham Jail*

DEAR MRS. HENDERSON: [1]

I have received a letter from Mrs. Evans the other
day, and I leave it to you to imagine how badly stroke
me the sad announcing of the death of your poor husband.   Here the life in this terrible hole cell, is so
thoroughly loneliness that I couldn't describe you how
sad it is, but through all my struggle life, since my
young adolescent till today, through all these long
segregation years away from all the beauty and joy
of liberty, away from all the heart caress and affectionate care of my dearest family, and from the smile
sincere gaze of the friends and comrades that I love
and loved, here—in the heart of this humble reclus

---

[1] Mrs. Jessica Henderson of Wayland, Mass., a constant observer
at the trial of Sacco and Vanzetti, who was early convinced of
their innocence.

were always a place to embrace the pain of the other sufferant. Yes, and especialy the mother pain because I do sincerely believe that they are more sensitive and the ones who swallow the bitterness and the sufferance of all the family . . . Therefore, please Mrs. Henderson, let me join together with my family for the loss of your companionship and the father of your dear children, with hope that it would bring you relief as much relief your letters have brought to me. Therefore, comfort yourself between your lovely daughters that you love and love you so dearly, and don't you forget that late and first one after another we all have to pass to the eternity world; and for the unfortunate creature that they have been condemn to suffering all their life long, more than once the death has appear more sweet than the life itself. . . .

November 28, 1926. *Dedham Jail*

DEAR FRIEND MRS. JACK:

Those beautiful clove flowers surprised me so deeply in my unrest heart that I could not describe you how deeply touch I felt. Really, I do not remember to have seen so big size and beautiful clove flowers like those in my life. I do remember very well that my father had several plant of cloveflower—but not so large size as those you sent me no, not so large, but they perfume immensely, and if you could see the peasant when they come back home from the work at the night, you would be surprise to see everyone of them picking every kind of flower here and there along the road side.

Then Monday, when Miss Betty [1] brought me the cloveflower and the bag of lovely and delicious apples with enclosed letter, I were reading *The Maritime History of Massachusetts* by S. E. Morison that Mrs. Evans brought me a few weeks ago, and I were immersed profondly in it with idea to get all the description of this particular history, because very often happen during the day that I have to re-read over and over again the same pages with a poor result.

It is true that all the best philosophers, the poets and the biologists—when they have the idea to write a good masterpiece of work, they untiring seek the solitude; yes, but not here close behind these sad bars, into an cold unjust walk where is not life and not hope; where all the making energy and the study passion are exhaust.   No, not here, indeed!   But there between all the harmonies of the mother nature, under the radiant rays of sun where everything grows so vividly in the human mind and in the heart, love, life and all the vegatation beautifully.   Oh life! . . .

December 27, 1926. *Dedham Jail*

DEAR FRIEND MRS. JACK:

After the good and unexpected visit that Miss Betty paid me, I thought to sent you those few lines to tell you that Miss Betty she does look perfectly fine; and full of an bright health that I have remember seeing

[1] Elizabeth Jack, daughter of Mrs. Jack.

in her. Moreover, in her lovely big eyes are always full of thoughts and dreams, but her dreams are still resting in her sweet and gay adolescent.

The lovely apples, the candy, the nice sort primture for my dearest darling Inez and the beautifully pink flowers that Miss Betty brought me for the Christmas gift did please very much my sad soul. That brought me new ideas toward always the beauty and oppressed humanity!

P.S. I hope from the bottom of my heart that the new year would bring us a pardon and in the embrace of mine and in the great human family.

CHAPTER II

THE last eight months of Sacco's imprisonment disclosed his convictions more firmly rooted than ever. The second refusal of the Supreme Court of Massachusetts, early in this period, to reverse Judge Webster Thayer's denial of the motions for a new trial left Sacco outwardly unmoved. Saying that he expected nothing else, he requested counsel to take no further steps in his behalf.

At the sentencing in the Dedham Court House on April 9, 1927, he utilized the permission of public utterance granted men by the state immediately before they are sentenced to death. He addressed the Court briefly, reiterating his innocence and his insistence that Judge Thayer knew before the Dedham trial began that both he and Vanzetti were innocent. As he had done seven years before when the jury brought in a verdict of guilty, he jumped up in the cage when pronouncement of sentence was finished and, before the guards could check him, shouted a repetition of his charge against the Court.

Thereafter he cheerfully but steadily refused to have any further dealings with the authorities on his case, either by signature or by word of mouth. Aided by Vanzetti, by Sacco's wife, and by all of Sacco's close friends, Mr. William G. Thompson and Mr. Herbert B. Ehrmann did their utmost as counsel for

40

him and Vanzetti to induce him to sign the petition to Governor Fuller based on the affidavits of prejudice against Judge Thayer.

With no hesitation, he resisted this attack of persuasiveness and argument marshalled in a final effort to save his life. He declared it futile and a denial of his principles to make any more representations to the authorities. He was smilingly passive in his willingness to have the petition presented with Vanzetti's signature alone.

The period between the sentencing and the removal of Sacco and Vanzetti from Dedham Jail to Charlestown State Prison on July 1, 1927, seemed to be the happiest for Sacco of all the seven years. It was the first opportunity since their arrest that he and Vanzetti had had to be together for so many weeks. Being sentenced to death, they were allowed certain privileges, including an hour or so daily in the courtyard of the jail. There they played *Bocce*, an Italian bowling game, with a set brought to Sacco by a friend. Judging by his conversation, these games and the discussions with Vanzetti were a source of deep pleasure to him.

The unexpected midnight transfer of the men to the Cherry Hill section of the State Prison—the antechamber of the death house where condemned men are placed several weeks before execution—abruptly interrupted this calm. The new surroundings (far less pleasant than Dedham Jail), the imminence of the execution, and the disquieting news, conveyed to him by his wife, of the attitude of the Governor and the Lowell committee which she felt was implied in their treatment of her and other defense witnessess, aroused violent rebellion in Sacco again. He began his second hunger strike. At the end of seventeen days he desisted because officials of the State Prison were about to feed him forcibly.

Shortly before issuing his decision on August 3, 1927, the Governor tried to interview Sacco. Sacco shook hands with him but refused to discuss the case. He was quite willing to talk about anything else. It was the same with the Lowell committee.

In the final legal moves, after the Governor's decision, counsel sought Sacco's signature for an application for a writ of *habeas corpus*. Sacco refused to sign, maintaining the same position he held regarding the petition to the Governor.

He and Vanzetti were in the death house twice during this interval—for several days preceding their execution soon after midnight of August 22, 1927, and for several days preceding August 10. Judge Thayer originally sentenced the men to be electrocuted the week of July 10, 1927. After the Governor on June 1, 1927, appointed President Lowell of Harvard, President Stratton of the Massachusetts Institute of Technology and Judge Grant as an advisory committee to supplement his investigation of the case, he reprieved Sacco and Vanzetti from July 10 to August 10.

On the night of August 10 they were made ready for the execution. Their trousers were slit for the electrodes and their hair was cut for the cap. A half hour before midnight, the official execution time, the

Governor announced a further reprieve of twelve days
—to August 22.

Sacco's letters in these last months give an insight
into the state of mind which enabled him to with-
stand the great pressure brought to bear upon him.

He was thirty-six years old when executed.

February 4, 1927. Dedham Jail

DEAR BARTOLO:

Here am I always in this narrow sad cell walking
up and down, up and down, while I were trying to
give an idea to each one of the dear images that very
often they crowd my mind, I were thinking that after
all these long persecution years instead to open our
prison door, the storm continues to pass upon our
shoulder one more cruel than another. But there between these turbulent clouds, a luminous path run always toward the truth, and here under the blue radiant
skies a little beloved sweet home in my eyes appear,
while two lovely children seeking and calling their dear
father; and at the high top a worn and tired but young
holy dear mother sitting there looking at the children
and smiles with warm gaze waiting to embrace her dear
comradeship. And not far off but near this dearest
vision, at the cypress tree, where the sun light were
shining, your loyal and faithful picture of yesterday.
Today in my eyes appear as a martyrdom. The vision
of this picture were none but the idea that I had in my
mind for several days to send you these words. Therefore, this morning just soon I were sitting I took my

pen and I begin to write you these lines, with certain that you would be pleased to get it and to know that, through all these long way cross road, I am still alive, and how I live I do not know, but I live as always I have done in the struggle fight. As you see, if I didn't write you in these few past months that doesn't mean that I have forgot you, no, not at all, because, on the contrary, I do often think of you, and then everytime I do see my family and the good friends and comrades I always asking about your health. . . .

Regarding to our case, I have no idea—because the experiences of the years past has taught us to not delude ourselves any more, but it is the end of the struggle, and let it hope so.

I have read with very carefully your pamphlet about your first trial, and I enjoyed reading it. It is a good work, it is the light through the history of an infamous frame-up to begin at your first trial to the end of the second trial. . . .

February 9, 1927. *Dedham Jail*

DEAR FRIEND MRS. HENDERSON:

Since the day that Mrs. Evans had announced me in one of her good letters, that you were going to come over to see me, I have been waiting every day by day, and the day did come, but that day . . . was too sad! But nevertheless, to have seen you together with the mother and had talk with you were please for me. Yes, because you, like all the great good mothers that just soon their painful soften down, just soon their struggle pass away, they open their hearts to receive the pain of their other brother sufferance. Therefore, that is why your welcome visit brought me pleasure, for you are not only one of those noble good mothers that knows and embraces the sufferance of their oppressed brothers, but you have the strength to preserve yet your sensibility toward your dearest and toward the victims of the oppressed humanity.

Four years ago next month, I remember that my companionship Rosina, she like you were sensitive— so much that everytime I used to describe her my prison life, you could see the tears run throughout her beloved face. But from and since that date, since my hunger strike, I have not told her any more my prison confinement for not to see this beloved brittle soul suffer. . . . By the way, Mrs. Henderson, you remember that I was saying to you how much injustice and cruel persecution is in this free society of today, and specially for the poor people. Yes, it is nice and noble to be rich and be kind and generous towards the poor exploit people, but it is much more noble the sacrifice of those who have none and divide his bread with his own oppressed brothers. Pardon me. Mrs. Henderson, it is not for discredit or to ignore you, Mrs. Evans and other human generosity work, which I sincerely believe that is an noble one and I am respectful; but it is the warm sincere voice of an unrest heart beat and a free soul that loved and lived amongst the workers class all his life. . . .

February 22, 1927. *Dedham Jail*

DEAR MISS BLOOM: [1]

I do not know you personally but Mrs. Evans she have talk of you always, and personally, I have not ignored your good soul. You worth while to be loved by Mrs. Evans, which I believe that she does love you.

I would have write and say to you lots of more things, but the sad soul of this life . . . far off from the life and from all my dearest that I love, has worn little by little all my kind and human ideas; but, nevertheless, I thank you ever so much for these continuous favor you do to me and for have been good hitherto toward Mrs. Evans.

Therefore, you will be good once more, Miss Bloom, to bring this note to Mrs. Evans that you will find enclosed, and I am sure that in your continuous visit that you do to Mrs. Evans you will give always my best wishes to her even when you have not letter to bring to her. . . .

March 3, 1927. *Dedham Jail*

DEAR FRIEND MRS. WINSLOW: [2]

. . . . The unexpected visit that you and Mrs. Codman [3] kindly have gave to me, though that person-

---

[1] Anna Bloom, secretary to Mrs. Evans.

[2] Mrs. Gertrude L. Winslow of Boston, who labored earnestly for Sacco and Vanzetti.

[3] Mrs. E. A. Codman of Boston, another believer in the innocence of Sacco and Vanzetti.

ally we never know before yesterday, it were welcome to me.

Our conversation were rather short than long and yet, the describe of vineyard, the remembrance of my sweet days of adolescent, the good soul of my poor old dear mother and the family that I loved, it re-enjoyed this sad life of today. Moreover, today, the remembrance of this noble soul of mother has renew in my soul the joy for I have find here another old dear mother, that in the struggle of these long years past she have been always near me and my family sufferance; and today, even when she is lying in bed with broke ankle she find the way to sent me the flowers and her warm greeting by her good friends.

I have received your good letter the other day, and I were please to hear that you enjoyed the visit and that Mrs. Evans is going to come out all right. Therefore, please let me say thank you ever so much for your kind expression words and the solidarity fraternal you have toward our case, and for the good news you have from Mrs. Evans. . . .

Yes, I have read very carefully the article that Prof. Frankfurter wrote in the *Atlantic Monthly* magazine, and after all the bitterness of these long way cross years, I enjoyed to see an competent lecture man to demolish all the frameup and flat one by one all the falsehood witness, who had try to sent us right straight to the electric chair. It is the truth flash of light that will remain forever into the history of tomorrow, it together with *The Brief* that Mr. Thompson wrote a year past. . . .

March 16, 1927. *Dedham Jail*

DEAR MRS. EVANS:

It is sad the life in this cross way road, sad as can be for a little dear mother away from the warm caress affectionate of her dear comradeship, and I feel in my soul as always I had wish in the past, the immensity of ardent wish to see the end of this dreadful case.

But this morning is lovely and the tepid ray of sunlight warming my heart while the idea run through these sad iron bars toward the good old dear mother image.

I have your letter of March 8, and the good news that you went back home almost better were *so* please to me, and would have cheer me great deal if were not for an letter that I had the other day from my poor dear Rosina, which she tell me that she have been very sick and lay in bed at the hospital for one entire month. Therefore, you can imagine how sad and bitterness this soul can feel to-day. . . .

March 25, 1927. *Dedham Jail*

DEAR FRIEND MRS. JACK:

The clove flower are always lovely and vivid to my heart, and I want always to thanks for this kind sentiment of sensibility that warmly you have toward me and my family.

So, after all, Friday Rosina together with Ines they were out here to see me, but indeed, I felt so badly to have find my poor companionship so depressed that I do not remember to have seeing her in all these dreadful long struggle years past so depressed; and naturally among other things, I forgot to give it to Ines. But today I will sent it by maile. Therefore, above all I hope from the bottom of my heart to see this monstrous case sooner the end.

April 1, 1927. *Dedham Jail*

DEAR ABBOTT:

Here the life is so monotonous and sad, away from the freedom of life, from the men and from all the friends and comrades that we love and reloved. But today, the spring April ray of sunlight re-warms the oppressed fallen soul, while into vision vivid come one by one all the warm remembrances of my dearests and the pleasure visits I had from the good friends and comrades. Today I feel that I could not go without sending regards and ideas to them. I have your welcome letter of March 8th, and I thank you ever so much for the kind thoughts you have towards me.

I see that you are quite a busy man, requested here and there, which proves that you have nothing to excuse yourself to me for your long silence, because, on the contrary, you that have been a teacher and understanding the prison psychology, will forgive me for not having answered your letters before. . . . In regards to me, I have love for nothing else than faith, which has given me courage and strength in all these terrible long years of struggle, and today and yesterday, I feel to be proud to have loved this faith. . . .

By the way, I have read also the pamphlet that the comrade John Dos Passos has written for the Sacco-Vanzetti Defense Committee, that is *Facing the Chair,* and it is a good bright piece of work, which will awaken all the intelligent human minds and the narrow-minds of the race and cast prejudice. . . .

April 26, 1927. *Dedham Jail*

DEAR FRIEND MRS. CODMAN:

It is very sad to be doomed and waiting for the electric chair today, after we have wait for seven long years segregate in this hole cell behind the sad bars for see our right justice. It is a shame for the Massachusetts law to step upon all the tradition of freedom of the United States.

But, however, we still live and we have our eyes to look above and down, we see the spring come always more vivid and blooming and the flowers grow always nice and free; while the perfume of the beauty blooms gayly arise in the earth, in my vision appear one by one all the remembrance of mine beloved and the old and new friends and comrades warmly.

I saw Mrs. Evans together with my companionship last week, and she always talk about you and Mrs. Winslow—which I appreciate very much your and Mrs. Winslow kindness and sympathy that you both have toward our case and my family.

Meanwhile give my best regard to all, to Mrs.

Winslow and special to your doctor—the good bright man as Mrs. Evans describe me. . . .

April 27, 1927. Dedham Jail

DEAR AUNTIE BEE: [1]

I have received your last with enclosed the cuttings yesterday, and my comrade Vanzetti and I took great deal interest reading these bright news, of course. But you should send us also the one that talks against us, so we could see what the narrow mind they have to say about. From the last issue of *The Boston Herald* you sent me, I was interest seeing the good fight that the ribel student girls of Smith College, they had put up in the mass meeting protest that they raise in our favor against the town people of Northampton, Mass.

But let me tell you right now, dear mother, that I do not believe that the people of Northampton are against us—no, for I have passet all my life amongst the worker class; but it could probable be, and I am sure that is it, that the people of Northampton they are victims of an false propaganda of an group that dominate and live on the shoulder of the poor exploit people of Northampton year after another. Therefore, if you happen to see anyone of the institution and the ribel girls of Smith College—and also the people of Northampton for I am convinced what I have said above, my and also my comrade Vanzetti warm sincere greetings for all their sympathy they have towards our case. . . .

[1] Mrs. Evans. This is a name used by some of her close friends.

May 3, 1927. *Dedham Jail*

DEAR AUNTIE BEE:

It is a beautiful morning and the gay tipped ray of sunrise warming the hearts of the full sad soul, while the most dearest thoughts running toward you and my beloved ones. . . .

Courage and be of good cheer!

May 8, 1927. *Dedham Jail*

DEAR AUNTIE BEE:

Next Thursday will be seven years that I have been segregate day after another in this narrow sad cell, and after I have been inexcusably persecute all these long years past, I and my poor family, here am I waiting to the ignominous execution. But however, this morning suddenly after I wake, my gaze were turn with the smile towards the bright and beautiful blue sky, while the gold sunrise were shining the flowers of the little pear tree and the leaves of an oak trunk that beginning to blossom, I was breathing with joy the perfume of these flowers that the friends sent to me, the vivid sweet atmosphere of another day that the gay breeze were blowing in my neat cell. It is sweet to me the date of this day because it remind me, warmly in my heart, the remembrance of my first and second old dear mother; the comradeship, the confidence of all the sudden pain of your life that stick to you, to her, and of the grave yonder, and with it all the other poor sufferince mothers. In the *Herald* issue of May 5th—cutting that you sent me—it weren't pleasant news, when we read, Sacco has refused to sign his name to the Fuller petition because— fanatic and—insane. puff! oh yes, it was also like that alway in the history of past . . . if his act would hurt the purse of an spiteful and tyrant class, after they had crush him to death, they call him felon-fanatic and insane. But in spite of all, in the right part has remain always the pride of an sincere faith which one have love and for it suffered and know to fall as he have suffered and loved, while at the other side is the ignominous shame for the humanity.

I felt very sorry when Rosina had tell me that the guards have refused to let you in to see me. Well I hope and I please the authority of this institution that next time, I would like that they would let you in anytime you should come to see me. . . .

May 14, 1927. *Dedham Jail*

DEAR MRS. WINSLOW:

I have received your welcome letter of May 5th and also the other before it was a lovely one, and you forgive me for I have not answer the one before last. . . .

You are very kind when you say that you went to see Rosina to bring her good news and to see her how she was for she was troubled the day after that I refuse to sign my name at the petition that Mr. Thompson sent in to the Gov. Fuller. I thank ever so much for this very gentil idea especially, and for all other and the sympathy that you are showing towards our case. Pardon me, but please can you tell me what is the good news that you brought to my companion? I did not sign my name because I am positively that the Gov. Fuller and also any other legal step of law they would have refuse to give us any square deal. Many friends and comrades of mine like you they hope and they have always the hope, and that is too bad to see them today sleeping in that same illusion optimism, while we face to the electric chair. My hope, the only one which I had always that today rest in my heart, it is that only the friends and comrades and the international proletariat can save us from the iniquitous execution.

Do not be afraid! When I think all this poor stupid, oppressed humanity, the sufferance of my belove Rosina and all the persecution for along these seven years segregate in this hell hole cell, I really forget what fear means. If the conscience of Massachusetts justice have the chance to hang us, don't worry, dear friend, they will inexorably execute us. . . .

May 22, 1927. Dedham Jail

DEAR AUNTIE BEE:

I knew well how you longe to have one of my poor letter once in a while, and I do write it everytime I do have something dear to say to you when I am sure that it will bring joy into your noble heart.

. . . . This morning sudden after I wake—as ever, I turn toward the window cell and I was looking the gold ray of sunrise that were shining the top branch trees of the vivid green leaves, and above, between the lovely running white clouds—the splendid sky, has appear to my eyes bright and blue than ever; while my thought were run toward you I thought to seeing there the image head of your lovely gray hair. Oh, life how sad is to live here and in this bad society! . . .

Yes, last Wednesday we have past a good hour in company with my dear Rosetta and Mrs. Winslow. . . . They brought each one of us . . . two beauty black red rose which they are dearest to me. . . .

All the flower has the perfume and the bright beauty, but the black red roses has the most perfume and the vivid beauty above all the flowers. There I report you one poem as example of beauty and also demonstration that I do like specially the black red roses. By C. Jacobs Bond—.

> There's a rambler on the trellis
> And a wild rose in the hedge,
> With a gay and golden Marechal Neil
> Upon the arbor's edge.
> There's a sweetheart bud a-tapping
> At the window of my room,
> And my heart is singing . . . singing
> For the roses are in bloom!

Well, mother, is not it a lovily little poem? . . .

June 14, 1927. *Dedham Jail*

DEAR FRIEND JACKSON: [1]

I know that these few words will surprise you, but

---

[1] Gardner Jackson, former reporter on *The Boston Globe*, who became a member of the Defense Committee early in 1927.

you should not feel that way at all because, since I have know you and I have been told by comrades of mine about the sincere solidarity you are gave the Defense Committee, I had always in my mind to write you these few lines as a thankful for all your sincere interest that you are give for the sure of our freedom. Although knowing that we are one heart, unfortunately, we represent two opposite class; the first want to live at any cost and the second fight for the freedom, and when it come to take away from him he rebel; although he know that the power of the first, of the opposite, class will crucify his holy rebellion. It is true, indeed, that they can execute the body but they cannot execute the idea which is bound to live. And certainly, as long as this sistem of things, the exploitation of man on other man reign, will remain always the fight between those two opposite class, today and always. But whenever the heart of one of the upper class join with the exploited workers for the struggle of their right, in the human sentiment is the feel of an spontanious attraction of an familiar affection and brotherly love one to another. Indeed, your last visit together with the comrade Felicani, Moro [1] and Georg Branting [2] were a familiar one, and even the most cheerfully one that we have had among the friends since the sentence day.

[1] Joseph Moro, Italian shoeworker, who became secretary of the Defense Committee in 1926.

[2] Georg Branting, son of Hjalmar Branting, former Premier of Sweden and President of the Council of the League of Nations. Mr. Branting, a member of the Stockholm bar, was sent to Boston by Swedish labor organizations in June, 1927, to study the case at first hand.

I was glad to hear that you went to see my little ones. I love Ines so dearly, as much as I love Dante who was always my comradeship around the house, and wherever I use to go. . . .

June 23, 1927. *Dedham Jail*

DEAR AUNTIE BEE:

Yesterday morning, the day were bright, and the green vivid leaves of the trees they were sweetly move under breeze waving gay, while the gold ray of sunrise were warming the magnificent atmosphere, the kind little birds they were singing very cheerfully. But at noon—in the night—and this morning the weather and the wind—has been change so sad in this soul that I wish that it stoped at once.

I hope from the bottom of my heart that you understand it—of course that I am tired to swallow all this —dregs and the old sweeping that I don't know what to do with it. I am tired to listen your little story today for tomorrow and do not forget—that the cruel inquisition and persecution never was in any time in the history an instrument of the affection and the education, never was and never will be, poor companion! I am telling you that I am tired to tolerate this cowardice persecution of the men law that you are faithful to; none other should suffering no pain but I only should suffering and crusifice from this iniquitous law, because I . . . have try to hit at the centres of this decrepid society, toward always the conquest of an integral liberty and happiness of all the exploit. . . .

I want that it should be understood! as I said above that for hereafter none other should suffering no pain because I am tired to tolerate it and your little unuseful story any long.

I knew that it will bring you a painful, and I suffer for it; but I want you mother! to think of me as always you have thought in the struggle of these years past, that I love you as I loved my poor dear mother. If I fall, remember, that this mother affection will be buried with this humble soul that have loved you as an good mother can be loved. . . .

June 25, 1927. Dedham Jail

DEAR FRIEND MRS. HENDERSON:

As you know I am still living at the same hotel, the same room, and also at the same old number 14—but on the first of July probably, they will bring us to the death house, and from there to the—eternity. That is the eager wish of all the inquisitors also the Gov. Fuller . . . but nevertheless, even today the perfume of the withered red roses revive often in my soul, the remembrance of friends and comrades and the old friends warmly.

Here the Sunday is always more monotonous and sad than the weekly days, and today is much more gloomy than ever, but it must be lovely out in the country to see all the trees, the flowers, the vast prairies verdant here and there and all the bloomy fruitful, gardens, while in my soul gain always more joyous the life free wish today more than ever—but, woe is me!

Last week then, it was a great surprising for me to find these lovely four roses in jar, and I have asked myself who is that good hand that have put these here? Finally, after a while, Mr. Curtis [1] came along and had tell me that Mrs. B—— brought me these roses while I was in the yard. If you should see her, give her my best wishes and thanks for these lovely roses she brought me. . . .

June 28, 1927. *Dedham Jail*

DEAR AUNTIE BEE:

Close behind these sad bars in these dull day the life feel so much depressed that you can not imagine— but, nevertheless, here into my heart beat eager, for an good mother, I can always find an comfort idea, an warm greeting for her.

Yesterday in the Boston *La Notizia* [2] issue, I read the heroic speech that James M. Curley, ex-Boston Mayor . . . made at the Bunker Hill celebration day; poor celebration! . . . Yes, because you can so well see that instead to dedicate themselves at the celebration of the Bunker Hill day they criticise prof. Felix Frankfurter [3] for his human solidarity that he does give to Sacco-Vanzetti case. Of course—where is the better chance for them to influence the people against us? They do it in the celebration day as well as Thayer had influence the jury at our first trial. It is

---

[1] One of the deputy sheriffs at the Dedham Jail.

[2] A daily Italian newspaper of Boston.

[3] Professor Felix Frankfurter of the Harvard Law School, author of *The Case of Sacco and Vanzetti.*

a shame indeed, to have gave the chance to these two men like Curley and the Registrar Goodwin to celebration the great Bunker Hill day. . . .

In the same issue at the next page—press comments, I read the criticise that Lowell, Mass. *Courier Citizen* of June 8th they bring against prof. Dean Pound, [1] for his conviction toward our defense innocence. However, I want to tell you that, when you see that the adversary move their criticise it mean that prof. Frankfurter and Dean Pound and others they are doing a good work. . . .

June 29, 1927. *Dedham Jail*

DEAR AUNTIE BEE:

I have your graceful letter of June 28th this morning, and I see with enjoyment that even when unpleasant letter of mine reach to you, your heart remain sensible as much is noble toward the beloved ones. Thank you, mother! you are good as good and generous was my poor dear mother.

It is sad in these day the remembrance of her who was dearest to me, but, in these remembrance I do find also the joy so much I have find in you and others that I love and loved.

It was rather glooms and dark days today, indeed, I didnt feel very well this morning and yet, I felt something vivid in my heart that I could not describe you, but, nevertheless, it was a great day. Yes, in-

[1] Roscoe Pound, dean of the Harvard Law School.

deed, because Rosina was out here to see me together with the both childs and, though of all and the very short visit, it is to not be forgotten how surprised and great one it was. . . .

June 30, 1927. *Dedham Jail*

DEAR FRIEND MRS. WINSLOW:

Your welcomed farewell letter reach to me safely the other day, and I am sure that you will enjoy this journey through the beauty spots in Europe.

Let me once more thank to you for all your sincere disinterested sympathy you have towards our case and my family.

By the way, yesterday morning my companion Rosina were out here together with the children, both childs they were looking fine but Rosina she didn't feel very good, although was an enjoy surprised visit for me as it was for my family of course. Dante growing big every day, and in his gay child face he was showing the joyful smile of sun burning. I asked him how he was like the job, and he says that he does like it, indeed he seem to me that he was please as much enthusiastic at it.

Well, I have read this morning news that the Governor Fuller have gave us 31 more day reprieve, that is, the August 10th, so you see we have thirty-one more day living death.

I wish you all the enjoy in the world in your voyage. . . .

June, 1927. *Dedham Jail*

DEAR COMRADE BRANTING:

Here in the prison, the intelligent prisoners are always looking forward for something new and more vivid, something original every day, even if it is little thing. . . . How could it be otherwise? Closed in these four and narrow sad walls, away from the face of life, from my beloved ones, and from all the good and the beauty that the human eye can see in this gay of mother nature! Therefore your last visit, the cheerful conversation that we had with Comrade Felicani, Moro and Jackson, was certainly a grateful one. It is only the second time that we both saw you, and yet, we have become so familiar with each other, that it seems that we know for many years as old friends of ours; it is that noble free sentiment of faith that does re-embrace us in one reciprocal affection brotherlike.

Often our good friends use to bring me all kinds of beautiful flowers, but the beautiful cloves and the red black beauty vivid roses that you brought us Saturday last, which I liked so well, were certainly the most big and beautiful bunch of flowers I have ever had.

I was glad to hear that you went to see my family and had a fine time with my little ones. Yes, Ines is a good and brisk child, as good as her brother Dante, and both love so dearly their good mother, and without a doubt it is a great relief for me, for I do love them so much, as only love could have loved. By the way, Saturday, when we were talking about your family, I saw the emmotion which enlightened your face, and of course when I came back to my cell, I have thought of you and how dearly you must love your family. It was a relief to me because I knew, that when one loves another even in the torturous struggle, as in poverty, the love remains forever; moreover, here the love . . . goes further on, much far,—like the Anarchist love. That is why we are still living, and we will live, in spite of the inquisitor Thayer, and all his back stage that have sentenced us to death, because you generous people and the world workers want us to be free and to come back once more into life, in the struggle battle for the love and the joy of liberty and all. . . .

July 3, 1927. *Charlestown State Prison*

DEAR AUNTIE BEE:

The Sunday was always lonesome and sad at the Dedham Jail—but and yet the little warm of home made dinner that the dear friends used bring us were of cheer and relieve for our unrest heart, moreover there we could see the green grow, the trees, the beautiful red roses and flowers that the friends used bring us and the beauty blue bright sky of Dedham. But here life buried—where none we can see but four sad wall and a lap of sky that disappear under the wing of a bird, the Sunday is much more lonesome and gloome here than anyelse where. But, nevertheless, while the life buried remain here, the idea runs through this little lap of sky towards all the friends and comrades and the beloved ones warmly.

As you see after these seven years confinment I have thought sometime that the men law of today which you are faithful had made a progress, but woe is me!—that is not so, they go backward instead of forward, they go right straight toward the end of the old inquisition. . . .

Bartolo have past me your graceful letter of June 30th, and after I have reread it I was glad to hear that you felt more quite and much better and as ever I hope from the bottom of my heart that here the waving gay breeze of the sun along the shore of Chatham—near your dear friends, will sooner get all better. . . .

I imagine how hard it is for my poor companion and for all the beloved ones in these day, but courage mother, and be of good cheer because after us other will take our place, it is the tremendous struggle of the life and every struggle they have the end and I am sure that the end of this struggle your rest in peace. . . .

July 5, 1927. Charlestown Prison

DEAR AUNTIE BEE:

As ever your letter are welcomed to me and the one I receive yesterday of July the second, certainly was the dearest one, as a remembrance to have received it at the day of my last four July.

It is too sad to think of it I know, but and yet, the cruel blind persecution, the continuous seclusion of these years past have taught me that if the friends and comrades they but get themselves as ever in the old past weakness illusion, I think they will be too late and sorrow for it tomorrow. But, however, it does not trouble me at all as it would have not trouble any other free soul that have dream and walked straight towards the radiant pathway for the integral conquest—for the joy of liberty of all the exploit and the oppressed class, not at all because, when it comes to feel to have been deprived from the life freedom, from the development of his life dream, for the beauty and the good of all . . . the life does not feel none the sorrow for give the farewell at their decrepid old society.

It is true, indeed, that it is and remain deeply and immensely in my heart—the idea of the dearest beloved ones and specially the little ones, oh, yes! But the idea of it, the remembrance of the ceaseless affection of my dear companionship, it was also comfortant to know that it were the end and my last fourth July.

I was going to write you yesterday afternoon, but in my mind to finish to read the *Portrait Life of Lincoln* by V. F. Miller, which enclosed in it I find many of Abraham Letters that Bartolo told me years go that these were wonderful letters. Indeed, I read these and I find so much worth of good as told in these letters that remind me of the old dear comrade Eugene Debs, and I will reread these ones more because by read these fine letters, I have forgot that yesterday was my last fourth July. . . .

July 10, 1927. *Charlestown Prison*

DEAR FRIEND MRS. CODMAN:

Your welcomed letter of July the 6th reach to me safely Friday late in the afternoon, and though of this hot day and the segregate living death of this life, I thought to send you these few lines because I am sure that after the last pleasant visit you gave to us together with my little Ines and Rosina, you will like to hear our news directly.

Yes, we also thought to remain in Dedham till the August the first, but, as you see they want get ready of our warm life before the monstrous execute date. However, let this date come if the brutality of the men law of today want, because it is really a shame and unhuman to remain here—and to tolorate any longer the sufferance of my beloved ones and the struggle sacrifice of our good friends and comrades.

By the way, the day after my companionship were out here to see us, and after while so to make the conversation little cheerfully, I asked Rosina what she was doing to her suffer face to make her cheeks so lovily smooth as roses, I think that Doctor Codman he must have find something for it! She smile gayly with that joyful smile that I long to see her smile. So, you see that when is the reciprocal affection of love even into the struggle sufferance we can always find something to relief the soul for a while of course, because once the old legend say that, from the heart every cheerfully come, but, when this cheerfully is not into heart, certainly it could not come through. . . .

July 19, 1927. *Charlestown State Prison*

MY DEAR INES:

I would like that you should understand what I am going to say to you, and I wish I could write you so plain, for I long so much to have you hear all the heart-beat eagerness of your father, for I love you so much as you are the dearest little beloved one.

It is quite hard indeed to make you understand in your young age, but I am going to try from the bottom of my heart to make you understand how dear you are to your father's soul. If I cannot succeed in doing that, I know that you will save this letter and read it over in future years to come and you will see and feel the same heart-beat affection as your father feels in writing it to you.

I will bring with me your little and so dearest letter and carry it right under my heart to the last day of my life. When I die, it will be buried with your father who loves you so much, as I do also your brother Dante and holy dear mother.

You don't know Ines, how dear and great your letter was to your father. It is the most golden present that you could have given to me or that I could have wished for in these sad days.

It was the greatest treasure and sweetness in my struggling life that I could have lived with you and your brother Dante and your mother in a neat little farm, and learn all your sincere words and tender affection. Then in the summer-time to be sitting with you in the home nest under the oak tree shade—beginning to teach you of life and how to read and write, to see you running, laughing, crying and singing through the verdent fields picking the wild flowers here and there from one tree to another, and from the clear, vivid stream to your mother's embrace.

The same I have wished to see for other poor girls, and their brothers, happy with their mother and father as I dreamed for us—but it was not so and the nightmare of the lower classes saddened very badly your father's soul.

For the things of beauty and of good in this life, mother nature gave to us all, for the conquest and the joy of liberty. The men of this dying old society, they brutally have pulled me away from the embrace of your brother and your poor mother. But, in spite of all, the free spirit of your father's faith still survives, and I have lived for it and for the dream that some day I would have come back to life, to the embrace of your dear mother, among our friends and comrades again, but woe is me!

I know that you are good and surely you love your mother, Dante and all the beloved ones—and I am sure that you love me also a little, for I love you much and then so much. You do not know Ines, how often I think of you every day. You are in my heart, in my vision, in every angle of this sad walled cell, in the sky and everywhere my gaze rests.

Meantime, give my best paternal greetings to all the friends and comrades, and doubly so to our beloved ones. Love and kisses to your brother and mother.

With the most affectionate kiss and ineffable caress from him who loves you so much that he constantly thinks of you. Best warm greetings from Bartolo to you all.   YOUR FATHER

August 4, 1927. Charlestown State Prison

MY DEAR FRIENDS AND COMRADES: [1]

From the death cell we are just inform from the defense committee that the governor Fuller he has decided to kill us Aug. the 10th. We are not surprised for this news because we know the capitalist class hard without any mercy the good soldiers of the rivolution. We are proud for death and fall as all the anarchist can fall. It is up to you now, brothers, comrades! as I have tell you yesterday that you only that can save us, because we have never had faith in the governor for we have always know that the gov. Fuller, Thayer [2] and Katzmann [3] are the murder.

My warm fraternal regards to all,

NICOLA SACCO

August 12, 1927. Charlestown State Prison

DEAR AUNTIE BEE:

I am still extreme weak—but, this morning I could

---

[1] This letter was sent to the Defense Committee from the death house through counsel for Sacco and Vanzetti.

[2] Judge Webster Thayer, who presided at the Dedham trial and heard the eight motions for a new trial based on new evidence.

[3] Fred G. Katzmann, prosecutor of Sacco and Vanzetti at the Dedham trial in his capacity as district attorney for the South-eastern District (Norfolk and Plymouth Counties).

not go without write you these few lines and to tell
you that after the death house, has remain still vividly
in my heart the free spirit of an sublime faith to sent
this good old dear mother, that I like always and in
the death house more than ever.   I often thought of
you, my first surest heart eager greetings.   Meantime
give my best wishes to all the friends and comrades,
to the beloved ones, kiss to my little darling one if
you see her, with my most hearty affectionate embrace.

August 18, 1927. *Charlestown State Prison*

MY DEAR SON AND COMPANION:

Since the day I saw you last I had always the idea
to write you this letter, but the length of my hunger
strike and the thought I might not be able to explain
myself, made me put it off all this time.

The other day, I ended my hunger strike and just
as soon as I did that I thought of you to write to you,
but I find that I did not have enough strength and I
cannot finish it at one time.   However, I want to get
it down in any way before they take us again to the
death-house, because it is my conviction that just as
soon as the court refuses a new trial to us they will
take us there.   And between Friday and Monday, if
nothing happens, they will electrocute us right after
midnight, on August 22nd.   Therefore, here I am,
right with you with love and with open heart as ever
I was yesterday.

I never thought that our inseparable life could be

separated, but the thought of seven dolorous years makes it seem it did come, but then it has not changed really the unrest and the heart-beat of affection. That has remained as it was. More. I say that our ineffable affection reciprocal, is today more than any other time, of course. That is not only a great deal but it is grand because you can see the real brotherly love, not only in joy but also and more in the struggle of suffering. Remember this, Dante. We have demonstrated this, and modesty apart, we are proud of it.

Much we have suffered during this long Calvary. We protest today as we protested yesterday. We protest always for our freedom.

If I stopped hunger strike the other day, it was because there was no more sign of life in me. Because I protested with my hunger strike yesterday as today I protest for life and not for death.

I sacrificed because I wanted to come back to the embrace of your dear little sister Ines and your mother and all the beloved friends and comrades of life and not death. So Son, today life begins to revive slow and calm, but yet without horizon and always with sadness and visions of death.

Well, my dear boy, after your mother had talked to me so much and I had dreamed of you day and night, how joyful it was to see you at last. To have talked with you like we used to in the days—in those days. Much I told you on that visit and more I wanted to say, but I saw that you will remain the same affectionate boy, faithful to your mother who loves you so much, and I did not want to hurt your sensibilities any longer, because I am sure that you will continue to be the same boy and remember what I have told you. I knew that and what here I am going to tell you will touch your sensibilities, but don't cry Dante, because many tears have been wasted, as your mother's have been wasted for seven years, and never did any good. So, Son, instead of crying, be strong, so as to be able to comfort your mother, and when you want to distract your mother from the discouraging soulness, I will tell you what I used to do. To take her for a long walk in the quiet country, gathering wild flowers here and there, resting under the shade of trees, between the harmony of the vivid stream and the gentle tranquility of the mothernature, and I am sure that she will enjoy this very much, as you surely would be happy for it. But remember always, Dante, in the play of happiness, don't you use all for yourself only, but down yourself just one step, at your side and help the weak ones that cry for help, help the prosecuted and the victim, because that are your better friends; they are the comrades that fight and fall as your father and Bartolo fought and fell yesterday for the conquest of the joy of freedom for all and the poor workers. In this struggle of life you will find more love and you will be loved.

I am sure that from what your mother told me about what you said during these last terrible days when I was lying in the iniquitous death-house—that description gave me happiness because it showed you will be the beloved boy I had always dreamed.

Therefore whatever should happen tomorrow, no-body knows, but if they should kill us, you must not forget to look at your friends and comrades with the smiling gaze of gratitude as you look at your beloved ones, because they love you as they love every one of the fallen persecuted comrades. I tell you, your father that is all the life to you, your father that loved you and saw them, and knows their noble faith (that is mine) their supreme sacrifice that they are still doing for our freedom, for I have fought with them, and they are the ones that still hold the last of our hope that today they can still save us from electrocution, it is the struggle and fight between the rich and the poor for safety and freedom, Son, which you will understand in the future of your years to come, of this unrest and struggle of life's death.

Much I thought of you when I was lying in the death house—the singing, the kind tender voices of the children from the playground, where there was all the life and the joy of liberty—just one step from the wall which contains the buried agony of three buried souls. It would remind me so often of you and your sister Ines, and I wish I could see you every moment. But I feel better that you did not come to the death-house so that you could not see the horrible picture of three lying in agony waiting to be electrocuted, because I do not know what effect it would have on your young age. But then, in another way if you were not so sensitive it would be very useful to you tomorrow when you could use this horrible memory to hold up to the world the shame of the country in this cruel persecution and unjust death. Yes, Dante, they can crucify our bodies today as they are doing, but they cannot destroy our ideas, that will remain for the youth of the future to come.

Dante, when I said three human lives buried, I meant to say that with us there is another young man by the name of Celestino Maderios that is to be electrocuted at the same time with us. He has been twice before in that horrible death-house, that should be destroyed with the hammers of real progress—that horrible house that will shame forever the future of the citizens of Massachusetts. They should destroy that house and put up a factory or school, to teach many of the hundreds of the poor orphan boys of the world.

Dante, I say once more to love and be nearest to your mother and the beloved ones in these sad days, and I am sure that with your brave heart and kind goodness they will feel less discomfort. And you will also not forget to love me a little for I do—O, Sonny! thinking so much and so often of you.

Best fraternal greetings to all the beloved ones, love and kisses to your little Ines and mother. Most hearty affectionate embrace.

YOUR FATHER AND COMPANION

P.S. Bartolo send you the most affectionate greetings. I hope that your mother will help you to understand this letter because I could have written much better and more simple, if I was feeling good. But I am so weak.

Part Two

BARTOLOMEO VANZETTI

CHAPTER I

VANZETTI landed at Ellis Island in 1908, at the age of twenty. He had come from a comfortable, middle-class home in Villafalletto, province of Cuneo, in northern Italy, where his father was a substantial farmer.

As both parents were devout Catholics, Bartolomeo had a strict bringing-up. He attended the local schools until he was thirteen, when his father put him to work in a pastry shop at Cuneo. He remained there a year and a half and afterwards worked also in Cavour, Courgne and Turin as pastry cook and candy maker.

Six years after he left home, he fell seriously ill and returned to the care of his mother and sisters. He was then nineteen. During the years spent away from home, he had read and studied whenever opportunity afforded. It was during this period that he turned away from Catholicism and became interested in radical social theories.

His mother's death, which occurred about this time, after a lingering illness, left a deep and permanent impression upon Vanzetti. He decided to leave home again and soon set out for America.

His first two years in this country were spent as a dishwasher in restaurants in New York. Brief snatches of employment on Connecticut farms, two years in the stone pits of Meriden, Connecticut, and a period in the brickyards of Springfield, Massachusetts, intervened before he again returned to New York and secured temporary work as a pastry cook. Five months of unemployment sent him back to Springfield where he joined a railroad construction gang. He went from there to Worcester and finally, in 1915, to Plymouth, where he remained until his arrest, except for an interval during 1917-1918 when he went to Mexico to avoid the draft. He was variously ditch-digger, pick-and-shovel man with a road gang, laborer in the plant of the Plymouth Cordage Company of Plymouth, ice-cutter and fish-peddler. Active interest in a strike of the Plymouth Cordage workers in 1916 marked him in the region as a labor agitator.

Wherever he went, Vanzetti continued his studies with increasing fervor. His two most thumbed books were copies of *The Divine Comedy* and Ernest Renan's *Life of Jesus*.

Vanzetti was thirty-one years old when he and Sacco were arrested. No criminal charge had ever before been made against either of the men. A summary narrative of the circumstances of their arrest, their conviction for murder on July 14, 1921, and the events which after more than seven years ended in their execution, will be found in an appendix.

During the period covered by the letters of this chapter (1921-1924), Vanzetti was taken from Charlestown prison to Dedham jail three times. Each time arguments were heard before the court on motions for a new trial.

Meanwhile, among guards and wardens at the

State prison, he had gained the reputation of a hard worker and a constant reader and writer. Immediately after entering the prison in August, 1920, he was assigned to the paint shop where the state automobile license plates are painted. Early in 1923 he was compelled to seek a change of work because the paint gases affected his digestion. He was then placed in the prison tailor shop where he worked until near the close of 1924.

January 10, 1921.[1] *Charlestown Prison*

DEAR ALFONSINA:[2]

I had received your letter dated Jan. 6–21. I heartily laughed to hear that the finger-nails of the little cat have scratched the Zora's[3] nose, and I continue to laugh everytime I think about it. Surely it is a good lesson not only for Zora and other child, but for mankind. The little cat knows very well that it has a sharped nails, and that when a little girl molests it, it is enough to scratch a little her nose for be let free. People too has sharp finger-nails, and the noses [of] tyrants and oppressors is make of flesh too, but it look tho the people ignored this notion. Oh how much less sorrowness and misery would be among the mor-

---

[1] This letter was written before the Dedham trial of Sacco and Vanzetti on the charge of murder.

[2] Vanzetti was living in the home of Mrs. Alfonsina Brini in North Plymouth at·the time of his arrest.

[3] Mrs. Brini's small daughter.

tals if they know just what a little cat knows. As for Zora, I know that she loves the cat, and is not cruel amongst it, but she played with it too much violently and insistantly, and so hurts and troubles it, with the well merited consequences that she knows now pretty well. I am sorry for her nose, but when I thought that the cat had anticipated my advice, I can't help but laugh. Tell Beltrando [1] that I received his callender; much oblige to him. I hear that the woolen mill has stopped to work, and you are without job. Certainly, owed to the high price of everything, and your familiar circumstances, it shall trouble you. But take it easy. After all we cannot become rich by the work of our arms. . . . Take this opportunity to enjoy sunshine and open air. . . .

I am glad for your good news. I too feel very well. Thanks for all.

Kisses to the children, best regards to Vincenzo [2] and all those who love me. Cheer up, be careful for your health.

P. S. One more order: If you have yet that callender with the world map, send it to me. I shall smile, in spite of the chain, in looking our gradual World's conquest.

---

[1] Mrs. Brini's son, who helped Vanzetti deliver eels to his Italian customers the morning of December 24, 1919, when Vanzetti was charged with participating in an attempted hold-up at Bridgewater, Mass. Beltrando was Vanzetti's chief witness at the Plymouth trial. He is a member of the Class of 1929 at the College of Liberal Arts, Boston University.

[2] Mrs. Brini's husband, an old friend of Vanzetti.

July 22, 1921. *Charlestown Prison*

MY DEAR MRS. GLENDOWER EVANS: [1]

I was just thinking what I would to do for past the long days jail: I was saying to myself: Do some work. But what? Write. A gentle motherly figure came to my mind and I rehear the voice: Why don't you write something now? It will be useful to you when you will be free. Just at that time I received your letter.

Thanks to you from the bottom of my heart for your confidence in my innocence; I am so. I did not spittel a drop of blood, or steal a cent in all my life. A little knowledge of the past; a sorrowful experience of the life itself had gave to me some ideas very different from those of many other umane beings. But I wish to convince my fellowmen that only with virtue and honesty is possible for us to find a little happiness in the world. I preached: I worked. I wished with all my faculties that the social wealth would belong to every umane creatures, so well as it was the fruit of the work of all. But this do not mean robbery for a insurrection.

The insurrection, the great movements of the soul, do not need dollars. It need love, light, spirit of sacrifice, ideas, conscience, instincts. It need more conscience, more hope and more goodness. And all this blessed things can be seeded, awoked, growed up in the heart of man in many ways, but not by robbery and murder for robbery.

[1] Mrs. Elizabeth Glendower Evans of Brookline, Mass.

I like you to know that I think of Italy, so speaking. From the universal family, turning to this humble son, I will say that, as far as my needs, wish and aspirations call, I do not need to become a bandit. I like the teaching of Tolstoi, Saint Francesco and Dante. I like the example of Cincinati and Garibaldi. The epicurean joi do not like to me. A little roof, a field, a few books and food is all what I need. I do not care for money, for leisure, for mondane ambition. And honest, even in this world of lambs and wolves I can have those things. My father has many field, houses, garden. He deal in wine and fruits and granaries. He wrote to me many times to come back home, and be a business man. Well, this supposed murderer had answered to him that my conscience do not permit to me to be a business man and I will gain my bread by work his field.

And more: The clearness of mind, the peace of the conscience, the determination and force of will, the intelligence, all, all what make the man feeling to be a part of the life, force and intelligence of the universe, will be brake by a crime. I know that, I see that, I tell that to everybody: Do not violate the law of nature, if you do not want to be a miserable. I remember: it was a night without moon, but starry. I sit alone in the darkness, I was sorry, very sorry. With the face in my hands I began to look at the stars. I feel that my soul want goes away from my body, and I have had to make an effort to keep it in my chest. So, I am the son of Nature, and I am so rich that I

do not need any money. And for this they say I am
a murderer and condemned me to death. Death? It
is nothing. Abbominium is cruel thing.

Now you advise me to study. Yes, it would be a
good thing. But I do not know enough this language
to be able to make any study through it. I will like
to read Longfellow's, Paine's, Franklin's and Jefferson's works, but I cannot. I would like to study mathe-
matics, physics, history and science, but I have not a
sufficient elementary school to begin such studies, especially the two first and I cannot study without work,
hard physical work, sunshine and winds; free, blessing
wind. There is no flame without the atmospheric
gasses; and no light of genius in any soul without they
communion with Mother Nature.

I hope to see you very soon; I will tell you more in
the matter. I will write something, a meditation perhaps and name it: Waiting for the Hanger. I have
lost the confidence in the justice of man. I mean in
what is called so; not of course, of that sentiment
which lay in the heart of man, and that no infernal
force will be strong enough to soffocate it. Your assistance and the. assistance of so many good men and
women, had made my cross much more light. I will
not forget it.

I beg your pardon for such a long letter, but I feel
so reminiscent to you that hundred pages would not be
sufficient to extern my sentiments and feelings. I am
sure you will excuse me. Salve.

1921. *Charlestown State Prison*

DEAR MRS. EVANS:

The "wake up" rings here in Charlestown at 7
A. M. but yesterday morning, the officer call me at six
o'clock. "Go to put on your own clothes," he tell me
with hurried way. I went and I found my old clothing
horribly wrinkled. There were nobody at the work,
at such hour, so, after a useless protest I was compelled to put them on as they were. Well, I was saying to myself, returning to the cell: There is, after all,
something worse than this. Sure it was: On the table
I found my breakfast, a cup of coffee, three slices of
bread, two frankforts and mashed potatoes, all so cold
as ice cream can be.

After such a breakfast, an official took me in the
"Guard Room." The little chauffeur, an old officer,
and the bravest one were waiting for me. I was
chained with the last one, and all four left the room
and went down to the street where the automobile was
ready. Six or seven officers stood at the door, with
their right hand near the back pocket, ready to protect
me from any attack. One must be most ungrateful
man of the world for not feeling quite reconoscent.

As the machine start I asked for tobacco. They
stop at the nearest corner and the old officer went to
buy some of it. A young policeman begin to speak with
the remaining officers, he leaning himself in such a
manner to put his head in the automobile. His eyes,
dark and clear, look at me with an ill-concealed curi-
osity, and I perceive his wonder at my common harm-

less presence. Surely he had expected something different. Meanwhile I was looking at the people going up and down of the streets. I can tell which of them are employed and which are not by their way of walking.

The former went straight ahead as men who know where he want to go and when he must arrive. The second look around, above, and below, as a man who lost himself, and do not know what he has to do. Little farther I meet a little compatriot. He is a little fellow of the South, with yellow pale face dry by a copious dayly sweat, but his mustachs are well curled up. He is very petty, and it look like if he were the centre of the world. I cannot help but smile. I never see him before but I know where he go, what he thinks; his hopes. I knew him, as I know myself; probably better than myself. "Take that way; avoid civilization," the brave officer is now crying to the driver who obey silently. Surely enough this man hope that such high language is incomprehensible to me.

So we enter now into a Park the name of which I already forget, but the beauty of it, I will never forget anymore. If I were poet and know the metre, I would write a song of it in third rhyme. I am not a poet, but neither so profane to disturb such splendor with my poor ink. The concerned officer point to me a big brick building, saying, "It is the Fine Arts Museum." He point many other buildings saying that they are almost all a private schools. I was then regretting to have only a pair of eyes, able to look in one direction alone. I observe everything, the trees, the bushes, the grass, the rocks, and the brook along the way, on which I was raptured. The drops of dew look like pearls; the sky reflects himself in the waters of the brook, and let one think that it is bottomless. But beauty over all tell to me a wonderful history of one day, far away, a day when the waters in a gigantic and confounded waves, left this place suddenly.

I look now to those which pass at my side in automobiles. But what a difference between these men that I meet now, and those I met a little while ago, a little far away going to work, or walking round about; what a difference! The big buildings had now give the place to a more modest ones, which become more and more rare, until only a little, humble, odd, funny houses, rise here and there from the accidentated soil. O, funny, humble, old, little houses that I love; little house always big enough for the greatest loves, and most saint affections. Here I see two girls of the people going to work. They look like to be sisters. Their shoulders are more large than those of the girls I meet a little before, but little curved. On their pale faces are lines of sorrow and distress. There is sobberness and suffering in their big, deep, full eyes. Poor plebian girls, where are the roses of your springtime?

I found myself in front of Dedham jail. We enter. A little ugly Napolitan barber has such a care and zeal of my looking, as if I am the Mayor of Naple.

They locked me at No. 61. Now the news of my arrival is known by all the human canaries of the place. The poor boys do their best to give me a glance, a word, a cheer up. Little after I was brought to the

Court, protected by a numerous American Cossack, as if I and Nick were a Russian Czars.

At last we come back to Charlestown, and I have had the opportunity to look at the sky and see the stars, as in the old days at home. The workers were then coming back home. Still in their confused forms I can see the "little of abdom and much of heart" as Gori sang. One of them appear to be a Latin, strong and noble. This is one of those who will win the battle that the citizens had lost, I say to myself.

Few minutes after we stop in front of the Prison, and little after I found myself carefully closed in my room, where a supper, something like tea and coffee, boiled beef and mashed potatoes with few slices of bread, wait for me, all as cold as ice cream can be.

Early Spring, 1922. *Charlestown Prison*
DEAR MRS. EVANS:

Your welcome letter of the 27th Feb. was received. My delay in answering was due to causes indipendent to my will. I was very beneficiated by your last visit and English-lesson. In a letter received tonight, one Friend tells me that my English is not perfect. I am still laughing for such a pious euphension. Why do not say horrible? Nevertheless, I can made a better translation than the one in argument. I did it as I did for an experiment, to prove if an almost letterally translation is intelligible. I show it to some friends, asking them if they understand it. The answer was "yes," while it should have been "no," that I might have remade the work with much profit and better result.

Of course, as the writing is beautiful in its original, and as I labored very much at the dictionary, so I was thinking to have accomplished something worth, and the disillution was, as almost all disillatin, rather cruel. But when a poor one is surrounded by many great difficulties, the small ones appear always a joke to him, and after your visit I found myself in the best of the mood—that is, I was decided to do in the future as much more good than the much bad I did in the past.

I analized attentively the original—it is almost impossible intellectual pleasure—which for hours has made me forget myself, the cell, and the others sorrowy things.

I am reading an English prose translation of *Gitanzaly* by Rabindranath Tagore. Except the beauty of language, the wonderful style and grammatical correctness, there is nothing new, nothing of unknown in it. Of course, great sentiments, sensibility; a liric panteistic feeling of the great mystery of which we are a part. But nothing else.

I value more the natural sciences that give us little but positive knowledge—which teaches better than anything else the great epic wrote in every square inch of the universe. Emotions and sentiments are maibe the greatest part of life, but too often, when alone, they lead mankind astray. Not a word in all these Tagore's beautiful poetries about social problems. Maibe a remote, so to say, incitation to freedom. But what one? He do not mention it. So his words maibe use by the Indian Patriots to excite the Indian masses against the actual, principal oppressor: England. But it would be a useless consummation, for India, with her cast of nobles and of priests, is simply criminal. Nor her people will enjoy peace and health before to annihilate this great social injustice and shame.

Otherwise we Italians know from tragic experiences the results of the Fatherland Indipendence. After half century of such a bless, we are now facing this terrible dilemma, to throw down every things and re-build upon other bases, or die. I suppose that you are informed of the present conditions of my native land. I know the details; they are horrible.

I am sorry for Nick [Sacco]. After a serious consideration I decide to not do the hunger strike now, although I am ready to recur at the hungry strike if and when it would seem reasonable to me.

Today the sun is glorious, and my cell more lighten and my heart more glad than the usual. The same I hope of and wish to you.

April 13, 1922. *Charlestown Prison*

DEAR MR. BIGELOW:[1]

Last week I received *Vita Nuova* of Dante, that you sent to me. One could not be more fortunate than you in the selection of a book present, because I al-

[1] Francis H. Bigelow of Cambridge, Mass.

ways wished some secondary works of that great man. But, apart from the high estimation that I have in the teaching value of the book, your intentions give to it an inestimable value.   In fact, a man in your condition, that spends and works for his sympathy and solidariety to a man in my condition, can only be moved by noble feeling and good-will.   The fact that I have not the pleasure of knowing you personally, so adds to the agreeableness of your gift.

I hope I will yet be free, thanks to the generous solidariety of the many, but, anyhow, I will conserve zealously your book, as I do with the many other books and correspondence.   If I have to die for a crime I never committed, I will send all these things to my father and sisters and brothers, sure that they will be much consolated.

December 25, 1922. Charlestown Prison

DEAR MRS. EVANS:

I was in thought for you, because I do not receive your missives.   Your silence had made me fear of something wrong.   I am glad after having learnt that it was due only to your work, saint work.   I wish to you the sweetest rest, and may your good actions be spring of life for you as they are for others.   I have also almost finish the reading of Mr. James' first volumes.[1]

With affection your Bartolo.

1 William James's *Psychology.*

December, 1922. Charlestown Prison

Dear Friend Bigelow:

Your long silence is always broken up by the presence of *Vita Nuova.* So, while toiling and thinking for answers to the many who, at this conventional date, had written me, I remembered you, and decided to write.

When one has passed through a trial as mine, and, amid such sorrows has had the comfort of such vast and deep human solidariety; when one has a principle, (liberty)—and at his side all the believers of liberty, and against him all the supporters of the tyranny, for him mankind is divided into two legions, and he loves as himself those who stand with him for the good cause. I think more, you have proved to be one of those of good-will. For this reason, I send to you in this tragic dreadful hour, the senses of my faith and of my gratitude.

April 14, 1923. *Charlestown Prison*

Dear Comrade Blackwell: [1]

. . . . The really and great damage that the fascism has done, or has revealed, is the moral lowness in which we have fallen after the war and the revolutionary over-excitation of the last few years.

It is incredible the insult made to the liberty, to the life, to the dignity of the human beings, by other human beings. And it is humiliating, for he who feels

---

[1] Alice Stone Blackwell of Boston, Mass.

the common humanity that ties together all the men, good and bad, to think that all the committed infamies have not produced in the crowd an adequate sense of rebellion, of horrors, of disgust. It is humiliating to human beings, the possibility of such ferocity, of such cowardness. It is humiliating that men, who have reached the power only because, deprived of any moral or intellectual scrupols, they has known how to pluck the good moment to blackmail the "*borgesia*," may find the approbation, no matter if by a momentary abberration, of a number of persons sufficient to impose upon all countries their tyranny.

Therefore, the rescue expected and invocated by us must be before all a moral rescue; the re-valuation of the human liberty and dignity. It must be the condamnation of the Fascismo not only as a political and economic fact, but also and over all, as a criminal phenomenum, as the exploitation of a purulent growth which had been going, forming and ripening itself in the sick body of the social organism.

There are some, also among the so-called subversives, who are saying that the fascisti have taught to us how we must do, and they, these subversives, are intentioned to imitate and to exacerbate the fascisti methods.

This is the great danger, the danger of the to-morrow; the danger, I mean, that, after the Fascismo, declined from internal dissolution or by external attack, may have to follow a period of insensate violences, of sterile vendettes, which would exhaust in little episodes of blood that energy which should be employed for a radical transformation of the social arrangements such to render impossible the repetition of the present horrors.

The Fascisti's methods may be good for who inspires to *become a tyrant*. They are certainly bad for he who will make "opera" of a liberator, for he who will collaborate to rise all humanity to a dignity of free and conscient men.

We remain as always we were, the partisans of the liberty, of all the liberty.

I hope you will agree my bad translation of Malatesta's words. They are words of one of the most learned, serene, courageous and powerful mind, among the minds of the sons of women through the whole history, and of a magnanimous heart.

May 6, 1923. Charlestown Prison

DEAR COMRADE HILLSMITH: [1]

The reasons for my delay are many; but the principle ones are two. I expected to go to the court the 30th of April, and consequently, I have worked much in collaboration of our abdomadari [weekly],[2] which, I am glad to say, acquire continually more readers, and steadily grows better and better. The second, and more serious reason is, that your two letters are very contradictory to and against my personal opinions, beliefs, criterion and principles. They have provoked my Italian and my partisan impulses—my passion. So

---

[1] Mrs. Elsie Hillsmith, Ragged Hill Farms, South Danbury, N. H.

[2] Vanzetti wrote frequently during this period for an anarchist weekly, *L'Adunata dei Refrattari*, published in New York City.

I decided to wait for calm and serenity before to answer.

The price to perfection is high, sorrowful. I suffered more in making my conscience, than in facing my trial. I am a bitter polemist, a merciless theorist, and I know to cause to others much anguish. With my letters upon "Syndicalism," I am actually causing sorrow to many. The same comrade to whom these letters are dedicated, has written to me, "Your opinions upon the syndicalism are unjust." But he does not produce a single fact or reason in behalf of his affirmation; while one of the most intelligent and learned comrades in his article, "What shall we expect from another Anarchist Congress," has shown many facts that prove the veridicity of my assertion; he has said also what I intend to say in my 4th and conclusive letter on the topic.

Undoubtedly, the words that I am writing will disturb you, will cause your heart to ache. But, would you prefer my insincerity to my sincerity? To be sincere is not only my duty toward myself, my fellowmen, and my Cause, but it is also the only way that I have to not repay your love, benefits, and sincerity with deceiveness and villancy.

Of course, we Anarchists are so because we differ in opinions from all the other humans who are not Anarchists. All the enemies of the workers and of the human emancipation, when they speak to masses in order to vilify us, and keep the workers under exploitation of the capitalists, they tell the masses not to let the handed false doctrine influence their mind. The deceit of bad shepherds among the workers, and the ignorance of the masses, has induced many sincerely but inexperienced friends of the workers to believe that we, proletarian vanguard of the Revolution, are mystified by false mirages and doctrines inoculated to our mind by the ill-intentioned propaganda of more educated rascals, propaganda blindly accepted. In verity, among us, those who blindly accept the propaganda does not exist. Why? Because we Anarchists; we, Peter Kropotkin, M. Bakunin, E. Reclus, L. Galleani, P. Gori, E. Malatesta, have been born in Prince's palaces, or in good mansions, and grown up in the Imperial Court, have been educated in the best colleges; we thought the same things that our enemies of the same social conditions thought; we have believed in the same things, acted the same acts.

And we humble worker Anarchists have been grown up without the confortation of the school, in poor houses, over working and suffering from the birth day on, we have done and believed as our enemy workers have done, believed and lived. We were as our enemies and adversaries are. Only by an incessant mental work, a long and terrible trial of conscience, we became different, as now we are. That is, we have analized, condemned, repudiated all conceptions, beliefs, the criterions and the principles that were inculcated in us from our infancy until the day of the beginning of our conviction.

I also believe that man has the faculty of reasoning, but that he can only exercise it upon what he can perceive, and by the way that he perceives. One cannot think in a language ignored by him. This is the cause of all the errors.

Now, I will begin to expose my divergent conviction upon your opinions. I have read the Bible and recognize some merits, but I believe wholly irrational to base upon it our works and hopes. I not only disagree from the global view and criterions of your letters, but it seems to me that they are self-contradictory, and that many natural and social phenomena are entirely left apart by you,—also incomplete and wrong.

This is why I decided not to enter into a discussion before these explanatory words, and the answer of the following questions: Are you contrary or in favor of the Anarchistic view and aim?—of a real physical equality in ownership, in rights and duties among the human beings? Did you mean to possess, relatively and humanly speaking, the whole truth and reason? If it would that humans should be compelled to the violence either for justice or for injustice, then would you approve those who would use the violence against the violence that compel them to be unjust and violent? Did you ever study Kropotkin, Reclus, Bakunin, Proudhon, or Tolstoy and compare their doctrines with those of liberals or authoritary Socialists?

[Unfinished]

Summer, 1923. *Charlestown Prison*

MY DEAR FRIEND MRS. EVANS:

Few days ago I received your two gladining post-cards, the more beauty of which told me of your intention to send me some shells. So I waited to have received them before to answer at your good words and better deeds.

I look more at your post cards, specially to that of the surf. Its colors glad my eyes and give me a sense of freshness. I will tack it on the wall of my room. That day I received four others post-cards; three of them are photographies of the farm of our Comrade Hillsmith. An Mapple wood; an old sleigh and strong man that take care of the farm; and two white horses attached to a sledge upon which is fixed a big barrel for the mapple syrup. The fourth one is not less original but much more rare to be seen: A Russian farm, under a tree the family eating the dinner, not at a table but upon the grass; a nice scene!

You said that you would like to have me help you to work in the garden. I would like to do it. I am not an expert gardener—but I think that you are so; and would it be possible, you would know what a worker I am, and what a garden I will plant and work out under your advice joined to some of my critersims. You would also know what a lighted heart the rough Bartolomeo has. In spite of all, I often feel yet as a child. I like to sing, to play and to foolish. But indeed, the water is rough now. Maibe, thanks to all the good ones, among whom you are prominent, we will reach the shore someday.

Summer, 1923. *Charlestown Prison*

DEAR MRS. EVANS:

I have so many things that I would like to tell you. I would like to tell you of me, of Italy, of my family, comrades, and so forth for hundred and more pages. But I send you the more hight and warmest sentiments. I hope that you are well, that the Ocean, the Sun, the great out of door, are giving to you all their treasures, so much and well merited.

Gratefully your friend forever,

BARTOLOMEO

August 26, 1923. *Charlestown Prison*

MY DEAR FRIEND: [1]

Your "special delivery" of yesterday noon has reached me the same evening, at the usual hour of mail distribution. . . .

Very well, I will read and give my opinion of *Mind in the Making.* [2] Thanks for this too.

No style is more agreeable to me than the simplest one. For this I love Reclus and Malatesta, and was delighted of the first volume of William James. (I have not read the second volume of James' psycology.) . . .

As I told you, I received five of my papers. Three

---

[1] Mrs. Virginia MacMechan of Sharon, Mass., who gave Vanzetti English instruction during much of the first six years of his imprisonment.

[2] *The Mind in the Making,* by James Harvey Robinson.

are of our "Assembly of the Refractary"[1] printed in New York, weekly. One is a special number; that of a manifesto in form of a journal, issued in behalf of the Italian Political Prisoner, and the fifth is *The Defense* printed in Paris, by our comrades in defense of Nick and me. From yesterday noon to early this morning, I read them all. Just imagine what it would be, for a man confined in a miasmatic, muddy swamp, to feel at once his chains loose and freely walk toward the summits, to dive in the first stream of living waters, and then proceed, surrounded and deluged by sun and winds, height and height, and drink at the alpine springs and reach the highest summit, and from there dominate the immense vista of lands, waters and sky. The same it was for me the lecture of these papers. Oh, friend, the anarchism is as beauty as a woman for me, perhaps even more since it include all the rest and me and her. Calm, serene, honest, natural, viril, muddy and celestial at once, austere, heroic, fearless, fatal, generous and implacable—all these and more it is. . . .

September 6, 1923. Charlestown Prison

DEAR FRIEND [VIRGINIA MACMECHAN]:

Osanna! Yes, it seem a long time since I have received letters from a friend of whose friendship I am sure and sorry for his silence. But now that I am regreting for the cause of it—I am content that you have done just what I like you to do in such circumstances.

---

[1] *L'Adunata dei Refrattari.*

A player of golf and of tennis, friend of mine! It is as a reconciliation of the *diavolo* with the holy water! Indeed, I never thought such a thing possible—but it is. *Pazienza.* Few years ago, when I fancy this world as a colleges of rascality, I used to look upon such players with the most stern and terrible of my glances. But now, [that I] experience the devine candor of their world, well now, I look upon them in a different position.

Do you know that I never lose the joy of that vagabond freedom of working and living in the open. There was a guitar too, and many pipes, and when I was tired of disperated effort to sing as a tenor, I used to indulge in those minor echos which, in case of waltzes run as follows,—um pa pa—um pa pa, and so on. Well, fulishness apart, that was life, and then I learned something that cannot be learned in the school.

So thank you very much for the vision that your description revives in my mind. The need of divagation is, I believe a natural need—which may not be subrogated by the work—viceversa it is envigorated by the work. All of your letters make me think what unnatural, irrational and foolish life mankind is living today, and how little the many who presume to be at the vanguard understand this fact.

When you were here the last time, I was just over one of the most fierce organic reaction against disintegration.

Did you read *My Prisons* [1] by Silvio Pellico? If you

[1] *Le Mie Prigioni.*

read it, you know what he passed through. Such physical suffering happen, less or more, to every one, accordingly with his constitution and environments. That is what sure those who survive. . . .

October 3, 1923. *Charlestown Prison*

DEAR MRS. JACK:[1]

Few days ago Nick and I have received a big basket of beautiful and savorous peaches from you; and another basket last evening.

I remember to have received other fruit from you during the first trial. Nick told me of your goodness toward us—(and not he alone.)

I was also told, last Spring, by a good friend, the beauty of your fruit orchard in bloom. And now I enjoy what those flowers have ripened; and it is indeed providential since our appetite is not very sharp—and the prison food not very good.

These fruits also remember to me the home's garden. At the time I lived there this kind of peaches was very little known. I remember when my father planted the first tree of this kind, in my garden. I tasted few of its fruit before to left my native place. So, if you will consider that these, your fruits, give me life, remember me the most loved place—and prove to me (in this black hour, second only, in sorrow, to that of my mother's death) the sympathy and friendship of you—you may realize, in a way—how I appre-

[1] Mrs. Cerise Jack of Sharon, Mass., who gave Sacco English lessons in the winter of 1923-24.

ciate your present. But you have sent to many. I still have some of the first basket (though I must confess to have gave some of them to some unfortunate youths.)

So, while I pray you to not send any more fruit to me, I also pray you to accept my hearty thanks, wishes and regards.

October 4, 1923. *Charlestown Prison*

DEAR MR. THOMSOMP: [1]

I cannot help but write these few words to express you my gratitude and ammiration for the your masterly battle in behalf of my life and of my liberty (which I love more than the life itself). I have refrained from attest pubblicly my sentiments because of my actual condiction, and the difference between you and me, of social condiction. In spite of all I would have congratulated you, yesterday evening, were not because I was indignated by the villain conducts of the Court's guards toward a very respectable lady,—generous friend of us.

Today, one brother of a Bostonian lawyer has told me: "My brother said that Mr. Thomsomp is perhaps the most able lawyer of Boston to present a case to the Supreme Court."

I feel positive that if we have knew you from the

---

[1] Mr. William G. Thompson of the Boston Bar who became counsel on March 8, 1923, for the special purpose of arguing motions for a new trial based upon exposures which came to light after the verdict, affecting the misconduct of some of the jurors. He, joined later by Mr. Herbert B. Ehrmann, took over the entire legal defense of the two men on November 25, 1924.

beginning of this shame, at this time we would have
been fred.

I beg you, Mr. Thomsomp, to excuse my poor English, and accept my gratitude.

October 15, 1923. Charlestown Prison

DEAR FRIEND [VIRGINIA MACMECHAN]:

I will as soon as possible write again, and more extensively to you.   I will try to make more clear and
spontaneous those two periods.   Meanwhile, I beg
you to reconstruct them as you see more fit.

This evening I have received an answer letter from
E. Debs, plus some writings and his picture.   There is
a beautiful fragment of his speech on "Liberty."   I
am touched by, and shamely glad for his words and unmerited praises.

Now, I must tell you the two principle causes of my
pedantic style.   One is my not at all blessing ignorance
of the genius and of the dictionary of your language.
The other is that we, Italians, have an old phraseology
. . . which did not pass through similar historic events
of our nation.   Beside that, words of Latin and of
Greek origin are familiar to my native language, while
I ignore almost all those words of Nordic origin which
form the most of your language.   Some men here are
surprised of my understanding of the "big words" and
of my ignorance of the common ones.

But I will do my best to learn this language, and
your teaching is providential.   I will learn it and you

will see the gradual changing and improvement of my style. And if it even will happen, that I will find the good time to write a novel—it would be a paean. . . .

Of course the style of Voltaire is wonderful as his condition. I will never reach it. But anyhow, his style is that of a man that strike an old injustice. That of Marat was the style of a man that strike the old, the present, and all possible injustice. And the style of Marat I should prefer were I not determined to have one of mine own. As for the living man, I believe that Galleani is the strongest writer—I knew a little the best editors of several nations—they are gnomes when compared to him. This is not wholly a result of faculties, but also the consequence of the "better cause which make the better ones."

Now let me thank you for your visit, and accept my hearty wishes and regards.

Congratulations to your mother, to you, to Romolo, to the maid, and why not? to myself—since I feel better and better.

November 12, 1923. *Dedham Jail*

DEAR MRS. JACK:

The hearing [1] is over and, before to go back at Charlestown I wish to thank you for your presence at the court room, because I attribute a great value to it, in our behalf, and also, because I was glad.

Please give my regards to Mr. Jack.

[1] Hearing of arguments for a new trial based upon the testimony of gun experts.

Fall, 1923. *Charlestown Prison*

COMRADE PETTYJOHN:[1]

. . . . I appreciate everything that is done in behalf of the Russian People and Revolution. But surely, Anna Louise Strong is wrong if she believes in the progress of that revolution. The bolshevik government is giving up to the international capitalism, all Russia's natural resources, land, mine, forests, fishery, wells. The Russian workers shall work for the State and the foreign Company. It is disinherited by the revolution of its means of life. Surely the returning of the capitalistic system and the filtration of the foreign capital has brought to Russia a transitory, apparent emilioration, but it shall be paid at usury. Yet, the revolution has done and is doing, even in its failure, a great deal of good to this poor world, nor are the Bolsheviks guilty for all its evils. To be sure. But to speak of such an event in a letter, is almost tantalizing. It cannot be well done. Just for an example: the cooperatives. In a capitalist nation, the workers' cooperatives—with socialistic and revolutionary spirit and aims, are to be looked on, and helped as an embryo of a new world. But in Russia, now that she is returning by the joined forces of other governments and of the international capital, how can the cooperative deeds and spirits compete, overwhelm such preponderant forces, and become a preponderant historical factor? Kropotkin has intended to organize and revive the Russian Co-operatives at the beginning

[1] Maude Pettyjohn of Dayton, Wash.

of the revolution when it was possible to mold them in higher manifestations, but he was forbidden by the government.

I received a letter from our K—— D—— about a month ago. Yes, she has had a sorrowful life, and now is alone, poor, and not in good health. It seems as if god solace himself in torturing the better and good creatures. As far as I can see, if there is such a thing as "the god's justice," it is not better than the men's justice. My heart rebels and bleeds at such things as these. . . .

I see that you are really and deeply convinced in re-birth and in all of such doctrines. It may be true, and you have all the right of your beliefs, which may sooth and console the anguish of this poor life of ours. I only know that I do not know, that I cannot believe any of the many religious beliefs which came under my mind's eyes. Yet, I am a great mystic and I can't get along without any faith. I can laugh to all the evil, worship all the good, accept whatever destiny the imponderable shall impose upon me. Yet, using all my capacities and will for what might seem to be right. . . .

Winter, 1923. Charlestown Prison

DEAR MRS. EVANS:

When the hour given for a visit is past I feel to have more to say than at the beginning of it, and so it happen that I think always a long time upon what was left to be said.

Undoubtedly the great sources of Russian Revolution troubles are of extern origin; others of natural origin by which man's power is overwhelmed; but some must be in the nature of all those human acts which constitute a Revolution. I fear, I am rather almost sure that a great sabotage is practiced against the new order. Now, the only way to be victorious is to eliminate the cause which determined any hostil deed against the revolution. The confidence of the [Russian] people in a violent punishment [against the rest of the world], operated by a new constitutional force, is such a folly that lead to an abyss; and the best result of a revolution, I mean that mental and moral improvement that every real worthy revolution should operate over the people, will so be destroyed.

But many things one could say about this subject, and besides, the work of the critic is always the easy one: so I return on the old subject "Morals." Man call moral everything that is favorable to conservation of life, to happiness of the individual, as well of the race, and these things are virtues and justice. For this reason, I cannot believe in those philosophers, who speaking of morals, tell me about a categoric order, a revelation, an abstract principle, and so on.

For me, the moral sense come from the strongest instincts of every living being. I mean the instincts of conservation and happiness, which as soon as the intelligence come, generates a third instinct, the love of the race. As soon as any intelligent creatures begin a social life they are compelled to social duties: hence the notion of what is just and what is unjust, of what is good and what is evil. So, we can say that morals, as well as everything else made by man, has the purpose of conservation and happiness. That is why he who said that the fundamental nature of morals do not change, was right, and that is the reason why men breaks a moral relation to anythings or person as soon he stops believeing in their goodness and justice. And this is why every new idea that mark a progress has in itself a superior moral.

What Kropotkin said in his Anarchist Moral: "Do to others what you would wish that the others should do to you, in the same circumstances," can be the basis of the morals. Of course, many comrades had criticised him, but my little I, believe him very near to the reason. Nothing new in this, save a little modification which not only command to not do unjust things, but command also to do good. And this is progress. Every normal persons can be in accord.

The trouble and the differences begin when the moral values of our present institutions, of our social contract, of our customs are put in discussion. And more complications arise when we treat of details of the life, of the relativeness and absoluteness of it, because we all are individual, and, what is more important, determined creatures leaded in life by an influence of our personal life, amid a perpetual conflict between the mind and the heart.

But we have instincts that lead us, and intelligence that serves them, and after all, a nature fundamentally equal. Those things would be enough if man would not be susceptible of degeneration, as soon as he left his natural way of life. Here we face a gigantic problem; not a letter but a book will be necessary to resolve or better to prospect it.

Before concluding, I put to myself a question, and answer to it. What is the good, and what is the evil? Till now from the greatest luminaries to the last dagoes wandering over the land, the idea is "All what help me is the good, all the rest is the evil." It is as Gorki said about the moral of the savage, and it run as follows: "If I steal the wife of my neighbor that is the good; if my neighbor steals my wife that is the evil." To be exact there are many and enough of moral principles abstractly true, but they are vitiated by their application.

The anarchist go ahead and says: All what is help to me without hurt the others is good; all what help the others without hurting me is good also, all the rest is evil. He look for his liberty in the liberty of all, for his happiness in the happiness of all, for his welfare in the universal welfare. I am with him.

Well, I perceive I have been very incomplete and inexact in my words, but, there are no pretention in them. They arise out of the intention of reveal my thought and exercising in English language. I begun to read the bible!

Winter, 1923. Charlestown Prison

DEAR MRS. EVANS:

In my opinion the umane afflictions caused by umane faults are due, not so much for lack of morals sense, but to use wrong application of it. The sentiment of justice too can become a source of injustice when wrong.

The crusaids for example, were possible by the explotation of religious sentiment and love of freedom proper to individuals and collectivities. Most of the umble tools of the "Inquisition" believed to be fair with their victims because by thus torturing the bodies they will safe the souls of them.

Still today the umble justify punishment as necessary to check crimes. Indeed some so-called educated confess such belief, but not in good faith. This subject seem to be endless and tempt me to write something about it.

Your idea of the government is the one of every good people believing in it. I am for free towns administered directly by their citozins.

After reading many critics of government, the writings of Spencer, Stirner, Kropotkin, Reclu, Bovio and others, I wish very much to read the critics of the state made by the ancient Chinese, Greek and Roman philosopher. But after much reflection I tend to believe that the critics of the ancient must not differ much from those of the modern.

Last evening I read a chapter of the *Psychology* [by William James]. I perceive at once to deal with a really great one. He speak with simplicity as Reclu and others did. I will learn a good deal from this lecture. I feel the fever of knowledge in me.

Mr. A. Brisbane always trouble me. Several months ago I read in a book of physical culture, that to sit down is an unhealthy habit and that the more one stand the better he feel. I like to feel well and consequently I took the advice. But today Mr. A. Brisbane tell me that the more we lay down the better it is. So I do not know now what I have to do for my good health. Till now I used to read on my feet, more often leaning like an elephant against the wall; from now I will maibe sit down. Of course, the best way to prevent diseases and troubles to a man is kill him while he feel well.

Winter, 1923. Charlestown Prison

MY DEAR FRIEND MRS. EVANS:

Yesterday I wrote practically all the day long and finished the novel. [1] My other teacher, Mrs. V. M. M., has criticise a little my "pedantic way of writing." I told her that it is not due to pretentions of any sort, but simply and purely by my "blessing ignorance of the English language." Now I wish to finish a treatise on "Syndicates and Syndicalism," in Italian and before the hearing. I have obtained the promotion to work in the yard, and already feel much better.

This evening I have received a letter from our great sublime E. Debs. I am touched by his goodness and greatness. Proud, even if little ashamed of his friendship, appreciation and praises.

I am feeling better and better, and I wish and hope that this letter will find you in the best of conditions.

---

[1] *Events and Victims*, a story by Vanzetti of his experiences in a munitions factory at Springfield, Mass., before this country entered the war.

December 2, 1923. *Charlestown Prison*

MY DEAR BRINIS:

It is quite a long time that I wish to write to you, but many little contrary things has till now frustrated my intention. So, I hope you will forgive to me the long silence. I have received your letters and, lately, the two post-cards, very nice and appreciated.

I am glad to be able to tell you that I have reported a good impression of the last hearing, especially of Mr. Thompson and Mr. Hamilton. Mr. Thompson is a quick and penetrating intelligence, a tongue wonderful. With few words he was able to destroy the elaborated sophistry, the mixing and twisting to make a truth seem a lie, or a lie seem a truth, of Mr. Katzmann [and] of his worth successor, Mr. Williams. At least I have had the moral satisfaction to see my framers unmasked, called liars—as they are. As soon as I saw Messrs. Thompson and Hill at work and the difference between them and the others, I realized of the principal reason of our condamnation. Mr. Katzmann, helped by Thayer, may always when he please, in a case of such nature, deceit twelve good men of Norfolk's or Plymouth's County and induce them to find guilty an innocent,—if in his defense [the latter] does not have men who do not fear and are able to analize and reveal to the jury the lies and the inconsistence of the prosecuters. Would we have had Mr. Thompson at the first trial, we would have been in the open long ago. And I hope that, no matter how this farce may end, that this bitter experience will not have been in vain.

Mr. Hamilton [1] seems to be a competent theenic. He discovered that one State's picture was little more smaller than the others—and that another set of pictures was taken with the light extremely at the one side, so that the black and narrow shadow at the opposite side was very liable to be taken for a scratch. Mr. Hamilton is sure of his affirmations and measurements, and he told us strong words of confidence and of victory.

But with all this, Mr. Thayer can use indiscretionally his discretional power and answer as he likes. Therefore, excessive optimism would not be a wise thing—after the conduct of this man during the two trials.

I dislike to vilify human being and would be more than glad, happy, if he, by a just act, would compel me to change my opinion—but there is no reasons till now.

I am very well and strong. I work outside, read, write and study as always, and sing too.

I also saw and spoke with many friends; am confident and determined to win.

So my dears, be of good cheer and strong heart—I love the courageous—those who know to banish the black and sorrowful thought. To know my friends and my loved ones brave—is the sweetest to my soul.

Give my hearty regards to all my friend and their

---

[1] Albert H. Hamilton of Auburn, N. Y., gun expert for the defense.

family—to the Plymouth folks. Kisses to the little ones, and a train of good thought to all of you.

With great heart, yours,

January 7, 1924. Charlestown Prison

DEAR COMRADE BLACKWELL:

Your first letter of 1924 brought me proudness and gladness. Thank you and good health and victory to you for all the 1924 and many others years, that you deserve life and its goodness, and we need you.

When you speak of Mazzini, you spark with life. I am glad that he happened to be born where I was born. Nature knows not the artificial bounderies and divisions made up by the stupidity and greedness of mankind to afflict herself. Nature bestows her gifts freely to her creature. Even in genious the people are equivalent. But the humble are kept ignorant of other people's virtues and poisoned with absurd conceiveness of themselves, by those who speculate in patriotism. We children of the heart, citizens and members of all the countries and of the Race—ought to toil in order to illuminate the humble of the unity of the Race. The bounderies shall fall. . . .

I am very grateful to you for the beautiful post card. I never get tired looking at it. It reminds me of my native place. The old shepherd's white hair reminds me of my grand-father. He was just like this man. And everytime I look upon this scene, my heart is gladdened. . . .

January 24, 1924. Charlestown Prison

DEAR COMRADE BLACKWELL:

Your letter of the 19th reached me at proper time. Lately I received a copy of our dear Friend Evans' pamphlets in the rear of which I have read your comment on Sacco and Vanzetti, and thank you very much for it. Each word of the narration is the truth. It sounds bitter because it is bitter, and we must be heroic with the truth, the only Liberator. I forget if I wrote in the narration that I remember a time in which the bosses used to spit upon the feet of the work-seekers. Then it was necessary to present ones self with unbuttoned shirts, because they wanted to see what one was like, they wanted to see the hair on the chest of the worker, and good for me that I am a Latin with haired chest. They used to say: "You are too small—you are too old." . . . Otherwise all false, that is the way thing grow worse instead of growing better. The fools are told by the deceiver that fire destroys—Fire purifies and represents life—it does not destroy.

I am writing a letter to Judge Thayer. The first part of it dealing with the first trial, is ready, both in English and in Italian languages. It is written for the world. The second part will deal with the Dedham trial. It will sound greasy and sacrilegious because it voices the truth, which to be such must be wholly and not fractional. But I do not care, because I disdain the greasiness of the wisdom and the profanity of the official sacredness which have cursed the passed centuries and are dooming mankind. If there is still life and little of good in it, both exist in spite of the so-called wisdom and sacredness. And I do not fear the consequences of my utterances. I am in their hands, let them crucify me, if it fitted them. It is in these conditions that I am now that I like to take my ground and assume my responsibilities—no matter how dreadful.

Each period of my letter is an axe or a mace when not a wedge—but always the truth. It seems to be my destiny to wrestle continually against the wrong, the errs, the unjust, the half truths more fatal than a whole false.

Once, a dear Friend, anarco-syndicalist, wrote me a letter on anarchy and syndicalism. Hence my essays in epistolar form on *Syndicate and Syndicalism.* Seven letters on the topic are already written and published. Two or three letters will be written to close the argument. My friend was shaked, his heart teared by the truth—but he wrote to me "you are deep on such matters—write, write, I dream of your idea and when you will come out we will beat one another." And my comrade also said "Write, write, in spite of all what was said, the syndicalist have not yet said what they are and many who call themselves anarchists, do not know what anarchy means." But believe me Comrade Blackwell, it is love that moves my lips— that makes me speak.

Lenin has passed away. I am convinced that unintentionally he has ruined the Russian Revolution. He has imprisoned and killed many of my comrades. And yet, he has suffered much, toiled heroically for what he believed to be the good and the truth and I felt my eyes filled with tears in reading of his passing and his funeral.

And to the prostitute scribes of the capitalist system, who are twisting and falsifying facts and truths, and throwing the mud of their miserable souls on the fresh grave of my great adversary—I roar with a mute gesture all my disgust and contempt.

Now I close because I wish to write to my sister this evening.

February 27, 1924. *Charlestown Prison*

DEAR COMRADE BLACKWELL:

Yours of the 23rd has reached me. You are right. Neither do I expect any good from that letter to the judge. I have never expected, nor do I expect anything from him, other than some ten thousand volts divided in few times; some meters of cheap board and 4x7x8 feet hole in the ground.

No matter how much sympathy I try to bestow upon him, or with how much understanding I try to judge his actions; I only and alone can see him a self-conceited narrow-minded little tyrant, believing himself to be just, and believing his utterly unjust and unnecessary social office to be a necessity and a good. He is a bigot, and therefore, cruel. At the time of our arrest and trials, his peers were seeing red all around, and he saw red more than his peers.

He was ready to kill us even before the trials, for he deadly hates the subversive, and he believed to have become judge of the State Supreme Court by eliminating us via Law. For he knows that the servants of Capital were always remunerated by the Bosses for a crusifixion of some rebel or lover.

I do not know if his conduct during the trial was determined by his preconceptions, hate and ignorance, or if he consciously murdered us by details of bad faith, double playing, simulation, etc. I know that he did it. I know that even now he does not want to give us another trial though he could not deny it. And this is why he delays so much to give the answer. . . .

And if I am wrong, if according to his own standard, he is fair; if he wishes to be just, ('til now he is very unjust) then he could be hurt by my letter, but also enlightened. And if he would not forgive the crude defence of a man extremely wronged, then, not even a sparrow would I submit to him as arbiter.

An almost centenial struggle against every form of exploitation, oppression and fraud, taught us that "the wolf eats him who makes himself a sheep."

I am not sure, but I believe, that there are no pamphlets in Italian language, which treat with detail the case. This is the second reason of my letter and the 3rd reason is, my wish to say what no one else can say—silence would be cowardness—and treat the case accordingly to my own criterions. This may hurt me, but will help the Cause. Otherwise, if it means a life sentence, I prefer to be burnt away once and for all, and I also know that those in height, upon the back and the heads of the slaves, are against me. . . .

There is no spirit of sacrifice in this deed. I simply realize to be in merciless hands, and do my utmost to say to my enemy that he is wrong. In a way that helps the cause. The great one, not the small. My only hope remains in the solidariety of friends and comrades and of the workers. After having spent $200,000, we are still at the beginning. The work of the lawyers are useless before the law.

It has helped only because they brought the fact to the conscience and consciousness of the People. That is why Nick and I were not yet roasted. Authority, Power, and Privilege would not last a day upon the face of the earth, were it not because those who possess them, and those who prostitute their arms to their defence do suppress, repress, mercilessly and inescapable every efforts of liberations of each and all the rebels.

I abhor useless violence. I would my blood to prevent the sheading of blood, but neither the abyss nor the earth, nor the heavens, have a law which condemns the self-defense. Not every woman has sacrificed to bring forth one more rufian, idiot, or coward to the world. There are yet some men. And if tragedy is compelled to us, who knows; who knows if to speak now is not my duty?

The champion of life and of the liberty should not yield before the death. The struggle for the liberty, between the oppressor and the oppressed, shall continue beyond the life, beyond the graves. I know what they have done and are doing to me and to thousands of others, rebels and lovers. And I know that they are and will always be ready to do against us. I know the millions of youth that they slandered, the virgins that

they have torn in the breast; the millions of wives
that they have widowed; the millions of bastards that
they let to miasma of the gutter, or grown to the
fratricide. I know the old fathers and mothers whom
they killed by breaking their hearts; and all the children that they starved and are starving to death; and
the hospitals and the crazy-houses filled of their victims, and the little criminals, victims, irresponsible and
semi-compelled to crime that they mercilessly executed
or entombed alive. They have never had pity for our
children, our women, our dear, poor old fathers and
mothers—and they never will have it.

The sorrow of their victims torture me in blood and
spirit. As for me, I would forgive them, but I could
not, for I would be a traitor of the race. Until not
a man will be exploited or oppressed by another man,
we will never bend the banner of freedom.

Are they not ready to do with other comrades what
they are doing to us? Are they not more willing than
ever to squeeze out the worker's blood for more gold?
Are they not preparing a greater war?

I will ask for revenge—I will tell that I will die
gladly by the hands of the hanger after having known
to have been vindicated. I mean "eye for an eye, ear
for an ear," and even more, since to win it is necessary
that 100 enemies fall to each of us.

The only vengence which could placate me is the
realization of freedom, the great deliverance which
would beneficiate all my friends as well as all my enemies: All. But till that, the struggle goes on, til we
are breath to breath with the enemy fighting with

short arms, till then, to fight is our duty, our right, our necessity. For, one of the two. Either we must go on and win, or we must ask for an armistice. And who will grant it to us? Since the enemy has no scruples nor pity, to ask pity of him is to encourage him to slander our fellows, to try to grant to him the immunity for his crimes against us; it would be as a matricide.

The more I live, the more I suffer, the more I learn, the more I am inclined to forgive, to be generous, and that the violence as such does not resolve the problem of life. And the more I love and learn that "the right of all to violence does not go together with the liberty, but that it begins when the liberty ends." The slave has the right and duty to arise against his master. My supreme aim, that of the Anarchist is, "the complete elimination of violence from the rapports (relations)."

To be possible, we must have freedom and justice. Now we have the opposite of them, because through errors and consequent aberations, men have risen as tyrants, deceiters and exploiters of other men, believing to gain their personal, familiar and cast welfare by such deed. Through both tyranny and servitude, we have lost our capacity of liberty and we are making life evermore miserable, operating our own ante-distruction.

Since "only the liberty, or the struggle for liberty, may be school of liberty" and since mine is but self and racial defence, why should not I use the truth to defend myself? It is supremely sweet to me—my consciousness of superiority, of righteousness, to know that I can judge and that the future shall bow to me, the doomed, and curse my judges.

Well, I have said many things which I sincerely believe to be so. But there are surely some mistake! Who possesses the absolute, or even the absolute-relative truth? So your point of view may be right, and I also realized that you spoke exclusively for my own good.

Wisdom is not only comprehension, but also many other faculties together; among which discrimination and sense of measure are prominent. I will try to be wise! ! ! ! ! ! I will think it over and over again.

This month I have had no visits, a little mail, and waited in vain for Mr. Moore and company, Mrs. Evans and Mrs. V. MacMechan. . . .

Altogether, sometime, in my solitude, I think that the world is gradually forgetting this son of it, entombed alive. But, I will bear my cross. There are those who will never forget me. . . .

P.S. I began to study arithmetic, and I find that my mind works in the same way. A Mathematic mind then? I asked it since I wonder that during 36 years no one else had perceived it, and the one who did it, fear to [do] me wrong.

May 4, 1924. Charlestown Prison

MY DEAR COMRADE BLACKWELL:

Thank you for you congratulation. I will try to deserve them ever more; have also communicated them to my teacher. And thanks for the [picture of the] Niagara Falls—and for your faith in the human destiny.

The Falls brings into my cell a glance of the immense awe of Nature, and an echo of its idiom into my soul; and your faith feeds my faith—now that life's oil is far from my lamp. . . .

June 1, 1924. *Charlestown Prison*

DEAR COMRADE BLACKWELL:

I beg your pardon for having delayed so much to write to you.

I have read the Magazine about Mexico; there are so many things that I wish to tell you. But, I cannot do it well now, because I am tired, and I would not have sufficient time, because it is late and I have two other letters to write. But soon, I will write you a long letter.

Most probably, I will begin to fast tomorrow, in order to have the definite answer of the judge, as soon as possible.[1] I want you to not suffer for this thing. I have the reason; I considered this thoughtfully. I can fast without suffering, and I assure you that I am serene and master of my mind.

In the next letter I will tell you the reasons of this

---

[1] Vanzetti was distraught by the delay in Judge Thayer's decision on the first five supplementary motions for a new trial which had been argued the preceding fall and early winter. Judge Thayer rendered his decision on these motions on October 1, 1924.

act. I am quite well, and hope and wish the same of you, your Cousin, and all the good ones.

June 3, 1924. *Charlestown Prison*

DEAR COMRADE BLACKWELL:

Since I have now a little time, I will write and try to say something, at least, out of the much that I think of, and would like to tell you about many things. As always, I will be a grumbler.

I have read the most important articles on "Mexico," and read them with all the earnestness, attention, and analitic faculty that I possess. I liked the writings written by the Mexican, and disliked those written by the American; and though I know very little about Mexico, I have learned very much from the lecture of these writings; yet the little that I knew and know, suffices to make me aware that the story is not really how they tell it. The major sincerity and nearness to the truth about the topic—*The Real Emancipation of the Mexican People* of the Mexican authors are the reason why I prefer them to the American ones. The publication is a communist propaganda for the communists' aim to capture the power and to gain the sympathy of the American more open-minded people to their cause in Mexico. . . .

This distortion does not educate the people; does not [make] for character or consciousness. It only serves to prompt bloody sacrifice to fall from one tyranny to another. . . .

The communists want power, and this explains all:
the ruin of the revolution. But, returning to Mexico
and the *Survey Graphic*, all in all I am optimistic.
The mankind is such a thing that turns to good many
bad intentions and deeds of its members and to bad,
many good deeds. And surely the magazine contains
good faith, good will, and parts of truth; it assured me
of a momentous good thing. Through its tragic travail, the Mexican is gaining self-reliance, and acquiring
self-sufficientness. For I left that people which I love
so much, with a doubt that was a thorn to my heart.[1]
I was saying, Mexico must depend upon the United
States, so a real emancipation of these people will not
be possible until the actual American regime will have
been burnt to ashes; and this is a hard job, because the
United States is the stronghold, as they will be the last
asylum and the final grave-yard of the Capitalism.
Poor Mexicans.

But now, I have learnt that Mexico is becoming
self-efficient. Not for the merit of the revolutionists
alone, as they believe, nor for the Providence, Obregon
Government, as the social bugs want others to believe
—No! Mexico is becoming so, because its nature per-
mits it—because it is the goal towards which individuals and collectivities always strived, and more than
for anything else. . . .

[Unfinished]

---

[1] Vanzetti was in Mexico in 1917 and 1918 to avoid the draft.

July 20, 1924. *Charlestown Prison*

DEAR FRIEND MRS. C. C. JACK:

I pray of you to be strong, and bravely resist to sorrow. Weighing the unpleasing incident—one can clearly see that it shall not be offensive, because it is determined by misfortune and not by ingratitude or advers feelings, sentiments, or thoughts.[1]   And, oh, how worth of sympathy and forgiveness the poor Nick is, even in his horrors. The imprisonment is for a lover an inefable martirdoom—therefore one must excuse, and also understand that certain acts or words— in such case—means and reveal just the opposite of what seems to be. I hope that with the coming of a cooler atmosphere, Nick will feel much better, and retake his good attitude toward you and those who deserve so well it.

No, his believes are wrong but justified by an appearence of a strange situation—and momentary results—and yet he is undoubtably beneficiated by the love of his friends—no matter if it seems that he does not feels and perceive it.

Of the case I prefer not speak, for, though much of good I could say of it—I am tired and disgusted. But I want to win, Soldier of Liberty, I will win or die.

P.S. Dear Friend, He that humiliate himself, exalt himself. In a way I appreciate your sentiments—but who of the two shall be more grateful and apprecia-

---

[1] Sacco refused to see Mrs. Jack when she went to visit him. He was temporarily hostile to all his "philanthropist friends." Later he apologized to them.

tive? he who have always received? or you who have always given? Who of the two is worthier? To have lived in material comfort is a punishment in itself because it weaken—but it is not a demerit to one who never abused of it; indeed it is written that you have not tresspass—yourself prove it. While to be of the rich and for freedom is the greatest of the merits for he who possess wealth and, if he wish, license. Honor to you—while so many disinherited are slaves of themselves, blacguards of the priviledge and tyranny—you are for freedom.

Let me say that we must not protest against the wreched regime to which we are compelled: we must destroy it. Destroy, annihilate its evils—to give back to latent life its atoms—for new manifestations. . . .

September 15, 1924. *Charlestown Prison*

DEAR COMRADE BLACKWELL:

About two weeks ago I have sent you a letter and till now, no answer came. I am a little anxious for your silence, because it may signify that you are not well. But, I hope with all my heart that you are well.

I think that Moore has left the Defense, but I am not sure of it. [1] If so, it may be better for us, but I lost the opportunity to deliver and receive correspondences.. A painful loss, which deprives me of the only

[1] Fred H. Moore, counsel for the two men at the Dedham trial, officially withdrew from their defense on November 8, 1924. The disagreement between him and the Defense Committee had been brewing some time before Vanzetti wrote this letter.

life manifestation of which I was not yet deprived. I do not know the least simplest thing about the case, save the babblers, which count nothing.

I am tired, tired, tired: I ask if to live like now, for love of life, is not, rather than wisdom or heroism, mere cowardness. And in my conscience, has riped the moral sanction to die and to kill for freedom. I am ready, and I may be mistaken, but most probably I will not die as a rabbit or a worm.

My heart is the tabernacle in which my mother, and she was brave, lives. If a good hour will strike me, I will tell you of her. Not now, it is impossible now.

Italy is weeping tears of blood, bleeding her best blood. The fascista's crimes, especially their crime against Matteotti alive and Matteotti dead, have precipitated the events—the historical Nemesis. . . .

Please let me speak of Italy of which destiny I may be more interested than my own. . . . Grossly speaking, Italy is split in two parts: fascismo and antifascismo. But the situation, the reality is far more complicated than it appears.

The "opposition" is composed of the Liberals, Democratic, Demo-socialist, the three differing Socialist Parties, the Republican, the Communist and the Anarchist, and the Popular (Catholic party).

The Fascismo has on his side the Pope, the King, the financier, industrial and Rural Capitalism.

Now, the liberals who have helped the formation of the fascism are swinging. The Democrats are steadily against the fascismo; the republicans are also swinging, and the Anarchist are firm; but the reformist are ready to betray again if Mussolini would be so gentlemanly to cut with them the power-pie.

But there is more and worse: the socialist are feared by the liberals, the democrats and the republican, while they fear the communist who fear them and the liberal, the democrat, and the anarchist. And the Anarchist distrust all the others.

Let us look at the other side: The king dislikes the pope, and the pope, the king. But a common danger makes them allied. The king who has the army and officialdom faithful to him, dislikes the fascismo and Mussolini, but he must stick with them or end in the Rome's main sewer. Mussolini and the most intelligent head bandits would like to get peace, and ask the venal adversary to partake of the Power's pie—but the dreadful condition of the people, the daily violence of the fascisti-thugs do not consent any normalization, and Mussolini is practically black-mailed and slave of the Capitalists who he has black-mailed and enslaved, and of the scum of his own band, to which he must obey or be stabbed. That Mussolini shall be killed is fatal, but most probably killed by his friends than by his enemy. Historical nemesis cynical as he deserves.

What about the Italian People; the great masses in the fields, the navy, the shops and the studios?

The lower are the best. The unpolitical masses who make life possible, are naturally well gifted, relatively good, purely good in all that survives in them of primordial. But they are dwarfed, brutalized, corrupted, cowardized by thousands of years of slavery, servilism, bestial toiling, sordity, poverty, unspeakable suffering, ignorance, and worse of all, by honors. But in spite of all this shame, horror and disgrace, they are the only ones who look to the stars and not the mud. Nor are they guilty. Guilty is the church, the monarchy, the capitalism, the militarism, the Burocrasy, and the yellow, pink, red, scarlet bad shepherds, demagogues and politician.

The political proletariat is very heterogeneous: Mazzinian, demo-social, socialist, communist and anarchist.

Mazzinian and anarchist are the best blood, and they are surely superior to the gray masses—unconscious and idealess—but they are few. The others have been too domesticated by their leaders—"plenty of eat, little of work," belly of mine become a hub; safety first, gradual conquest, historical fatalism, and fascista blackjack over all.

Besides that they look for power, are much servilized and *"imborghesiti."* Yet, they have fought heroical battles, and would be capable of great acts, were the worms so good to eat the leaders alive. Gigi Damiani has raffaelistically painted these truths in his *The Problem of Liberty.*

Thus Italy's condition is equivocal, comic, but over all, tragic. And no worthy son of a good mother can look at it without sorrow, aggravation and anguish. There is death and even worse than death, all round. The task is titanic, the mean men are gnomes and dwarfed.

How will be the future? It will be tears of blood, crimes, degeneration, diseases, insanity and death—

or the life and its liberation reached through a terrific lavacrus of blood, through aspiration, heroic sacrifice, and fire. This is the truth. Hard even to look upon.

Republicans, democrats and socialists have a program. The re-establishment of the constitutional grants: freedom of press, speech, and association; annultation of the past election and new election; the abolition of the fascista Militia.

The communists are for "the power to themselves," the name don't matter. And they are playing Don Quixottes.

You will surely admit that we, poor, hated, dispised, wronged, exacrated anarchist have a hard job to get a straight way (straight to our criterion) among such an entanglement.

People in general are not yet capable of liberty, others are contrary to it, so that it would be impossible to establish general anarchist order after the fascismo vanquishment. On the other hand there are places whose population is almost totally anarchist. Also the first necessity is to crush the fascismo now, and it is a work that requires the cooperation of all the parties contrary to the fascismo.

[Unfinished]

November 13, 1924. *Charlestown Prison*

DEAR COMRADE BLACKWELL:

I have in the *La Notizia* that you are going to speak somewhere in Boston, at a meeting in Sacco's and my behalf.

What a labor, what troubles and cares of the few to advocate a case of which the great masses care but little or nothing, and the powerful detest, to finance a useless work of civil thieves. When I think of it, of all what has happened and of how the present is and I am, I dispise the words. And this silence is a thing which cannot be said.

I always remember my promise to you of a writing on "incoherence" still to be fulfilled.

It is, that beside to have little time at my disposition, I seldom feel that way, or in that mood, which consent one to express a little of himself. When one is killed, or is dying little by little, as I, the happy moment of self-expression becomes always less and more weak, so that even if there is time enough one can do nothing, of what is only possible to do quickly, in a slow manner. Yet, sometime I will try it.

I am going to school now, and reading many newspapers and few books. Also, I feel quite well and strong, only that my native me is dreary for what it is becoming. I have cut down trees with a sense of sympathy for them, and almost a sort of remorse; while now thinking of my axe, a lust seizes me to get a mad delight and exaltation by using them on the necks and trunks of the men-eaters; on the necks of those who seem to have the evil in their head and on the trunks of those who seem to have the evil in their breast.

It is good for them if they succeed to loosen me, splitted and crushed in flesh and in spirit—a shadow of a man, a human rag—and still better to them if they will turn me out well nailed amongst six cheap planks. Yet, I am still well and strong enough, going to school, reading many journals and some books, writing a little for the case, and for the great cause, and planning how to destroy a world.

I know that our comrades are fighting, laboring, preparing, and that different days are near at hand. The *Thought and Will* and *Faith* are simply sublime —Malatesta is a saint.

. . . . Thus while hope is still alive in me, desperation is growing powerful, and it is good, as sane hate is good. They are providential. And since I reached a good point I will stop at it, temporarily. Hoping to find you well, I send you my regards and good wishes, to your cousin also.

November 30, 1924. *Charlestown Prison*
DEAR COMRADE BLACKWELL:

I have received both your letters, one of Nov. 22nd and the other I received at the same day, November 25th.

Thank you for your participation and your description of the meeting. I read something about it in the *La Notizia,* but it is from you that I learned of our dear Eugene Debs' message, and brave Larkin's cablegram. I am glad and proud of it for Debs and Larkin are estimated very dearly by me. Two of the really good and brave are they among the many of this side of the barricade. . . .

I do not know, but I heard several times of Miss Donovan—how many good souls are working in our behalf and suffering for our pains and sorrows who we do not know. Human nature is good. I would assert it even I burned a hundred times, or chained for hundred lives.

Thank you, dear comrade Blackwell, for the nice post card. Your letter has made my Thanksgiving day a little better than it would have been without your messages. And your friendship makes each of my days a little better—it daily gives me sincerity and joy and life.

I beg of you to have care of yourself and to do all what the oculist prescribes to you. We and our race need you, and you have to preserve your faculties and gift for the common welfare and little of happiness.

Now I am busy. Yesterday, I finished the first of a series of articles (three) and I hope to write the other two, tomorrow. After, I will finish my letters on "Syndicate and Syndicalism." I am really ashamed of my long delay. After I will write a series of articles on "In Defense of the Revolution" a topic very much discussed now. For this reason, I am going to close my letter, but with a promise. I will write to you of my mother at the first good hour.

December, 1924. *Charlestown Prison*

DEAR MRS. EVANS:

For the water in liquid state, freedom is, to flow from a relative up to a relative down; or vice versa when the water is in vapor state. For the fire, freedom is, to expand and to arise. In short, freedom is, for each and all the things of the universe, *to follows their natural tendencies*—and to fulfill their own virtues, qualities and capacities.

This,—and not at all an abstraction, nor an abstract right which enable someone to say of a man, dead for want of food, that he has not die of starvation, but for not having exercised his right and his freedom to eat—is my idea of liberty.

Please, permit me to prove you the trueness of this true conception of freedom by applying it to Nick and myself. Am I without a lover? Yes, but I would like to have a lover. Have I not, by nature, the instinct, the faculties and, therefore, the right of love? Of course yes, but it would be better if not, for having them but not the freedom to realize them, it all become an excruciable laughing stock.

Has Nick a wife? Yes, and a good one; but not being free, he must either thinks that she is consoling herself with somebody else, or that she is suffering the unspeakable agony of a loving woman compelled to mourn a living lover.

Have I no children? Well—I would like to have or to generate some children. Have Nick some children—yes, and what his heart experiences when he thinks of them—is a thing known by him alone.

O the blessing green of the wilderness and of the open land—O the blue vastness of the oceans—the fragrances of the flowers and the sweetness of the fruits—The sky reflecting lakes—the singing torrents

—the telling brooks—O the valleys, the hills—the awful Alps! O the mistic dawn—the roses of the aurora, the glory of the moon—O the sunset—the twilight—O the supreme extasies and mystery of the starry night, heavenly creature of the eternity.

Yes, Yes, all this is real actuallity but not to us, not to us chained—and just and simply because we, being chained, have not the freedom to use our natural faculty of locomotion to carry us from our cells to the open horizon—under the sun at daytime—under the visible stars at night.

CHAPTER II

BY almost uninterrupted application of mind, Vanzetti had withstood the first four years of prison routine and the delays and disappointments incident to Judge Thayer's denial of the first six motions for a new trial.

Early in 1925, however, his resistance temporarily sagged. Persistent digestive disturbances indicated that he might be suffering from stomach ulcers, and it was thought that this organic trouble explained the excitability which characterized his conduct at this time. He was accordingly taken off work in the prison tailor shop, and placed in the prison hospital for observation. After several weeks, he was removed from the hospital to the Bridgewater State Hospital for the Criminal Insane. Here he stayed four months, regaining his health completely, after which he was returned to Charlestown, this time to work in the paint shop.

During this year there were no days in court for him or Sacco. Towards the close of 1924, Mr. William G. Thompson, later joined by Mr. Herbert B. Ehrmann, superseded Mr. Fred H. Moore and the other counsel for the men. Vanzetti was profoundly pleased with this change, and waited out the year 1925 in relative patience while the necessary steps were being taken to carry his case to the Supreme Court.

February 17, 1925.
Bridgewater Hospital for Criminal Insane

DEAR COMRADE BLACKWELL:

It has been very hard for me this forced silence,
yet, for a while I have been unable to get paper, and
after a while I had been compelled to spend my weekly
letters (2) for answering my family and others, for
urgent necessities.   This is a special letter which I
asked after having received your dear Valentine.   Indeed, it seems that almost all have stopped to write
to me, since my coming here—for, except some mail
addressed to Charlestown, which I received the first
week of my new residence (not surely Royal) I have
received but one from Mrs. M—— who promised
to visit me, but has not yet come; few other missives
from a friend family, and your letter and post card.

I have not answered to those who cheered me the
last Christmas and New Years.   Nor have I been
able to answer to the last heartfelt letter of our great
Eugene Debs.   And just think—I am knowing myself
—I wish so intensely to tell him my ideas of the Italian
conditions and other things.   Also to you I would like
to tell.

I am not allowed to use paper or write.   This intellectual compelled idleness is crucial to me, now that
so many ideas whirling in my brain and sentiments into
my being, give me a yearning for expression—most
all because of my understanding of the nature and
needs of our times.

Lately, I read in a review, a few letters of Eliseo

Reclus, written while he was in prison for a 1st of May demonstration in Paris. These beautiful letters, though brief and familiar, voice the genious of their author. Could I translate them in English!

Because here the visits are allowed daily, I have seen many dear friends and their children since I am here and they brought me some particular Italian dish. A festival of the heart and of the stomach. They are doing to me what Caserio, the killer of Carnot, used to do with the more poorer than he; baker and anarchist, he spent all his money to give them some bread, and some books, "the bread of the spirit," as that hero used to say. . . .

I hope I will be able to fulfill my promise to you, about my mother, in the near future, and to send you writings which may interest you. . . .

April 4, 1925.
Bridgewater Hospital for Criminal Insane

DEAR COMRADE DONOVAN: [1]

This very sheet of paper tells you that I have received your two copies of *The Nation* which you promised to me in your letter of March 30th. Much obliged, comrade Donovan, for the papers and more for your letter, which came to me as a flash of light. . . .

So, you are studying Dante's language, and will

---

[1] Mary Donovan, at this time an industrial inspector for the Massachusetts Department of Labor and Industries, became recording secretary of the Defense Committee in 1924.

write to me in the *"Idioma gentil sonante e puro"* of the *"Bel Paese aue il 'si' suona"?* Very well—I proudly congratulate you. There is something in the Italian literature worth while reading, studying and ponderating by every person of good will—not mentioning a revolutionist. And of this we shall speak later. Of Dostoyevsky, I only have read some letters —'til then unedited, published by the *Culture* issue of June 1924. So I am most eager to read his *Poor People*. Next I would read his *Prisons*. And I believe that it would suffice to give me a proper idea of this famous writer's spirit and soul. Next I will ask for the Barkman's *Memories* in Italian translation. I have already read twice *My Prisons* by Silvio Pellico, which and who you may know. I think that I could have something to say on this subject, some future day, and it is the reason why I wish to learn what others have said upon the topic. I will also pray my friends to order for me some of the books—very interesting—which I have seen in the book of *The Nation* at five cents each. Now I have *Resurrection* by Leo Tolstoi and an American volume of poems to read. *The Nation* is a reading issue. A good mental divertion and stimulation to me. You speak of physical exercise. I do a little daily. Today I played ball in the yard. I need, and will exercise more. But not to keep thin. By gosh, no! A strenuous life of work and rebellion has left but skin and bones since my arrest, and I am lucky enough to have saved them from the worms, during five years of exceptional good times. . . .

April 6, 1925.
Bridgewater Hospital for Criminal Insane

DEAR COMRADE BLACKWELL:

This week I have asked [permission to write] a special letter which was given me, and now, with this second letter, I am at last able to write to you.

As I told you, our Eugene Debs has also written me, and I answered him, but I am rather pessimist about the case, and am convinced that they will do all they can against us. Most probably, you already know that the case discussion has been postponed to next Fall. Yesterday, I had a visit from Mr. Thompson, and he explained to me the new delays causes: the judge's operation, Williams' promotion; a new district attorney, etc. I have not the least hope or trust in laws and law-traders; and you know what it is of which I trust and hope.

My hand writing progress was due to a comfortable table in the hospital at which I wrote while I was there.

Something is gradually dying in me, and what remains is just all right. I'm beginning to believe the Bible "The tyrants should be stabbed," and I am working out a philosophy proper to me and to many a millions of people; the philosophy of the new actual revolution in act: its moral sensation; for it was that which Victor Hugo used to call "the revolutions' god."

A comrade told me: "Alas to him who in the hours of revenge would raise his voice for pity and forgiveness. His same comrades would kill him, after what we have suffered from the fascisti. They did neither beat or kill me, because the fascisti of my town were ashamed and afraid, and because I ran away from the others. But I have seen my wife hungry and my children crying for bread. I am more offended than if they killed me."

Enrico Malatesta is against useless or not necessary violence, and he may be right.

As for me, I have suffered these last few days a terrible heart-burn, and I have said, and maybe I may have, or I may not have ulcers in my stomach. If I have ulcers, it is alright, though I will fight against it. If I have no ulcers, it is still better.

April 10, 1925.
Bridgewater Hospital for Criminal Insane

DEAR FRIEND [MRS. MAUDE PETTYJOHN]:

Your letter of April 3rd with the enclosed scientific historical thesis received yesterday morning. They brought me joy and delight. . . . Scientific progress is one of the few encouraging things of these wretched times. Nevertheless, there is great confusion, contradiction and an always more rapid discovery of perceived former mistakes in this field than in the Labor Field, which is to say all. . . . Sometime ago Enrico Malatesta has written an golden page about what should be the mental attitude toward science, religion, the little knowledge of the enormous mystery encircling us and from which we sprang—of those who, as I, have Anarchistic principles and aims. And, if possible, I will translate it to you, some day; then I will speak further on the topic.

I cannot share your confidence in "better government," because I do not believe in the government, any of them, since to me they can only differ in names from one another, and because we have witnessed the utterly failure of both the social-democrat governments in Germany, and the bolsheviki government in Russia. At least, such is my honest and sad opinion. But I wholly share of your confidence in Co-operatives, and, what is more, in real co-operatives, free initiative, both individual and collective. Mutual aid and co-operation and co-operatives shall be the very base of a completely new social system, or else, nothing is accomplished. . . . But when you tell me that the only consolation you give to your complaining friends against economical difficulties, is "that the times will be much harder," then I cannot help but clap my hands in great approval. So much so, that it is but the truth. And not only in economy, but in life's problems this will be true. We are galloping towards misery and wretchedness. Life grows miserable by each second, and he whom the gods have not yet wholly deprived of understanding, far from being surprised, should indeed wonder if it were not so, for, man is today his own greater enemy, and the slaves are, more than the powerful, the slave-keeper of themselves. Crucial truth for the libertarian, truth that drowns tears from our eyes, and curses from our heart, curses to those whom we would also deliver for their own sake. . . . Just this morning, I finished the lecture of *The Penguin*

Island, by Anatole France who masterly slaps, in this book, the pretentions, proudness, hypocracy, stupidity and ferocity of the humane, and shows the uselessness of religions, and the venom of the clergies. The last chapter is entitled future time and is naturally drawn from the present conditions and state of mind and emotions. And it is said "after having destroyed the present curse called civilization, the people return to a certain primitiveness through which they gradually build and return to the present state." Thus the revolutionary Anatole did not superate any of the great writer of the past, for he reached the same con- clusion which has 'til now been the truth. . . .

Even before I came here, I was the cause of much disturbed fear; distrust of keepers and doctors who have their jobs, love them, and believe me and my friends the worst and dangerous criminals. The higher of them, the more jack-asses.

So it follows that I was kept in solitary confinement for five weeks, after which I was allowed to the day-room, where it is forbidden to speak, and watched by eyes always. A few days after that I was admitted to the common table; knives and forks were taken off from circulation, and we compelled to use the fingers as table-tools. Meanwhile, every good day, the other patients were compelled to go into the yard, and I had to stay in. It is five years that I have been de- prived of all that makes life worth living. Sunlight and open-air is what is greatly needed after five years of shadows and miasmatic dwelling. So I kicked and I kicked: I want my rights, and I have the right of a daily hour in the open air. The State so splendidly framed us, cannot it give me any rights? Meanwhile, I began to perceive abuse and wrongs to the patients and, therefore, to protest and rebel. Were I alone, they would, for this, have me die within this wall. Well, after my protests, I was allowed to go into the yard; once a day, early in the morning, when none were there, and together with the biggest attendance. Thus, in three months, I went 7 times into the yard, and only the 7th I stayed there one hour, all the other, less. I used to clean the floors, help the patients take off the dust, watering plants, etc., so that the head assistant proclaimed me to the doctors "his better patient." And yet they kept watching, fearing and distrusting me to the point that the head assistant said that I should write in English my letters to my sister, to which I answered in rhymes.

Then they began to send me two times a day in the yard, where I began to play ball. Color was returning to my cheeks and fire to my eyes, and it happened that a strong Italian patient was brought here that time. So the keepers were trembling. Then, the ugly Monday of three weeks ago, while returning from the yard, I was arrested!!, compelled to undress myself, take a bath, change all the clothes, and to go to a worse ward of the institution, where the dangerous were. Here I can see but a fragment of sky, walls and a bare yard. I am allowed twice a day in the yard; one hour in the morning, 1½ hour in the afternoon; the rest of the time, in the room. I asked the director the reason for this change. He did not give me a single word of explanation, but answered "Oh, we make the people go 'round." Indeed, he laughed so heartily at me. They also try to dispute and find difficulties with those who come to see me, so that to tire them. And I have only a letter a week, and I do not know when I will be able to send you this one, or a regular one. You will excuse me. Next time I will tell you more. Hoping this finds you and your family in good health and spirit, and I send to you, your family and our common friends, my regards and greetings.

April 14, 1925.
Bridgewater Hospital for Criminal Insane

DEAR COMRADE BLACKWELL:

I wrote the last letter in a fit of humor, and my actual regret cannot change it now from what it is. But I have improved and am improving from heartburn.

Naturally, in the age of franctic competition, as ours is, those who have a good job think themselves lucky, and thank their stars, for it means a good roof, table, bed, reputation, good living, for them and theirs, so that no matter how much of spirituality and christianism they feign to themselves and the other to possess, they look for themselves, which means: a world based on privileges, to abuse their neighbors. Many of us have a blind faith in science, and they believe in science, because it must be good.

For me, I have already experienced that in name
of "Psychopathy" may be committed the same, if not
more, cruelty, injustice and partiality, as in the name
of the law.   Psychology is still more subtle and in-
definable than Law itself.   And a doctor may be as
mean as lawyer or a keeper even more, though, both
may be good.   We would not have advanced an inch
toward justice, progress, liberty or happiness, by
simply and only shifting from laws to medicine or
psychology, because the real progress represented by
the "curing" upon the "punishing" may become, by
environment and men's vices, a bloody insult to misfortune and truth.   To progress, even a little, we have
to destroy a world. . . .

April 16, 1925.
Bridgewater Hospital for Criminal Insane

DEAR COMRADE BLACKWELL:

I bite my tongue 'til now, not to tell you a thing
which will make you sorry, but I cannot help but tell
it.   They took me away from the hospital and brought
me in the east north ward, the worst of the wards, for
the most dangerous or the punished.   While other patients enjoy all day long the sunshine and open air in
spacious yards, we have one hour of yard in the morning, and one in the afternoon, and our yard is narrow
and shadowy; closing the sight, except to the sky.   The
door of my room is kept open during the day, and I

have a chair and books in my room.   But I stay in because the other prisoners are kept in.

Now, they cannot say that I am dangerously insane, nor can they claim that I deserved punishment by my conduct.   So they say that in a letter to my sister, I told her that "I wish to go out soon, and get rich quick, and return to Italy."   I answered that it is not true, and, not knowing if they were saying it for a second end or very uncertain of its truth, I had believed to have convinced them.   But two weeks ago Mr. Thompson was here, and they told him the same thing, and said that they cannot give me more liberty because I am a dangerous man.   After that, I was declared by the Prison authorities "A model prisoner;" the best one, and after my conduct here, really exemplar.

They believe me guilty; they believe my principles to be aberration and insanity; they believe my friends (I mean the comrades and Italians) arch-criminals; they believe, (and told me so) that the Americans in our behalf are fools and cheaters.   But, what is worse, they asked me if I believed in God, in the golden rule; if the murderers shall not be punished.   If they do not nail me, I will answer.

P.S. Yet they are not naturally bad, and they let my door open, give me two cups of milk a day, and the permission to keep books in my room.   These are privileges which few are given here.   I feel ashamed and my heart aches for them, yet I shall help myself, even when I cannot help others, and appreciate what I receive.

April 17, 1925.
Bridgewater Hospital for Criminal Insane

DEAR COMRADE BLACKWELL:

Your letter has reached me today. I am improving and I don't think I have stomach ulcers. Now, I have milk at each meal and it does me good.

Yes, I can read Spanish, and it would be great to me, the poor Mugoni's letters. Please, in writing to those comrades, tell them that I salute them brotherly, and with them also the Mexican peasants, workers, good men and women, whom I love so dearly, give them my greetings.

Your letter is alright, sweet as nectar to me.

I fear a little for those of F——, because, as the letters of any prisoner to his friends, are not written for publication, that is without care, and are heart-crying soul's notes, burst out spontaneously and without pre-co-ordination, they may appear incomplete and orderless. Yet, they are humane documents.

April 26, 1925.
Charlestown Prison for Criminal Insane

DEAR FRIEND BRITE:[1]

I do hope that you have had news of me during the last few months. If so, I feel sure that you have understood the causes which have unabled me to answer to your Christmas letter and gift, and, therefore,

[1] Mrs. Mary Brite of Cincinnati, Ohio.

that you have never blamed me for my involuntary silence. . . .

I am very grateful to you for your solidariety to both Nick and me. I understand what the sum that you have sent me may mean to you, and I appreciate it beyond the meaning of words. Thanks to you and all my friends whom I received money from this last Christmas, I have this day an account of $102.23, which shows how many small ones together will make a big one. This money will suffice, I hope, 'til the day in which the case will be however set, and an end came. . . .

May 11, 1925.
Charlestown Prison for Criminal Insane

DEAR COMRADE BLACKWELL:

I have read in the papers the strong plea that our Eugene V. Debs has made in our behalf, and yet your letter has filled my eyes with tears. Oh, indeed I would have been with you, near, honoring the grand old young man. I love him as I love my father and my masters. . . .

How happy he must have been of the welcome that you all have given him. One of my friends who has not known him before, spoke to me of him, almost weeping. I shall be happy forever to have seen and known him, and have his friendship; such a superior man. But I wonder of his and your optimism. Also our dear and noble Mrs. Evans wrote me a letter filled, vibrating of optimism. I cannot understand from where and from what are drawn the reasons for your optimism.

It may be the effect of my captivity—but to me the world seems all black and tragic. Of this I will speak in another letter, after having received your promised, and very much wished, further account of the Teacher's words.

I have a letter for him, in which I said that "they are trying to break me morally and physically, so that if they shall not be able to kill me, or keep me in chains 'til my death, they will make a living wreck out of me." I also told him that at the worst, I will make my own little revolution before the close of the book, that is, going, but flinging the doors.

I came near tearing the letter to pieces, when I thought of the sorrow that my words will cause to the Teacher's heart. But, I had thought and felt so, and I shall tell the truth to you and to him. Death for death, I think that the times require to bring with us some enemies, some black-guards—I should say the more that is possible. It is my reason, not my heart, that is speaking so. I think I do not feel so now, but sometimes. I still abhore the blood now, as always before.

Yes, my heartburn is gone, and I am quite well, so well that I feel to write a treatise on sociology, which I have not yet begun, because I wish to hear some friends in its regard.

June 10, 1925. *Charlestown Prison*

DEAR COMRADE BLACKWELL:

I have just read your welcome letter and the enclosed one of Comrade R———. Thank you for both of them. I will return you the latter, and write to its author. . . .

Now, dear Comrade Blackwell, I spoke with you pessimisticly of others' optimism, because of Comrade Debs' optimism and Mrs. Evans' great optimistic letters from England. This I have intended, since we, you and I, had not discussed yet on that subject.

It may be the prison, the paint's gas, and my conviction that I am comically doomed, that makes me rough and difficult—but I cannot help a reaction when a note of optimism vibrates into my dark prospect of this mad world. This in spite that I wish and like that people be optimistic and have faith. It is that I belong to the volontaristic, to which "faith" only means strong life and steady will. History shows an gradual advance, you say. This opinion of yours is shared by the greatest part of the comrades, and by many scholars and thinkers. I doubt it. . . .

One beautiful morning, a young bandit, a lifer, with a young wife and two children, looked through the window of our shop, and said to me, "What a wonderful good world this will be 5,000 years from now, if it will yet exist." "Yes, then it may be, 5000 times better, or as well, 5000 times worse than it is now. It depends on the people's will, actions and capacities."

Thus I answered and explained to him—because I had seen at once that he believed that the world must get better by force—I mean by its fate.

But enough of this poor theorizing. I have faith and I am optimistic—we ought to be so, and I have intended, previously, an impersonal discussion or judgment in these sentiments. Yet, of course, nothing is worse than these sentiments based on fallacies—it becomes horrors, illusion, and paralysis. This is the reason why we anarchist are often vexed with the reformist, even if, as Malatesta, we recognize to be ourselves reformist at the same time that we are revolutionists. . . .

June 18, 1925. *Charlestown Prison*

Dear Comrade Blackwell:

Well, well—I had thought it impossible; an antecedent publication of such a directly and really radical book as is *The Peace and the War*, by Proudhon, in this free country. Now that your letter proved to the contrary, I am only glad to apologize for my "temerity" and mistaken "judgment." Well, I will translate it, and a learned American Comrade will re-touch the translation and publish it. I have learned that only the first of the several letters which I wrote to my family from Bridgewater, has reached them. Also a letter concerning the translation was kept by my keepers, without a word of warning. Maybe my keepers have decided to make the translation as well. . . .

Kropotkin has been able to write inspirational remembrance because he escaped from his keepers.

I cannot see how our stupid contingence shall inspire and fortify future revolutionists and prisoners. It is indeed so stupid, that it cannot be told at all. I have been found guilty two times, of two crimes of which I am innocent in the complete sense of the word. . . .

But, if I make them pay dear for my life, if instead to rot or to be killed beastlike, I will choose to die beautifully in an open and heroic rebellion, that would signify something, inspire and create. The enemy would ponder a little before to frame others upon the already framed.

It would be the old and yet the best way to teach— to teach with the example greater than all orations. If generalized, it would free the world of all the tyrants and their black guards.

When the hopes of freedom are gone forever, better the death than the chains, better for both the chained and his beloved—for, to mourn a living one is the most excruciable of the sorrows. This I say, serenely.

So please do not worry—all the hopes are not yet gone—by them I realize the possibilities. And I am quite well, capable of a long resistance and of a longer feat. And I laugh. . . .

The shame about China may develop in a world wide shame and crime. There is no choice, either to destroy or be destroyed.

June 20, 1925. Charlestown Prison

GREETINGS AND GOOD WISHES TO MY DEAR COMRADE: [1]

Just this evening I have received your two postcards greeting and good wishes on my birthday. You say you would like send me roses and peonies from your garden. I would appreciate them immensely—for I love flowers, living fragments of heaven, rising from the earth. You seem to ignore that you have sent me something even more sublime than flowers and stars, your loving, noble spirit, the woman spirit. It revives the flames of my withered life. I am in the twilight, the sky is dark, there are lightnings and thunder. But I like the storm, I am fearless and serene.

To have your friendship quickens the life in me and sweetens my soul. The spirit of your words reaches and thrills the innermost sources of my life.

What am I doing? Well, reading, writing some articles, corresponding, translating *The Peace and War* by Proudhon, hoping and thinking.

The hot waves of which you spoke have reached us here, three days of very hot weather—about a hundred degrees, but it does not bother me at all. The trouble with the weather in this state is that the season is short and the weather variable. Many poor Italian immigrants troubled by the new place's very different way of life used to joke: "Crazy weather and crazy peoples in America." It seems to me the whole world is crazy. In my native place in northern Italy the

[1] Irene Benton of Granada, Minn.

weather warmed up in April and keep increasing steadily and slowly. It acts the same way in the fall. Winter has more snow and less freezing than here. The results are that we raise corn, wheat, beans and cut hay three time a year. We cut hay the first time in May and when the season is rainy we cut 4 crops, after which the mountaineers come down in the autumn and put their herds to pasture in the meadows and return again in the spring.

Forgive me if I cannot write oftener as you deserve.

June 21, 1925. *Charlestown Prison*

MY DEAR COMRADE BLACKWELL:

. . . . Now, everytime I think of you, I remember your wish to hear of my mother, indeed I sense it—and my promises to speak to you of her. And each time I feel a little ashamed and regretful for my conduct, but also gladdened by all of this. But, my good Comrade, how can I speak to you of my mother, while in this present physical and moral condition, when homicide impulses are hammering into my very heart and skull? I hold my mother's memory as the sacrest thing to me. I feel an unspeakable responsibility at the very thought to speak of her to you, and my conditions do not allow me of it. It would be a torture to me now, for I would really like to speak of my mother with the tongue of an arch-angel.

I will do my best to improve myself and I promise you that when the good hour will strike, you will be told by me of my most good and adorable mother. . . .

P.S. I may have been crude and cruel as ferocious in my posteriour letters, but, do not let it bother you. Mankind needs the acquisition of the faculties and forces to discern the truth and look into it.

June 28, 1925. *Charlestown Prison*

DEAR COMRADE BLACKWELL:

Your letter of June 23rd was welcomed as all your letters are. . . .

It happened that I remembered the words of our Debs which follow the others: "good things are ahead, if we will be faithful to our highest duty." These latter words alter the affirmation of his optimism. He bases it, not on events, but upon our deeds. And thus I would sign it with both of my hands.

I am quite well now; I labored all the day long, describing one of a series of articles about Russia and the Bolsheviks. As soon as I will have it finished, I will begin the translation of the book.

This year, the season is quite late, and the weather irregular. Yet, I hope you will enjoy the country and the sea, and wisely, treasuring their treasure.

July 8, 1925. *Charlestown Prison*

DEAR COMRADE DONOVAN:

I write with little hope to reach you on this shore,[1] before your sailing, but it may be possible if our com-

[1] Mary Donovan went to Ireland in the summer of 1925.

rades will come here with Mr. Thompson. So, I do not know exactly your inner opinion about the outcome of our case, though I believe you to be more optimistic as to how the real chances should allow. It is natural and also good of you, such opinion.

Yet, I pray you to tell our friends that all the probabilities are that a new trial will be denied, this is my firm conviction. It is better to be pre-warned than to be taken by surprise and found unprepared.

And now, with hope to reach you yet on this side of the big pond, I would like to make hundreds of accommodations about your trip, to wish you an good voyage, to bid you a hearty farewell and a vigorous handshake. . . .

July 21, 1925. *Charlestown Prison*

DEAR COMRADE BLACKWELL:

I have just finished reading your letter dated July 18th, which arrived a few minutes ago. . . .

The Defense Committee is about to publish a financial account, and I have been asked to write a letter, also in Nick's name, to be printed in the first page of the account. In 1923 a similar account was published by the Committee, with a letter written by me and signed by both of us, which was much praised by our comrades, and by the readers. The comrades know my actual psycologic state. There is venom in my heart, and fire in my brain, because I see the real things so clearly to utterly realize what a tragic laughing stock our case and fate are. So my comrades exercised a gentle pressure to induce me to simply translate in English the old letter to be printed, in the new financial account about to be published in English.

Miss Mary Donovan has been here last Thursday. She will soon sail for Ireland for a six weeks trip, and she said that some friend will come here soon to take my translation, which is now due. But it would be necessary the presence of Mr. Thompson. For this I think that my friends have pre-arranged with him a near future visit, and I hope to see them soon.

But, returning to the letter, it was written three years ago, when the condition of the case and of ourselves were not so bad as they are now, and for this reason, it is no longer truthful, as it was then.

I have thought and thought, tried and re-tried to add to it a statement of facts and a confession, but having never satisfactorily succeeded, this morning I resolved to do nothing more, just use the translation of the letter. Now, your letter had inclined me to add something. Well we will see.

Here is another bad story. Only three weeks ago, I have received my books from Bridgewater, in frail and bad condition. All that I had left in my room there, was not received. Hence, a letter from me, with a list of the objects left there, to the Medical Director. This evening the following answer came: "Dear Sir: I have had Mr. Tallman make a very careful search for any property of yours which may have been left at this institution, and so far have been unable to discover any of your books.   Mr. Tallman states that he is sure that everything was boxed and returned to you at the State Prison.   If anything does turn up in the future, I shall be only too glad to forward it, as you have requested.   Very truly."

Well, I have been taken out from my room without being warned of my returning to the prison.   It was said to me, "If you have something to eat in your room, take it with you."   Being in the worst ward of the institution, I thought that they were about to have me changing the place.   I was led to the store-room, seeing my old plain suit, I realized that I was about to be sent back here, and I said to the assistant, "I have left many books and things in my room."   He replied, "Never mind, we will send everything to you. Your room is already closed with the key."   This they did purposely, because it is simply impossible to do it involuntarily.   If none had occupied my room, the objects should have been there and found.   If my room was occupied, in changing the bed, washing the floor, etc., as they always do when someone changes a room, they would have found the books.   I will give you a note of the books which I lost.   1st. A *Divine Comedy*, It was given to me by a far away comrade and friend, whom I fear, I will see no more.   The binding itself costed me $2.50 before the war. 2nd. *W. Emerson's Essays*, given to me by a most dear friend. 3rd. *The Meditations of Marcus Aurelius*, given by a generous soul. 4th. *Thoughts of Nature.* 5th *Friendship* by Thoreau. These are the only ones which I now remember. Besides

I have left other personal effects; a valuable pipe, given to me by a comrade; brushes, combs, etc.

What shall I do? Write to Mr. Thompson? All is useless; they are right, I am wrong. So I will consolate myself, thinking that they have done me greatest damages when I was in their hands, and that this sorrowful loss is a trifle, for one who, as me, is robbed of all that is worthwhile in life, and who will soon be robbed of his own life. And this is all. . . .

I think that Mrs. O—— T—— is a little too optimistic. Meanwhile, we are slowly executed by five years, and to be conservative, ¼ of our execution is already a fact—an irreparable fact. I cannot understand if Mrs. T—— means "by saving us" to obtain the commutation of pain, from an execution to a life long imprisonment; or if she is believing that, since it is inconvenient to the State to kill us, it will free us. Executive Clemency. That is what has been longly pre-established by our murderers, who are thinking to get square with everybody by killing us in 20 years, instead of in 8 or 12 minutes. That is what I expect. It will kill my father, and then me. To sign it would be worse than the three shakes for me. I have to see what Nick is thinking of such a signing. Were I fatherless, and alone in trouble, I would never sign the pardon, may be I will not. I do not know what I will do.

I cannot speak of my mother, having murder in my heart. I can only say that I am glad she died before my arrest. I think I will never be anymore able to speak of her.

July 22, 1925. Charlestown Prison

DEAR COMRADE BLACKWELL:

Since yesterday evening to now, this evening, I have read many times your letter, wondering if I understand it or if I utterly misunderstand it; its parts which treat of the case and the citation. I wish to elucidate it.

Our case is this: We were found guilty of first degree murder, which penalty is death. If the State Supreme Court will deny a new trial, we ought to be sentenced to death. Then the executive clemency *may* be obtained, but with what consequences or result? I believe that by executive clemency, you mean the grace by the Governor. Now, if it is that, and in our case, the result would be that the Governor will commutate our penalty (death) with a sentence of life imprisonment, and such sentence being already a "grace," it will destroy every hope, in future, of "Grace." If you think of this in the same way as I understand your words as follows: "You will not be executed, but life imprisonment."

And if Mrs. O—— T—— also thinks of the case as I have exposed it, then her words: "I am certain that they will be saved," means; by execution alone, and not by perpetual chains.

As you see, I am compelled to understand your words in this signification because I do not know any other procedure of the "executive clemency," except the above stated one. If there are other way of proceding and other power of the executive what I ignore, then your words may have all a different meaning.

Otherwise, people talk just like [that] about our case, no chair but life. The State is informed of everything, and of course, when it will be sure to satisfy everybody and to eliminate every danger by such a commutation, surely it will deny us a new trial and save us forever in prison. And consider, our accepting the *grace* would be equivalent to our confession of guilt. And this, after five years of struggle, after an expense of $300,000, a three-fold mondial protest; after our comrades have given blood and liberty in our behalf; after all that we have in our favor, in spite of our innocense. We have said many times that we want either freedom or death.

Please Comrade Blackwell, use your means in this direction, let everyone know that we prefer the death to the chains—that not a word should be said, not a cent given, nor a finger raised, if not to give us freedom or death.

July 22, 1925. *Charlestown Prison*

MY DEAR COMRADE M. DONOVAN:

. . . . Thank you very much for your happy idea and action to send me a picture of our John Larkin. He, Debs and Evel [1] are the three American men who have the admiration, love and respect of me and of my comrades, including Galleani, for, fanatic as we may be, we know a little about sincerity, character and faith, and those who have them. Nick will be as glad as I to have such a picture. . . .

[1] Hippolyte Havel, editor of *The Road to Freedom*, New York anarchist weekly.

I had understood at once why your letter was not signed—but the little note opened a vista to me: I see you typewriting, reading the letter, quite satisfied, closed it, went to the box, dropped the letter and— o my, o my, I forgot to sign it. I see your nose more than everything else. Do you see me laughing? Well, well. . . .

Yesterday, I also received a letter from Alice Stone Blackwell. She says: "I too, believe you and Nick will never be executed, even if the effort for a new trial will fail. I have good hope, if worse comes to worse, we may get executive clemency." And she quotes in a friend's letter: "I have not worried much about Sacco and Vanzetti, because I have felt all the time that there were too many people in Massachusetts who would never submit to the shame of their execution. I know it has taken, it will take, incessant hard work to save them, but I am certain that they will be saved. Even the bourgeoisie will get out and hustle now, rather then let them be murdered in the name of Capitalism."

It seems to me that the words of them both means; "they will be saved from the chair—the Governor will commute their sentence to life imprisonment." And I am sorry for such a letter through the official channel.

This is what the people are saying, and if the comrades and the prominent personalities begin to say it— showing that this result will satisfy them, surely a new trial will be denied. I wrote and told it to her.

You have already surprised me with your Italian— "In Morta del Bona"—splendid! But it takes a nose as sharp as mine to understand what it means: "In Morte del Boia."

But you are brave typist and letter-writer.

Now, before to close, let me give you some advises, about traveling and seasickness, which I forgot to tell you when you were here. Eat plenty of garlic. It is good against seasickness. Provide yourself with a wide linen strap and tie it straight around your obdomen (on the skin) as a belt. It prevents the shaking of the intestines, which produces seasickness. Have your stomach as clean as possible before sailing—have some green or onions with olive oil each morning before eating, and hot coffee after it does very good. And above all, be at rest and of good cheer.

I would be but too happy to accept your cordial invitation. I like the country. I need it, and I am sure I would like your father and your sister as I like you. But the chance is thin—getting thinner.

You looked fine when you were here, and I hope you will be even finer.

Farewell, Comrade Donovan,

BARTOLOMEO

July 31, 1925. *Charlestown Prison*

GREETINGS TO MY DEAR FRIEND [IRENE BENTON]:

Your card is here and read with joy. Thank you for the picture of the road. I would walk it barefoot and light as a butterfly in spring days.

Things seems to be taking a good turn. It may be some day I will tramp that road.

The picture of the moccasin flowers are beautiful. I saw and plucked some on a hill near home in Plymouth, Mass. The spot where they were was shady and moist, strange creature of brightness.

Our dear E. V. Debs has plead masterly in our behalf here in Boston as well as elsewhere—wherever he goes.

I have been reading *Vedanta Philosophy*, much foolishness and err, and much wisdom and truth in it. Anarchy is my beloved.

Every little good thing is good but to prevent another world war greater and bloodier than this one only a revolution or danger of a revolution can be effective. We have seen the Socialist movement of Europe collapse at the first rumors of war, and becoming a tool of war.

A whole Italian opera was radio-telegraphed. Sometime I have wished before it and hoped after it that you might have listened.

September 14, 1925. *Charlestown Prison*

DEAR COMRADE BLACKWELL:

Your letters of the 10th and that of Aug. 21st, and that of Sept. 5th were all received in due time. Before all, let me thank you very much for them. I am sorry to have been compelled to such a delay to answer. Even now, I cannot answer, as your letters deserves.

I have not been distressed, but a little enraged about the said "executive clemency." August 18th, Mr.

Thompson was here, and he told me that I am right, and I knew it before he told me, because it is six years that I am in prison, and I learnt something.

The loss of my books is but a joke. I am robbed of everything—and of life itself, and I do not worry for it all, so try to be of good cheer.

Nowadays are yet very many people who believe in witch-craft, and almost all of the people believe in something else not less absurd and bloody. Change of evils, errors and crimes, is taken as progress by many.

Your letter of Sept. 5th, has made me laugh. I will write longer letters to you as soon as possible. . . .

September 15, 1925. Charlestown Prison

DEAR COMRADE BLACKWELL:

I am again answering your later three letters, in order to express to you, more thoroughly, my thoughts about the case.

The cases of Tresca and Debs were different from my case—they were sentenced to a definite term of time—I will be, to death. In their cases "executive clemency" means, in a way or another, freedom. In my case it means life imprisonment, as Mr. Thompson told me August 21st. I knew it before then. There are five lifers here, whose death sentence was commuted by the Governor [1] . . . .

As a matter of fact, the Governor can free us, if

---

[1] Vanzetti means former governors of Massachusetts, not Governor Fuller.

he wishes it. But why should he? Why should I expect clemency, from he who denies justice to me? My enemies: the judge, the prosecutor, my former lawyers, the Supreme Court, honors the Governor, his council, the Chamber of Commerce, the Plymouth Cordage Co. The Governor and the President himself are all of the same parties—all of one ring. Given this truth, all that has happened 'til now, proves that they want to keep us in prison all of our lives, that consequently, they will repeal the appeal. I don't pretend to be infallable, to know the secrets of the hearts and of the conscience, but I have a certain experience and a sharp nose. Why should the presiding judge have refused a new trial if his ring would wish to free us? To give trouble to them, or useless expenses to the State? Why should the Supreme Court grant a new trial, if the ring has ordered to the presiding judge to deny it? . . .

I hate to deceive myself with foolish hopes: I prefer to face the truth, nude, crude, horrible as it may be; to look the eye into the eye, the reality. Not to shrink from, not to fear the reality, is my chosen rule. To think, but not to be crushed by the thoughts, is what I like. . . .

You wish that I may bear as well as possible my imprisonment—so you name to me men and women who passed, or are passing through the crushing ordeal of prison and exile (prison is also exile, and worse) keeping themselves mentally and morally healthy.

But also this fact I like to look at and see it just as it is—dreadful as it is—enough if I can bear the spectacle; if I don't yield and become coward. There are ordeals which shatter the flesh or the spirit or both of the men and women. Prison is one.

You speak of Ricardo F. Magon, who spent many years in prisons and in exile and kept his faith and courage and optimism to the last. To the last, for, strong and young he died in chains, maybe killed just because he was untamable, by his keepers, as the Mexican Comrade was chained, and since his death, the world became worse and worse.

Eugene Debs left just in time to care [for] and to recuperate his health; another few months of prison and we would have lost him. Bakounin, a healthy giant such as he was—died at 62 years—killed by the prisons, the exile, and the struggle. I wonder if Catherine Breshkovsky would have appealed the capitalist nations to invade the Russians and crush the revolution, were it not for her suffering in prisons and in exile.

Thousands, millions of the best men and women were crushed by the mercenary keepers, by the prisons and the scaffold. I would kill all the keepers of the world to save such as Debs or Magon. We fight for the triumph of a cause,—not to be crushed by the keepers—we will never win without vanquishing them. They are mercenary, we idealist; should a free man or a rebel allow them to do what they please to him? . . .

Yet, if I had renegated my faith, or become a degenerate, I would presently enjoy privileges and I could hope for freedom. But to the freedom bought at such price, I prefer the chains and the death.

I would like to answer to every argument of your

letter, also, to tell you many other things, but this letter is already very long. So I close with affection and with the most hearty regards to your cousin and to you.

P.S. I will write you something of my mother, in the near future, I hope. . . . Your last letter has made me laugh. I must laugh every time I think of it. Please take care of your eyes.

September 18, 1925. *Charlestown Prison*

MRS. L. N. RUSSELL:

Expecting a soon opportunity of mailing—I decided to and am writing to you, this evening.

My ancestors were farmers, my grandfather was an agriculturer and dealer in agriculture's products. My father is himself a land owner, gardener and an intelligent agriculturer. I hereditated their passion to the land. But I have no experience nor skill because I left home when 13 years old, to learn the trade of pastry cook, candy maker and liquorist. I only worked the land—some insignificant works—in my father's garden, when a boy, and afterward, few weeks, here in a farm of an American family.

My father own a beautiful garden and a good deal of land among the better veins and position of the town-territory, which extends itself at the feet of beautiful hills.

The most renditive crop of the place, is the hay, and, naturally, the land at meadow is the most valuable. Ordinarily, we have three yearly hay crops, but when the Summer is a little raining, we have four crops of hay. Consequently, we have a great many bovines. The largest farms has an herd of 300 cows. Several other farms have over 100 cows—many have 10, 20, 30 to 80 and 100 cows. Thus, the amount of dairy products is very considerable. There is a Swiss-cheese factory which produced tons of cheese daily, and raises many hundreds of hogs. At the Autumn, the snow-storms chased the mountaineers out from the mountains—down to the valley they come. The young men and women and their children—with great big herds of cows or of sheeps, they carry their furniture in carts pulled by a pair of mules. They take shelter in the farms in which meadows (after 3 or 4 crops of hay) they pasture their herds—until near Christmas—when a heavy snow-fall covered the valley in a thick mantle of white, and they begin to feed their herds with the farmer's hay. Only their old folks remain at the mountain, blocked for months in their houses by high walls of snow.

All this will prove to you that the farms-building must be very big in my native valley—in fact they are, in spite that those farmers do not dwell so comfortable as the American farmers generally do. Much less, indeed. In my father's house, we had a family of tenants—composed of 3 brother and one sister, all old singles, who live in one large room. The poor ones were very clean and decent persons. In spite of their poverty, the poor sister fixed the only room of their habitation, quite well. Two of the brothers sleep in the stable at winter time—in the hay-barn, during the

summer. Many of the peasants like to do so. Next
to the hay, the most important crop is that of the
wheat; then, that of the corn, then the clover. We
also cultivate beans, etc. We use the "rotation sistem"
in our fields. Also, since we raises a great deal of silk-
worms (a painful and hard work for the women),
every field is planted of lines of mulberry trees. The
fields and meadows' hedges are planted of wood trees.

In May, to cut the first hay, in June, to pluck the
mulberry's leaves, in July to cut the wheat, thousands of
young mountaineers come down to the valley—in num-
berous groups—riding in big carts pulled by mules. As
they approach the towns and the village, they begin to
sing—and they pass through the towns and the villages,
singing in choir, throat-full, with stentorean voices
their rough songs. They go directly to the valley's
bottom—where the crops ripe first. At the evening,
in the piazza, they bargain with the farmers about the
wage and the conditions. At three o'clock next morning, they are in the field, ready to the tremendous task.
The sun strikes providencially the soil of the turgid
valley—but the sun strikes also mercilesly and often
fatal upon the skulls of those poor creature, bended
upon furrows, seeing red, sweating blood, to give the
bread to the worthy and to the unworthy—alas!

Every years, some of those men fall into the furrows
—for ever. They went to their death—singing. The
valley's folks fear these groups of young mountaineers,
espécially the women. Once, they might have been
dangerous. They are men of appalling force and carry
with them the sharp, bright scythes—or the sacks, ac-

cording to the occasions. But, actually, my folks' fear is based only on leggends. I know what has past in my town for twenty years; not even a case of rape or an homicide was committed by these mountaineers during those twenty years. Yet, my father told me many a time to have witness those mountaineers commit bad thing when he was young and my grandfather hired many of them.

Once, says my father, 10 of them went in the hay-barn and begin to smoke—a joke with intention to burn the whole farm to the ground. My grandfather—well, my grandfather chasted them out of the farm.

Returning to the farms-buildings, you may perceive, by what I have told, that they must be big. But they are also little farms and some farmers who lives in the town.

With the exception of olives, oranges, lemons, and the tropical and semi-tropical fruits—we raises many fruits, apples, pears, cherries, grapes, plums, figs, peaches, berries, etc. etc. The nearby hills are all a fruit-garden, wine yards and woods of chestnut and of hazelnuts. Blackberries, strawberries and mushroom grow wonderfully up there. Each farm has a vege-table-orchard, tilled by the women. The women work very hard there—beside to their householding—they till the orchard, raise the silk-worms, help in the field during the height of the hay's and wheat's works, care for the hogs—and raise hundreds of chickens, besides the dairy works.

Well, is not my story a long one? I don't know why, but in re-reading your letter over again, I was seized by a strong desire to tell you of my valley, of my folks, of my native town. I love my valley and my folks as myself. I know their soul which is my soul. It is six years that I am in chains—I may suffer of prison psycosy—So I beg your pardon for my long letter, random and fragmentary, about such far away places and peoples—I carry it all within my heart—I would tell more of my native valley, town and folks, and of my home. But enough of it for now—If possible, I will write some other times to you, especially because in your later letter are arguments of great moment, of which I would like to express my opinion—humble or wrong as it may be.

With warm heart I salute you and Mr. Russell— wishing to you, health and peace.

September 25, 1925. Charlestown Prison

DEAR COMRADE DONOVAN:

Your good letter of the 25th just received and read. Beside to be good, it has other qualities which made me admire and thank you. I would bet my neck that you are Irish as well as cosmopolitan.

Yes, our last visit was indeed short and so unhappy. The weather always influences us—I was particularly sensible of it even when living more normally than now. Now, my given particular environment and conditions, it asserts upon me a stronger influence. When the atmosphere is heavy, the gas floats lower in our shop, and stays longer, accumulating itself around us, making us more blunt. The day was cloudy and wet, when you were here, and I was simply unable to think, to remember, and to speak. When you left, I was sorry for you, and sorry and shameful for me. But afterward, I consolated myself by the thought that it has been more worse for me than for you. Is not this a fair piece of philosophy. I know that you have understood and forgiven.

You are wise: I would not have lost your feeble attempts at writing Italian, for I would not have received it, and your letter freed my mind of a preoccupation. I am inclined to believe that you are progressing in Dante's language. Next time I will examine you. . . .

I knew of the many anti-fascist meeting held all over the Union, and I am glad to hear of the future one to be held in Boston. I would even write something to be read at the meeting. But I am so caustic, so violent, realistic and impartial, that sometimes my thoughts are dreadful, even to myself, and almost my utterances are *"spiacenti a dio e ai nemici sui"* (displeasing to God and to his enemies). . . .

No honor was ever more deserved than our invitation to Miss Blackwell to speak at the meeting, and none can honor it more than she. She has only one fault; that to flatter the undersigned a little too much —spoiling them. I have no words to tell of the good that I received from her friendship and solidariety. As always, I was rough with her, and with all, and by gosh, I have been sad for it. She wants me to write her of my mother. I cannot speak of my mother, I told her, but she insists. She says "that an exceptional man is always the son of an exceptional mother." Well, she might be right, at that—but I have never dreamt, proud as I am, to be an exceptional man, though I adore my mother. But if the moon and the stars and everything in between will be prosperous to me, I shall try to answer the generous request of our noble Friend. To you, if you please, I ask to forward to her, at the meeting, my highest sentiments.

The man wants to boss the woman and therefore, the man invented many bunks to replace the reasons and justify their wrongs. (As always has happened and will happen in such cases.) I have always believed (since I begun it) that you women are not less, but more, courageous than us men. Yet, we call you the fair sex, and that seems true to me. Seriously, moral courage counts far more than physical courage. This is one of those things which negative side is superior to the positive.

But beside that, you women are also physically courageous. Kropotkin, as an historian, has sung epics to the courage and the heroism of the French and Spanish women. And I know that the Italian women have laid themselves, holding high their babies, across the railroads, before the trains, which, carried of soldiers, were moving to the war—to stop the train. And the Italian women did the same thing before the squadrons of cavallery charging the people. And the Irish women—stop—you know better than I do about them. So three cheers to all the good women of the land, of every province of the land. But I feel sure

that politics would spoil them as it spoiled "us men."
You too? But our dear Alice is of a different opinion.
But she is superior; she is high above the "suffragism"
just as Eugene Debs is above the "socialist party."
And both of them have done and are doing splendid
and great works of education and of emancipation.

Now, I will stop before you say that I am loqua-
cious. Your good wishes are most welcome to me. I
do what the Galilee did with the breads and the
fishes—, sending you seven baskets filled with them.
Mia buona Maria Donovan. I salute you with great
heart. *Arrivederci.*

October 27, 1925. *Charlestown Prison*

DEAR COMRADE BLACKWELL:

I understand that you must have been very sick.
And I was about to write for information when Miss
Mary Donovan came here and told me, with some as-
suring words that you were in the hospital, where you
had undergone a serious operation. After her visit,
I waited eagerly for your news, and the morning of the
25th Oct., Mrs. Evans told me, shining with gladness,
that you were doing well. In the evening of that same
day, I received the letter which you dictated for me.
It shows that you are in good spirit, and I thank you
a thousand times for it. I am happy that you are
surviving after the operation, and for your doing well.

Yes, I have had to swallow things so bitter "that
little more than death." It reduced me to a boney

pile of perambulating bitterness. Nor is it a matter of the past. It is six years that all my thirsts are quenched with gall and vinegar, and what is worse, I believe that the worst is yet to come. For I know the heart and the mind of my murderers, and the rest— to nourish empty hopes. My dignity refuses them— nor I feel the need of the help of self-illusioning. I am yet man enough to look straight into the eyes, the black ghastly reality and the tragedy of my life. And I would have the deadly joke to end, no matter how, this very moment.

But now, I want to congratulate you of your victory—not repeat my lamentation. That in spite of all, I can toast to your health, even after the gall and vinegar, and with great heart tell you that your flowers and your toast are most welcome here. To the triumph of your life, a worthy life, I drink. As even a nihilist, knowing you, would drink; if it is true that "In its gesture of death, there is nothing but a great dream of life." . . .

Yesterday, I received a picture of Beltrando Brini, who was with me peddling fish the day and the hour in which the Bridgewater hold-up happened. He testified at the first trial—keeping the stand for over two hours in one day, and for over an hour the following day. I am proud of him for he is my spiritual son, and he is doing very well. At the age of 12, he bought a violin with the money he earned by picking blue-berries. He belonged to a Musicians' Union for 2 years. Last year he graduated from high school with an honorary record, and he is entering Harvard this year. He is teaching violin to 11 pupils in Plymouth. A magnific son of the people. . . . And now, three cheers to you, and my hearty greetings.

November 13, 1925. *Charlestown Prison*

DEAR COMRADE BLACKWELL:

Your most welcome letter of Nov. 4th reached me in due time. Its news about your health assured me of your recovering and its arguments rouse many thoughts and sentiments within my being. I am going to answer with an attempt to express myself—and this will be a long random letter.

You blame to me, anarchist, Miss H—— because "she hates politics and never votes." Well, these facts cause me to add my admiration and my gratitude to her; and I don't believe that you have written in the hope that I would have approved your "blaming," for, you should believe that I have changed my ideas, in order to expect it. And I cannot see any reason for such belief. I know that you are doing everything possible to my welfare. Therefore, I think that you have said it purposely to have me thinking of controvertial arguments and forgetting my personal troubles and my environment. Thus, to beneficiate me. Most good of you. But, I will not discuss about yours and my different beliefs about ballot, etc., because I have many other things to tell you and I know that you know quite well the reasons of my disbelief—reasons advocate by men such as Bakounin, Kropotkin, Proudhon, Malatesta, Emerson, Shelley, William Goodwin, Reclus, Galleani, Tolstoy, Spencer, and, it seems, also Christ, are named for the love of my beautiful anarchy, not for vanity or worse than that,—and, forgive me.

Now, something about hope, hopes and hoping. A Damiani's paradox says: "There is no faith without desperation, and no desperation which does not hope to the last." It is right, I believe. It is more than logic, —fatal, that my friends and comrades shall hope in my freedom. For, it is human, and honors them and proves to me their love. The hope would be the last goodness, were it not for the desperation. Our difference is a psycologic one of persons in different conditions and natures and beliefs, thus psycologically different.

To me, my life and my liberty are in the hands of enemies who can do what they please of us, because to give or to deny us a new trial is absolutely arbitrary to them. Which, in the world, and where are the reasons that make it reasonable to expect from them a new trial? All that could have been, or is, favorable to us, —in the sense to compel the enemies to give us, against their own will and wishes, a new trial,—has failed or is failing. So that such hope is contrary to all reason, knowledge, realities, facts, experiences, criteria and logic. The hope of the doomed. Our enemies know very well that by another trial we would be free, and this is the reason why they will forget it; save that they want to free us. I have hopes—but I hope in me and in others.

Yes, I am disappointed already, without having to wait for further damages and offences. How could I not be disappointed? I should be insane and vanquished, while I have the soul of a winner. People have taken the bread out of their children's mouths to help us. Many have dedicated all their energy to the case; other prisoners were wronged; the same great cause has suffered because of us; we are chained, all our beloved in sorrow; the case is lost. We did not come to be vanquished but to win, to destroy a world of crimes and miseries and to re-build with its freed atoms a new world. I am disappointed, but not crushed. I have not become a rat or a renegade. And I can carry my burden to the last, and only that counts.

A good communist girl wrote me from Milwaukee: "We are celebrating the 7th anniversary of the Russian Revolution, and you too, I believe." How can I say to her that at the very thought of the Russian Revolutionary's failure all the sores of my heart open themselves, and all the anguish of my soul arises? Without hurting, or maybe, offending her? Ah, my passion for the truth! What a cross. Yet, I am glad of it, and I carry it with a strong heart. I adore freedom, it is my divinity, and the truth is its archangel of liberation. . . .

November 18, 1925. *Charlestown Prison*
DEAR FRIEND PETTYJOHN:

I had believed that one of the causes of your delay was that you were overworking, but I had also feared that you or some member of your family might have been or is sick. So, your letter of October 30th has been a most welcome pleasure and relief to me.

To write me such a good and long reviewing letter as yours from amid your hardship, is most good of you, and commands all my appreciation and gratitude.

As for the political, economic means, tactics and actions to quicken the history toward our common good, your beliefs and criterion are quite different from my beliefs and criterion, so that, only to put clearly and exactly the differences, not a letter, but a book would be necessary.

The topics of your letter are so many, deep and vast, they involve so many problems, phenomena, beliefs and conceptions, that it is almost impossible for me to write enough in a letter to make my opinions clear and understood. Therefore, I will limit myself to say that your letters always make me thoughtful, which is good—and that I share with you, if not your conceptions about methods and means, all your ideals and intention, and the goal. Our beliefs and our minds may be very different, but our aspirations and our hearts are most akin.

I will soon begin the translation of *The War and the Peace,* by Proudhon, from Italian to English, and I hope that my labor will not be done in vain.

December 5, 1925. Charlestown Prison

DEAR COMRADE BLACKWELL:

Your letter of December 3rd was just read. Thank you for the waited *Unity.*

Well, I am laughing at the Matteotti's murderers' white-washing. My comrades are long tragically joking of it. One has said, "Not only the government will acquit his (Matteotti's) murderers, but it will prize them, and find out that the only and real guilty one of this atrocious crime is the victim himself. In fact, had not he permitted to be murdered, his assassins would not be such. And, since Matteotti's crime was a very anti-national crime, and his family has a discreet patrimony, we advice the fascista State to pass a big fine on the martyr's family."

Justice is suppressed with fire and iron, by the tyrants and their blackguards. And for iron and fire the liberation calls. For that Mazzini adviced the Italians to turn in daggers even the iron-cross upon the graves of their dead ones. . . .

All in all, the truth is that Italy has to choose; either fascimo, or revolution. And the oppositionists fear the realization of the socialism—to which a revolution would inevitably lead. Hence, their impotence, and the ruin of the People.

Well, I am translating the Proudhon's book about war. Today, Mrs. Evans has read and corrected the translation of its first chapter. She says it is well done.

December 5, 1925. Charlestown Prison

DEAR COMRADE DONOVAN:

. . . . You call my wish for freedom, a christian wish. It may be, but I know of so many Christians who have perjured and framed me, who would be so happy to burn me, who enjoy so much of my chains and are so distressed at the thought of my possible but unprofitable future freedom, who are so beastial towards little criminals and so servil towards the great criminals, that I doubt if you can call your good wish a Christian wish. I know of professional Christians who have written and are doing the dirtiest tricks against me to send me to the chair. Last evening I wrote you 10 pages on this topic, but later on in the night, I decided not to deliver them. Thus, this morning, Dec. 30th, I am writing this hurried letter to you.

I hope you are well and I hope to see you soon again. And now, dear Comrade, I want to wish you with all my heart, Health and Vigor to Fight Joyfully the Heroic Battle of Life and Win, and Conquer Pains, Sorrow and Fatigue with the Flame of Force and of Courage. To know, to suffer is the sole, real, heroism.

CHAPTER III

IN the year 1926, a series of important legal steps took place. Mr. Thompson was now in charge of the defense and on January 11, an appeal from Judge Thayer was argued before the Massachusetts Supreme Court. The decision went against the men. Then followed another effort to secure a new trial from Judge Thayer, based upon disclosures made by Celestino Madeiros, then confined in Dedham jail for another murder. According to Madeiros, he and a notorious band of professional criminals were the perpetrators of the South Braintree crime. Again Judge Thayer decided against Sacco and Vanzetti.

This increased activity had its effect upon Vanzetti. In previous years he had occupied himself by translating into English Proudhon's *War and Peace,* writing his autobiography, *The Story of a Proletarian Life,* completing a novel called *Events and Victims,* which was a first-hand account of his experiences in a munitions factory before America entered the war, and contributing articles to anarchist newspapers and to the Defense Committee's bulletin, often on matters not directly related to the case.

Now, he bent his energies to the task of aiding counsel and the Defense Committee. He began to translate Mr. Thompson's brief into Italian, for distribution in Europe. Most of his letters at this time indicate a steadier preoccupation with the case. He conferred more frequently with members of the Defense Committee on steps to be taken.

January 30, 1926. Charlestown Prison

DEAR, DEAR COMRADE BLACKWELL:

. . . . I am sorry that you were unable to hear the whole argumentation of Mr. Thompson. He has really been magnific. Also Mrs. Evans says so, but, and not wrongly, she adds, "I will believe it when it comes to pass." Yet, a denial of a new trial, after the work of Mr. Thompson would solely, most clearly and irrefutably mean: we care, we look, we consider, we want nothing except to doom the defendants. A dangerous answer to the conscience of the world. It could change the proletarian Jobs into a Sampson, the proletarian rabbit into a lion. There would be flames. Fatally. Nor I believe the five men capable of such monstrosity.

I am glad and grateful to the Mexican lady for her interest in our case, and sympathy to us. And if you please, tell her of these sentiments. . . .

February 8, 1926. Charlestown Prison

DEAR MR. THOMPSON:

Your letter of the 25th Jan., 1925, reached me at due time; and here, I wish, before all, ask your pardon for my delay to answer.

I was very glad that you like the little jewel-box, but your letter to me is hundred fold worth than that triffle, pleasend and artistic that it may be. Indeed, even if I could have filled the box of most preciouse jewels, your letter would be hundred time more worth, just the same. Jewels can be bought by money, but the contained of your letter is of such high and preciouse nature, that no money, not all the money of the world can buy it. This is very good and very great of you, Mr. Thompson; and very good and very great to me. Permit me to express my gratitude and my appreciation to you.

I understand that your work in our behalfe is underpaid; the most difficult test of you; the noble sentiments and impulse by which you were decide to take the side of two underdogs; this I understand. And I also hope to understand a little the brave, learned, beautiful fight that you are fighting in our behalfe, paying of it in peace, rest, interest and other universally desired things.

Ha! to have known you 6 years ago! I would never have been a convict.

Of what you are doing for us, Mr. Thompson, I am not only grateful and thankful for myself alone, but for my old father, for my brother, my sisters, for all those who I love and am loved.

Here, the men are wondering and enthusiastic of you.

February 13, 1926. *Charlestown Prison*

MY DEAR FRIEND [MRS. MAUDE PETTYJOHN]:

Your letter of February 3rd has reached me this very evening, and also the clipping, and I thank you for both. I receive regularly the *Daily Worker,* the weekly *Nation* and glance daily at many American capitalists dailies. I receive free for several years an Italo-American, Fascista daily of N. Y., one (neutral) from Boston, and glance occasionally at some other Italo-American paper. Beside those, I receive the Socialist, communists, syndicalist, anarchists and Italo-American weekly. Their lectures, I mean the latest, makes my heart bleed, not to speak of the formers. ....

I am, with due recognition of an overwhelming cosmic force, a voluntarist and an anarchist, that is, the opposite of a fatalist, and all of the fatalist are Musselman. Some of them style themselves "evolutionists." . . .

I despair, it seems to me that the world is going to hell by radio. Just that. But I cannot articulate my ideas, in no way, and even less in a letter.

Proudhon has illuminated me. My pessimism is based on the blindness of the more, the rascality of the few, the dreadful unconsciousness of all, the tragic destiny and impotence of the exceptional one, the indirect evils of civilization overwhelming the direct benefits and the capacity, bad faith, ignorance, greedness and dearth of power of those who claim to be revolutionists. Evil cannot breed good, to my understanding.

Well, some other time, I will talk even more. We are still waiting for the decision. There is much optimism in Boston, not so much in me, yet, things are looking well. . . .

April 24, 1926. *Charlestown Prison*

DEAR COMRADE BLACKWELL:

I have received your letter and also your Easter card. I have wished to answer you, but I have been unable to write before this.

Comrade Rivera has requested me to tell him all about our case, or at least its last part. But I decided to tell him of the first part of the case and furnish him with all the literature and documents of the Dedham trial. So I wrote him an outline of the Plymouth case and a list of statements of facts on the causes and factor of the whole case, and its outcome; 53 large sheets of paper. I was very eager about that writing, which I deemed important and urgent, and meanwhile I was not in good mental condition: altogether I have had to toil long and painfully. It was the cause of my delay to write. I do not ask your pardon, because I am sure that you will forgive me.

I have heard about our dearest Eugene Debs going to Bermuda and his friends claiming for the restoration of his civil rights, and his refusal to ask for pardon. He was always great. Always a master of human dignity and bravery. But what a shame, what a shame for his nation to deprive her best child of the civil rights. The future generation will blush with shame in remembering the present ignomy of their ancestors. I wish to send a word to him, and I will. . . .

The delay is terrible, but I hope it will end soon.

The poetry on your easter card is really beautiful, but a bit too fatalistic. I would like, but I cannot believe, that the triumph of the good in this world is predestined. Yet, there is but two possible suppositions; either that we will be doomed, or else, by ourselves and other things, redeemed. The latter is hope no matter how foolish it may be; the former is despair, and better, a hundred times better, a foolish hope than a crazy desperation, for, all desperations are insane. But to keep myself near home, within the fence of the relative, I believe that a little more of voluntarism, and a little less of fatalism, in all what concerns the human powers and possibilities, would be more salutary to all. . . .

May 13, 1926. *Charlestown Prison*

DEAR COMRADE BLACKWELL:

Your letter of today has reached me this evening, when I returned from school having obtained the permission to stay in my room this evening. I asked it, not because I am over-sorrowed by the refusal of the Mass. State Supreme Court, but because I expect to see Mr. Thompson tomorrow, and wanted to do my work.

Your letter cheered me; it proves how careful and

mindful you are in our behalf, in this black hour of vanquishment. [1]

Yes, I have been a facile prophet—no wonder of it—after my previous experience of what justice, law and their bosses are. Yesterday, we got the last stroke. It ends all. We are doomed beyond any kind of doubts. I am sorry for myself. It is cruel to be insulted, humiliated, wronged, imprisoned, doomed, under infamous charges, for crimes of which I am utterly innocent in the whole sense of the word. But more than for myself, I am sorry for my father, my sisters and my brothers, and for poor Rosa and her two children.

My friends and Mr. Thompson were so optimistic and confident in the decision of the State Supreme Court, that I have been affected by it, and fool enough to write words of cheers and encouragement to my family. Now more sorrowful the news of the denial will be for them—now—after having hoped for my freedom and rehabilitation. Last night I wanted to write to them, but I was unable to begin it. I do not know what to tell them.

Mr. Thompson has been here yesterday, and three comrades were here today. Mr. Thompson has new evidence to present to the Superior Court and he could appeal to the Federal Supreme Court. But, what is the use? We would only ripen new affronts and de-

[1] The first decision of the Massachusetts Supreme Court refusing to over-rule Judge Thayer's denial of motions for a new trial was handed down at this time.

nials. And if we give up the fight, the electric chair will be at hand. I would spare the people and my friends and comrades of other expenses and troubles —vain as I know that they would be, and, on the other hand, I hate to give up the struggle and surrender myself to the executioner.

They have started just now the prison electric plant, which they use for the electrocution, because the Edison Electric Company refused to provide the State with electric power for the executions. My new room, very much better than the old one (I can write on the table now) is very near to the electric plant. I am hearing them now, preparing for an execution, maybe for my execution—and that noise cuts my being all over. I suppose they are preparing it for Madieros [1] or for the convicted car-barn murderers. [2] (No, I broke the rule and asked another prisoner, in the next cell, about the engine noise. He told me that it goes every night, and that we did not hear it before because the windows were closed.)

I expect nothing more of good from the so-called men's justice. . . . Of course, its deadly outcome does not minimize my gratitude and my love for all those who have been so good to me, during my ascension to the Golgotha. They and you have done very much in

---

[1] Celestino Madeiros, convicted of murder in connection with a bank robbery at Wrentham, Mass. In November, 1925, Madeiros had confessed that he had a part in the South Braintree payroll murder and that neither Sacco nor Vanzetti was involved in that crime.

[2] Three young men convicted of the murder of a guard at the Boston Elevated Railway carbarns at Waltham, Mass.

my behalf, much more than I deserve, and only the death will kill my reconoscence to them, and to you. If I have to die for a not committed crime by me, I will pass confiding in a future re-vindication of my innocence and of my blood.

May 15, 1926. Charlestown Prison

MY DEAR FRIEND [VIRGINIA MACMECHAN]:

Your letter of yesterday morning has reached me this evening and it was even more good to and for me than it had been for you, my dear friend. The refusal of the Mass. State Supreme Court has been an hard and most cruel blow to you and to all my friends and beloved ones, especially after the words of hope and of optimism which I had written to you and to them. I would never had written so, and you are begged to forgive it to me.

The confidence and optimism of all my friends, the strong proves and evidences of my innocence, of unfair trials, the magistral presentation and peroration of the case, made by Mr. Thompson; all this has induced me to believe that at the last I would have obtained justice by the State's Court. But there have been more and greater reasons and happenings than the above mentioned ones, to induce me to confidence. In Dedham jail is a man, Madieros, found guilty of first degree murder committed at the robbery of the Wrentham Bank. That man is a professional highway robber and his record is terrifying. He struck a guard at the Dedham jail, in an attempt escape,

There is no doubt of his guiltiness of murder: two of his partners pleaded guilty of second degree murder, and are now my companions of chain. Well, Madieros appealed to the State Supreme Court which, about a month ago, granted him a new trial on the ground of the presiding judge ommission (I do not know if intentionally or not) to tell the jury that *"The defendant shall be retained innocent until he is proven guilty."* Now, the defendant had, previously to his trial, confessed to have been the one who killed one of the bank's men, and asked to declare himself guilty of 2nd degree murder—which the Commonwealth refused.

Now, just compare his case with ours: he is an habitual robber; we were two real workers enjoying a good reputation. His record is most taint; ours were spotless. His conduct in prison was bad; we were publicly declared "model prisoners." There is no possibility of doubts on his guiltness; there is at worse, many doubts on us. The State has not a single testimony to prove that I have been seen on the crimes place,—I have never been there. His exemption is of purely technical nature, insignificant before the certainty of his guiltness; we have 35 reasons, unrefutable reasons of the most grave and vital character in our behalf.

How could I, before the State Supreme Court's granting of a new trial for such reason, to such man, have expected that the same Court which granted it would have denied us a new trial? . . . It is by all this that I have been decided and induced to write words of hope and of encouragement to my family in sorrow and in anguish, and to all my beloved ones. And I have not yet written to my poor sister and old father, since the decision.

The later Supreme Court's delay arised in me the suspect that they were following Judge Thayer's conduct; that is to being favorable—to decide and give confidence to all our ones, and to delay and delay in order to test the situation, and, at the deemed moment, stab us again at the shoulders. So I decided to begin a fast, in protest to the delay from May 1st. Mr. Thompson dissuaded me, and made pressure to the State Supreme Court. They told him that they will assemble on the 17th of May. . . . Then, they gave their decision on May 12th even without warning Mr. Thompson, so that the New York people learnt of it from the newspapers before the defense. . . .

Now all is lost. That was the last opportunity to have justice. We are at the arbiter of our enemies. Our friends wish to be told by us what they shall do. Nick, poor Nick, he has been so confident and trustfull —want to drop at once every legal defense. He won't do nothing more. I agree with him on the uselessness of any further legal defense as for to obtain justice. But why should we surrender ourselves to the enemy before to have exhausted every means of defense? I do not believe that the better people of the world are willing to let our hangers to burn us as two wild turkeys on the electric chair; and consequently I believe that the legal defense should be carry to the last. . . .

I suppose you have seen, or will soon see Mr.

Thompson. He has, or will tell you, about his intention. He is surely a goodly heart and a great minded man, so sincere in himself. He works hard for us—he accomplished a chief work of judicial science in our behalf. But he found his whole world against himself as soon as he assumed the defense of two poor Christs. Yet I trust and hope in him.

This is a bitterly reasoning letter, my dear friend. And yet, there is a great fortitude into my breath, my abdomen, and my spinal cord. And it is there that our soul dwells, not in the skull. And I am proud and happy of your sureness in my innocence. The truth is that not only have I not committed the two crimes for which I was convicted, but I have not stole a cent nor spilt a drop of human's blood—except my own blood in hard labor—in my whole existence.

But I was prompted by my nature to an ideal of freedom and of justice to all—and this is the worst of the crime to my enemies. The fact that for it and for consciousness I have renounced to a life of ease and of comfort, to wealth, to worldly ambitions, goods and honors, even to the joys of love—make me a terrible criminal to the eyes of my judges—a criminal capable of every crime. In fact, I voluntarily submitted myself to hard labor, poverty, dangers and persecutions. Had I renegated my principles after my arrest, I would not find myself, now, on the threshold of a death-house. I neither boast nor exalt, nor pity myself. I followed my call, I have my conscience serene, I regret nothing except the unspeakable agony that my destiny causes to my most beloved ones. And strange indeed, I cannot even hate my murderers and my diffamers. I even pity them. But oh! how they hate; how they fear; how unhappy they are! . . .

P.S. I am told that they burnt my anarchist journals which they found in my box in the store-house since my return from Bridgewater. By burning the symbols of thought and the thinker, they cannot destroy the thought itself—for it thrives and won in the ashes.

Mr. Thompson told me that Judge Thayer believes us guilty and that the well-to-do American people, whose will prevail, think very bad of us, that we are guilty and have had a fair trial. Nothing of more consequent and natural than their feeling and thinking against us and in favor of the harlots, the criminals who testify against us, of the jury, of the judge, and of the hanger. I understand it because having been myself one of them—I have been like them, and am shamed of it. But of Thayer—it is another thing.

May 21, 1926. *Charlestown Prison*

DEAR COMRADE BLACKWELL:

Your letter of yesterday received. This is your 3rd one after the decision. You cannot know how good your friendship is to me in this hour of passion.

I have been very busy these last days, writing letters on the case and conferring with friends. This is why for my delay to answer you, and of this brief note. I have so much to tell you—volumes. Your letter in the Boston *Post* is very good and beautiful, because it is truthful. . . .

P.S. Be of good cheer. We will fight to the last. Many people and reasons are with us. Augural greetings.

May 23, 1926. Charlestown Prison

DEAR BALDWIN:[1]

Your letter of May 15th reached me last evening, but I had been previously informed of your opinion. As you know, I accepted the hiring of a good lawyer to present the case to the State Supreme Court, not because I trusted in a fair and favorable decision, but to avoid the mockery and the damage, as the case would have been had we assumed an incompetent lawyer. Now we have at least an incontrovertable historical document in our side.

I do not know how it is that you repute the actual Massachusetts' governor a liberal, contrary to the universal opinion and all his public act. Well, the life and the man are so mysterious, I know so little of them, that I would not wonder that a reactionary might be liberal in some circumstances, or that a libertarian might be reactionary in some other occasion. Yet, I will not lose a second in conjecturation, for, now and here, to act is more urgent than to phylosofy.

What is it that you would ask the Governor? A

---

[1] Roger Baldwin of New York City, director of the American Civil Liberties Union.

commutation of the sentence, or a pardon, or deportation, or what? What do you know, either directly or indirectly, but positively, about the Governor's intention towards us?

If it is for a commutation of the death sentence into one of the imprisonment, there would be no use to talk. In this regard, the *less* is contained into the more, which is, in this instance, a fight for freedom.

But if you know that the Governor will free us, even if through deportation, then, I ask you as I would to a brother of blood, faith and arms, jump to this shore, or appoint a person of your confidence to obtain it. We will accept and spare to us and to others further toil, sacrifices and anguish. If it is not so, I will remain for the continuation of the legal defence to the last, though I am convinced that it will be useless and we, beated. . . . We will ask for revindication; we know that in digging our little graves, the reaction undermines its world, and anticipates its final collapse. . . .

We have still evidences enough to obtain a trial, but I know that all is useless in our case. So, let us fight to the last; if we will fall, thousands will arise, determined, implacable, daring of the supreme audacities and of the extreme perdictions. Let us fight!

Please answer me as clear and as soon as possible, if you know nothing positively. And act ever more quickly, if the other hypothesis is the true one. Another time, if you please, spell "coraggio" with a single 'r' and a double 'g'.

May 24, 1926. Charlestown Prison

DEAR MARY [DONOVAN]:

Thinking about what you said to me yesterday, it came to my mind last night, that Mrs. C—— of Plymouth is keeping a lamp lighted to her saints and Gods and Madonnas, for six consecutive years in her home, to receive from them all the grace of my liberation.

On April 15, 1920, at the very hour in which the Braintree robbery was committed, I was on the North Plymouth shore, conversing with Mr. C——, who was putting his boat in order. Before to reach him at the shore I went to look for him at his home where I found Mrs. C—— and their boy. They told me that he was at the shore preparing his motor boat to be put on the water. There I went and was, while the robbery was committed, and the whole C—— family are positive of my innocence—and keeping a lighted lamp for my liberty. I really believe that many others are doing the same thing. . . .

May 31, 1926. Charlestown Prison

DEAR MRS. EVANS:

Your letter of the 27 May is at hand and at heart. You are dearly eager to cheer me, dear Mrs. Evans and I will never appreciate enough your good friendship. That you and all my friends and comrades will never forgetting us—we are sure of it. It is our only confidence.

Yes, we still have more than enough proofs to obtain a new trial—were our case an ordinary one and not a pre-established legal lynching. Well, we will see.

June 5, 1926. Charlestown Prison

DEAR COMRADE BLACKWELL:

I was told that you wrote in our behalf in the Boston *Traveler* of June 3rd. How thirsty for our blood all of them are! Knowing that they can to us what they please, we know our fate,—but your solidariety is a balsamic dew to our dry leafs and exasperated souls— extremely disgusted with this most vile world.

With all my heart.

June 13, 1926. Charlestown Prison

DEAR COMRADE BLACKWELL:

Last Thursday, Mrs. Evans was here, and she gave me a copy of the *New Republic*, containing the editorial on our case, and indeed a splendid editorial. Oh, if everyone who wrote on our case would have had such a capacity and treated it so well as that writer, how much better it would have been for us. The indolence, the incapacity, the inexactness of those who have willingly or half-willingly wrote on our case, has always caused much disgust, and, often, indignation and wrath to me. I am sorry to say that the writings of the conservative or of the liberals have shown much more competence, sense of measure and of responsibility, than those of the more near to me. The writings of our Eugene Debs and those of the anarchist weekly,

Fede of Rome are the better of all; and good ones have been written by our affines. Yet, someone of our comrades made big errs and blunders. Thus the truth is spoiled, the seriousness of the case destroyed together with the trustings of the intelligent and impartial readers. What a contrast with the perfect, superfine ability of our enemies. Of all this I have spoken and lamented with one of the *The Masses* staff who was here a few days ago.

For several weeks I received *Il Nuovo Mondo*, an anti-fascist daily of New York, sustained by the American Clothing Amalgamated Union, and edited by the ex-Italian congressman, Vincenzo Vacirca, a unitario-socialist. I must say the following, even if it tears my heart. If we do not know to do better, we are doomed by our incapacity to a perpetual vanquishment —we will ruin even the most complete victory of a revolution brought first by other historical factors than ourselves. That anti-fascism has in itself, endemic, the fascism. It is as equivocous as that anti-clericalism which consist in fighting the clergy by revealing the priest's sins through pornografic expositions and in a false, unilateral historical philosophy, which consist in a wrong and partisan interpretation of the churches history. Equivocous as that atheism that affirms itself with blasphemous bravados, with dogmatic criterion on the creation and on the universe, with a trumpetting ignorance of the human nature and a self-imposing simpleton philosophy. And I could go on, on, and on.

Well, the *Nuovo Mondo* has talked a great deal about our case, within these last few weeks. But, oh, how badly! As for the Bridgewater explosion,[1] and the letter to Mr. Cox,[2] it limited its fatigue by copying from the American newspapers. Not a single rectification of the many voluntary inexactnesses divulged recently on our case by the capitalistic American press, and with many inexactnesses of itself. It even said that I was sentenced to 50 years for the Bridgewater robbery. In one writing it exposed the Braintree crime with an astonishing inexactness. It was most humiliating and painful to be compelled to recognize that the fascisti or philofascisti Italo-American *Progresso* and *Popolo*, New York dailies, have shown more earnestness and intensity of feeling in helping us, according to their character and thought and skillful journalistic ability. Well, I take it easy and am more displeased for the great than for my personal little cause.

I would like to read the anonymous letter that you have received. I am rather inclined to believe it of some police, as I feel was the one to Mr. Cox. The

[1] In the spring of 1926 in West Bridgewater, Mass., there was an explosion in the home of Samuel Johnson, a brother-in-law of Mrs. Johnson who claimed the reward for information leading to the arrest of Sacco and Vanzetti and who testified against them. The explosion, in which nobody was hurt, was never explained, being attributed variously to dynamite and to a still. Samuel Johnson later testified for the defense before the Governor and the Lowell committee.

[2] Cox was driver of the pay-truck in the attempted Bridgewater hold-up and was a witness against Vanzetti in the Plymouth trial, June–July, 1920.

contrary may be the truth in both cases, but the style and the words of the last letter smelt of the police station to the nostrils of my political nose. No, no, it is not the style and the phrasing of a presumable Italian radical. Not at all. Beside this, Mr. Cox did his best to have us convicted, but he was also the only one of the State perjurer at the Plymouth trial, who refused to identify me positively. He is therefore the less guilty one. Also, he had a good job; he was paymaster of the shoe company, and urged by it to hurt us. I was told that the public voice said that Mr. Cox lost his job because he refused to identify me positively.

I am sure that you will not be embarrased to answer to that letter, and sorry for the trouble. I hope and wish that you will do it.

That our framers and doomers might be afraid of punishment, it is well comprehensable. Moved by greed, hatred and prejudice, or compelled, they have determinedly acted against us and disposed to kill us. Being themselves actual murderers, they cannot help but to measure the others with themselves and to fear. And I not christian, am for vindication—but rather than to spill a single drop of innocent blood, I prefer to be electrocuted for a crime of which I am utterly innocent. In six years of wrong, abuses, outrages, persecution, revenges and of too slow murdering, none of our enemies have been touched. If they fear, the justification and the source of their fearing is in themselves. . . .

September 1, 1926. *Charlestown Prison*

MY DEAR COMRADE [OSKAR CREYDT] :[1]

Your letter of July 14th, 1926 has been received the day before yesterday, and I have no words, dear Comrade, to thank you adequately for the good that your letter has done and is doing me.

I count on you as one of those who will uphold the flag of freedom and justice when our dead hands will be no longer able to uphold it.

September 26, 1926. *Charlestown Prison*

MY DEAR BALDWIN :

Your letter of the 24th of September reached me last Saturday, and I was glad to hear from you and of the going on of our work. I hope to live long enough to read the printed book.

When you were here, I forgot to ask you several informations on things that I have at heart. Will you please tell me, if during your turn through the State, you have detected certain reactionary elements or associations to be against us? I remember to have read that you were hindered to speak, somewhere in California, by the American Legion. Were you to speak on the case? I pray you to inform me on all that you may know of this matter, and to do it without hesitations or regards. Because I am writing on the case, and need to know the truth. And since I am remem-

---

[1] Oskar Creydt of the Instituto Paraguayo, Asuncion, Paraguay.

bering: tell me if the Massachusetts American Legion has been or is against us.

Also, I am sure that you, together with the other friends and comrades of us, are doing everything possible in our behalf. But, alas! the case is too beaten, and I believe that we are lost.

No one here, who knows Thayer, believes that he is going to grant us a new trial.[1] The only way to kill us is to deny a new trial. And if you wish to foresee the "*crucifige, crucifige*" of the reactionary press, for when Thayer will give us "no," just read the editorial "Sacco and Vanzetti again" of the Gloucester, Mass. *Daily Times* of Sept. 23rd.

Saluti a tutti.

October 7, 1926. Charlestown Prison

DEAR FRIEND:[2]

Your letter of the 1st of October was handed to me the day before yesterday. I am grateful for all you are doing in our behalf, and glad that you appreciate the little pen-holder.

Your letter voices your hopes and optimism on the good outcome of the case. Would it be as you believe —but I cannot share your good expectations. I know too much our deadly arch enemy. Thayer, my experience, his words and behavior during the recent hearing,

---

[1] Motion for a new trial based upon the Madeiros confession and supplementary affidavits.

[2] Mrs. M. O'Sullivan of Kansas City, Kan.

his delay to give the decision, the fact that we do know nothing of what is going on, all proves to me that they are going to doom us.

I would already have began a hunger strike and give a declaration, had it not been because Mr. Thompson strongly opposes it with such arguments and reasons which sound to me as a death sentence. He has done wonders in our defense, and I dislike to contradict him so much. Of course, all his arguments, reasons and proofs, cannot compel the enemy to give us justice. Only the thunders of a mighty, world-wide agitation and protest could induce the enemy to free us. In Europe it cannot be done; in America it is not done—to explain why, would drive me crazy.

You speak of wheat farms . . . My Father has plenty of good land and a beautiful garden. They grow corn, wheat, sugar-beets, silk worms in my district, but the grass meadows are the more renditive and dear, fairly being the greatest resource of the place. . . .

As for our garden, it takes a poet of first magnitude to worthy speak of it, so beautiful, unspeakably beautiful it is. . . . We have fig trees, cherry trees, apple trees, pear trees, apricot trees, plum trees, peach trees, rhubarb shrubs, and three hedges of grapes in it—two lines of black and one line of white grapes. We plant one-third of it with potatoes, and make enough potatoes for the year round, even sell some sacks of them. Another 1/3 is planted with corn, also of it we produce more than we need yearly. The other 1/3 is planted with vegetables: onions, garlic, red and yellow peppers, carrots, spinach, cabbages, rhubarbs, anicettes, tomatoes, parsly, lettuce, asparagus, cucumbers, etc. We sell all these things and fruits also.

And the singing birds there: black merles of the golden beak, and ever more golden throat; the golden orioles, and the chaffinches; the unmatchable nightingales, the nightingales over-all. Yet, I think that the wonder of the garden's wonders is the banks of its paths. Hundreds of grass leaves of wild flowers witness there the almighty genius of the universal architect—reflecting the sky, the sun, the moon, the stars, all of its lights and colors. The forget-me-nots are nations there, and nations are the wild daisies. The blue, scented violets thrive well, the capel Venere are luxurious, the primtimes are at the vanguard. And the blue-blossoms erect themselves soberly dark blue toward the light blue sky, like breasts, turgid mother's breasts. And the white and the red clover and all the other scented, sky bestowed and beloved wild flowers of which I do not know the names.

You ought to see the king wasps, big velvety, lucid, ravishing forcefully on these flowers' calices, and the virtuous honey-bees—the wasp, the white, the yellow, the forget-me-nots, the hedge's butterflies and the variated armies of several genuses of grass eaters, the red conconcinas, the meadows gri-gri. Each of your step would arise from the ground a rainbow cloud of these creatures, with a multiphoned vibration of wings. Well, I have told you something about my native place. . . .

November 3, 1926. Charlestown Prison

MY DEAR COMRADE DEBS: [1]

Your letter of the 7th of October from the Lindlake Sanitarium reached me lately, when our unforgettable Gene was already very sick. Alas! of what I have to speak. I would have given my life to save him. I would have written to you during the agony of our Beloved and after His departure, but when I am sorry, I cannot talk; so forgive me my long delay. I ask this of you and of all your and His household. They killed Him because He was too good. And it is a long time since I realized that we would have lost Him quite soon.

To you and his household, I cannot find words worth enough to condol Him.

November 12, 1926. Charlestown Prison

DEAR COMRADE BLACKWELL:

Your letter of yesterday, mindful and heartful, as all of your letters, has reached me this very evening, with the enclosed letter from your niece. . . .

I hope I will not be entirely unworthy of him [Debs] in writing the memorial. It would (the work) certainly be original. A doomed man, saluting a great man, as an honorary citizen of his dreamed utopia—centuries ahead of our age. For this is the truth, Debs is not great to our time; he is great, will be great

---

[1] Theodore Debs, brother of Eugene V. Debs, living at Terre Haute, Ind.

in the future superior ages. The compliments that the capitalist scribbles are paying to him, after having bittered and shortened his saint life, because he is now out from under their feet, which have abused him—virtualizing, memorializing, naturalizing his real nature, the greatness of his heart and of his mind, and his doctrine, just as the mercenary, prostitute scribbles of all the ages have done of each great death. This is one of the greater of the many great crimes of inhumanity; to deprive the race of the real Genius of each great doctrine so to turn it in instrument of regression.

It is now customary to speak of objectiveness—as of a great thing. Relatively understood, it is a good thing, absolutely it is trash. A human being can perceive, understand, judge from and with his being and he can only be objective according to the very nature of his being, in respect to each and all the questions and the problems of life. Nothing is worse than a false belief of self-goodness or greatness. It is that which permitted Nero to kill his mother without remorse. . . . The convinced of the most bad belief may wrong everything and everyone, convinced to be objective.

Therefore, I will only try to be just and honest to each of my topics—this is the only possible and real objectiveness. Yet, if I will treat anything in a wrong erroneous way, by ignorance, I will be unjust and unhonest, *che fatto*, in spite of all my good will. The truth, then, is what matters. But in this regard too, alas to one who is too sure of possessing it, especially if more than relatively absolutely. . . .

Returning to the more good Man that I ever met, I must confess to have read very little of his own. And to me, few pages of a man tell more than a voluminous biography. The letters of Lincoln, for example, put me in war with almost all the biographic writings which I read of him. Another great difficulty for my text is that I am a European, while our Debs is an American. It is hard for me to truly understand you Americans, in many respects. This, of course, is reciprocal, it means just what it says, and you are prayed to forgive my open sincerity. I believe you can, and I pray you to inform me if our Beloved was deist or gnostic, or atheist. Also, if you please, the dates of the killings of the Presidents Cleveland and McKinley, and what was Debs' attitude toward those historical events.

I feel of a great responsibility in writing of the Man who has loved me more than my own father and whom I love with the heart of a son and disciple.

Was Debs involved in Pettibone's Trial for the murder, or more rightly the execution of a Governor of Illinois? Or was he only the bravest defender of those defended?

Well, I have gathered all the material and now, your information and the material which you have so goodly thought to provide me, will surely enable me to speak with cognition and cause—and love's fire is in me. If only the stars would be propicious!

As for the case, what you told me was certainly good, but we are beaten beyond remission. . . .

I rebel to the conception of an omnicient god, infinitely good and just, omnipotent, who foresees everything, who could make the human good and good-behaving, whereas he let them do bad and afterward punishes them. But history has a nemesis which does not forgive. . . .

To be sure the American people's attitude toward the case is turning better—though a little too late. I am glad that the honesty and exactness of the Defense Committee is recognized.

November 18, 1926. *Boston*

DEAR MR. LEARY, JR.: [1]

Your letter of the later Oct., 26, has reached me at proper time and, though it is an answer, I feel obblige to answer, if for nothing else to assure you that I understand and appreciate the great good that your own work and that of the *New York World* are doing to Sacco and I. I also wish to tell you that I agree that your way and Mr. Thompson's ways are the ways more apt to bring some good results—given that the U.S.'s Workers are as they are and the European condictions, desperate. So, you easily understand my appreciation for your earnest advice of conduct.

[1] John J. Leary, Jr., of the reportorial staff of the New York *World*. Mr. Leary had spent several weeks in New England investigating the Sacco-Vanzetti case and preparing a series of articles on it for *The World* shortly before Vanzetti wrote this letter.

I may or may not keep to it—but not because I do not recognize its sensibility. It would be because I do not care any longer of what may happen to me, and choise daring and defeat; a vanquished man, but a formidable shadow.

You alluded to my friends' impatience and to their lost of confidence in Mr. Thompson. I was surprised because I had never heard of such things before. I presume that you have took it from the *Boston Advertiser*, for I have been informed that it published some thing of that sort. You know that it and the *Boston American* are sadic toward us. . . .

All of us realize that no better man than Mr. Thompson could have been choised as our defender. Our pessimism is related solely to the sistem.

In the hope of having dissipated a confusion, I beg you to excuse my prolixity.

November 25, 1926. Charlestown Prison

DEAR FRIEND ABBOTT: [1]

Your letter of November 23rd reached me yesterday evening. . . .

You said, dear Abbott, that the Russian Revolution "has dethroned one class to put another in charge." I don't believe, in fact I am positive, that that was not done in Russia—that it is impossible to be done either in Russia or elsewhere. In Russia, this happened: The Czarism was destroyed by a revolution; part of

[1] Leonard Abbott of New York, an anarchist friend of Sacco and Vanzetti.

the owners were expropriated; a party took the power, stopped the continuation of expropriation and appropriated to itself that part of the social wealth which had already been expropriated by the people. From that moment the revolution began its regression and few leaders of a small party became the only and real rulers of Russia. They were immediately compelled to form a national army, and build a policy worse than the Czars' one; to uphold a new church, not better than the old one; and, given the conditions, to be more reactionary and tyrannic than the dethroned autocracy itself. Moreover, to hold their power and stop the natural evolving of the revolution, the few leaders of the small party, now in the government, were compelled to take in their service the officials of the Czar army and police, the burocrat, the bourgeois, and to repress and suppress all the people, workers and revolutionist who disagree with them.

So that it is now experimentally, historically proved what the "damn fool anarchist" are saying from a half a century at least: The proletariat cannot become a ruling class; it can dethrone the actual ruler and place its leaders in their place, but in so doing the revolution would be in vain and the workers exploited and oppressed as before, if not worse.

In fact, the outcome of the Russian Revolution, under the Bolsheviki Leaders' dictatorship, is an increased perfectioned exploitation of the proletariat, reached, achieved through the great and scientific industry. All boiled down, the actual crisis of the world is due to the industrial competition of the greatest nations and to the fevering development of the minor or retrograded nations, plus the fact that their rent of each of them become daily insufficient to the daily increasing social parassitism and the rampant development of new needs that our civilization (?) determine in each individual.

So that the ruling, owning classes of each and of all the nations find themselves compelled to a more extensive and intensive exploitation of the masses and to a more firm oppression of them. Hence, the fascism and the bolshevism compelled to the same policy, same means—though their opposite aims—and damned to same results. It is so perceivable that it seems idle to say that both of them are not only utterly unable to eliminate the social evils, but that they make them worse and lead to destruction and death. Yet, in spite of all our boasting and pretension of intelligence, radicalism, masternism, understanding, culture, etc., how few understand this palpable truth slapping all of us on both cheeks. . . .

I may be rough, but I am convinced of truism when I say that most of the self-styled radical are more superficial than many ridiculated or dispised backward people. And Proudhon's words "The Socialist have sinned more than anybody else of this craziness more crazy than all the crazinesses that they have all the pretense of curing," ring very often to my minds' ears. Proudhon was right, abused, ridiculated. I dare to say that even the anarchist have scorned at his stern truth. But the historical events, from his time to this

miserable Thanksgiving Day, have proven his asser-
tions—revindicated his genius.

You say you cannot any longer take as seriously as
you once did, the discussion on libertarian and socialo-
gic theories. Well, not even I; for never as now have
I been convinced of the veridicity of my beliefs and
of the necessity of their realization; action, then, not
verbosity, is what I am enthusiastic for. Are we alone
despised, hated, doomed? Ah! to see the world to
doom itself in dooming us; to see the enemy more
wretched than us—deprived even of the inner morals
prides, to see the rightness of our ideal confirmed by
the negative results of the enemy's triumph, is as sweet
as nectar to us, doomed, because it proves to us that
we die for the right while our enemies die of our
wrong; that we die as men, they as degenerates; and
that if the world and mankind is worthy of a laugh,
we, the vanquished, not our enemy, the victor, can
die with a laugh—and what if that is not so? If that
is not so, then everything is testifying that our defeats
are victories and the enemy's victories, vanquishments.

This almost bakouninian letter—in quantity, not in
quality—may seem to be wholly assertional, not docu-
mented. I believe that volumes would be required to
documentate my assertion or to develop my premises.
Volumes have been written on the touched subjects—
and you know them better than I.

And so, excusing my prolixity, with unbroken mind,
steadfast will, and glad heart, I salute you, friend
Abbott.

P.S. I too believe in "our release." Fuller boasts himself, making the liberals believe, to be a liberal. . . . Beside to be a liberal, some liberals know Fuller as an independent man, willing to the right thing as he sees it (which is as the Massachusetts reactionary plutocrats see it) and so, that he will do justice. See the *Success Magazine* of December. But, as the whole bunch is mighty but not almighty, let us hope and over all, will. *Salve!*

December 11, 1926. *Charlestown Prison*

My dear Friend [Mrs. Maude Pettyjohn]:

Our I—— B—— has told me that I will receive a letter from you. . . . I was pleased with the news, for it is quite a long time that I have heard from you, and I eagerly expected the letter, because I like your writing. Finally, I received it some days ago, and now I am trying to answer it.

Yes, trying . . .! for there is much understanding in your beautiful letter, strong beliefs, and hints to things so vast and deep, that I do not know anything about, not even how to begin my reasoning, before which however, I wish to thank you for the goodness of your letter and the pleasure that it brought to me— to us all.

Exactly talking, I am not busy in writing, but in trying to write. For, the prisoner's spell is telling its story also on me, and how so! It seems to be increasing my understanding and diminishing my power of expression. In fact, it is an experience alright; but an experience that undermines the life straight to its sources and centers so that as long as consciousness and memory are not yet weakened, you can realize something—but, as to express oneself at one's best, one has to be at one's best, while after such experiences one is no longer at his best; he can no longer express himself at the best of his power. These are the reasons why I am busy trying to write and writing very little at all. Oftentimes my mind is ravishing; oftentimes, it is blank. More often I cannot express my thoughts. Oftentimes, I manœuver hard to write down what I wish, then, reading it, I perceive that it does not say what I mean and I tear the writings in many little pieces. Many times, I feel lazy, indolent, malignant and cynic; asking myself what is the use to write and if it pays its troubles. If I still write it is to gratify myself, when I feel to write. At least, it seems to me.

The crux of this inner drama is not only about expression—it is that I doubt my own thoughts, my opinions, my feeling, my sentiments, beliefs and ideals. I am sure of nothing, I know nothing. When I think of a thing and try to understand it, I see that in the time, in the place, and in the matter that thing is, both before and after, related to so many other things that I, following its relations, both backward and forward, see it disappear in the ocean of the unknown, and myself lost in it. It is easy to create a universal system, to human minds; that is why we are blessed by so many of universal systems, while no one knows what a bed buck is. The sense of relativity and of measure is a progress on the sense of the absolute and infinite, for the former is a capacity of discernment, the second a mental abstraction, a symbol of the "abroad" of our senses and relative knowledge.

To be sure, I am not in any better support with the words, opinions, beliefs and ideas of others than I am with my own ones. I believe to have been [born] with the faculties of acquiring ideas, forming opinions, learning words, and express myself—but not with opinions, ideas and words already in me. Believing this, I must also believe that all my actual ideas, opinions, beliefs and words came to me from some other persons. Yet . . . only that part of their saying that satisfies my ego. But, even in this, I am not entirely free, for, to be the best that I could be now, I should have been, before my very conception, conscientious, intelligent, a power more capable and intelligent than the one I am now, so to begin my beginning in the best of the ways, and to impart continually to my evolving self only truths and normalcy. Evidently, it must not have been so, for I have not the least recollection of such a feast! Whereas, I am but too well aware, alas! to have begun as a miser to have inherited all the misery of the earth and of the race, called atavism— to have been taken to church when I was wholly unconscious and irresponsible, to have been spiritually raped by the priests, when I was wholly unable to defend myself, to have been intellectually warped and poisoned by the State school, when I was unable to discriminate—to have grown within a humanity so stupid, ignorant, vile, coward, arrogant, self-conceited, brutal, greedy, ferocious and filthy and falsely proud and humble, that the best of my essence was choked in myself, or, what is still worse, distorted and aberrated. To my parents, to my mother especially, I owe not only my life that she gave me by birth and cares, but all that is good in me. Yet, even my parents, in spite of their love and good-will, they teach me many wrong ideas, false principles, and a false divinity. It is by a rinnovation of [my] own previous self, through a self reaction, an inner tragedy which costed me the bleeding of my heart's blood, that I re-began and became what I am now. I brought it to myself and ever more to many humble persons and children who gave me fragments of truth and to the genious of the race. Thus I reached the present stage of my being.

All what I have said may induce you to believe that I am a so-called "Determinist." I am not so, though I believe in the existence of a "together of things" which we pass through and which influence is a "concomittant" factor of our individuality. That "together" is made of two different orders of things, namely; of the things of nature above the human-will and power, and the things which result from the human behaviors and their worksome matters. But that is not "all," for each of us differ from the others, though many spoke of conception, maternity, atavism, etc. Well, those things too are subject to changes and conditions that alter them,—still determinism. But, why are we? Why are we as we are? Why chances make differences? Here the "determinism" spring from something else—from the unknown. If we follow it, it ultimately opens in the unknown again.

To believe that hope, faith, optimism, confidence, are good to the individual, is part of the race wisdom; an historical experience. So we all are most grateful and appreciative of your motherly incitation to them.

Yet, life, happiness, health and goodness depend from things which are what and as they are, and not what and as we believe or hope them to be. So that wrong faith, absurd hope, unfounded optimism and confidence are or may be fatal or at least very deleterious to the individual, in spite of their real help to him as animators. For they mislead us and when we face evil, cannot help us.

I believe better, to try and look the reality straight in its face, eyes into eyes. The question is not to shift from barren reality by any dreams or auto-suggestion. It is: 1st—Not to let ourselves be overwhelmed by the adversity, scared by black prospects, but face them as bravely as possible. 2nd—Try to fight them with all our force. To destroy bad realities, to create good ones, lo! that makes gods out of men and women.

It is for such reason that I indict all the new and all religions. They dope the people so to eternate slavery, unequality, exploitations, crimes, vices and death. The new religions are not better than the old ones for this. . . . By these criterion I came to understand the phylosophy of "free will" and that of "determinism." According to the latter, none is guilty. The former is more wrong and deleterious than the latter, and it explains the mercilessness of the law, the dishonesty of the State, the ferocity monstrous of the churches, and the immorality of the pure moralists. The latter, too, has its weakness and bad consequences. It tends to weaken the human will, to incline its believers to an idle fatalism, to self-indulgence and irresponsibility in a way, for if things cannot be otherwise than how they are, or go otherwise than how they go, if we are what external factors determine, you can see the consequence of such thinking. As for me, I believe to a certain extent in both, as limited and changeable phenomenum, interdependent, and dependant from some higher phenomenism. So, I have no ultimate word on them and I remain a *Voluntarist*.

You are right—maybe it would be a rest to me, not to think of the case. But the case is turning badly. The enemies are determined to burn us as soon as possible, and therefore, I am compelled to write of it, while I can. You know that I am a revolutionist; dreaming, willing a Polygenesis of life. My own story serves my purpose, points to my goal magnificently. That is why I am in spiritual travail. . . .

M—— M—— is a dear little soul. A farmer girl too. . . . Her letters are bliss to me. Now, she may be sad for me, for she wrote me about religion. . . . The dear thing asked them to pray for me, to send her prayers to me and one for me. She sent it to me. I answered as kindly as possible, that I do not believe in it, but that I respect her belief, and appreciate her intention. Maybe, I told her, it is good to me, do it if you wish, but I don't believe. She must be sad for it for it is quite a long time since I have heard from her. . . .

I see that B—— L—— is quite a scorner and a pessimist. Well, the world will never have enough scorners. Pessimism itself, in a way, is good. Darrow said, "If you are not worse than your fathers, if you have progressed a little, you shall acquit these negroes." And the jury acquitted them. Had they thought their fathers to be holy, in spite of slavery, they would not have acquitted the Negroes.

Thayer and Katzmann always appealed to the jury pretence of superiority and goodness to induce them to convict us.

Of course, the saints have a better way; but the saints are few. . . .

I too, would be with your son, in the farm, through woods, on hills and mountains. I love farming more than any others works and nature over all. But I do dislike hunting, not as a sport, but for its killing. Bears must be damaging and dangerous if people are allowed to hunt them freely. Don't you think so?

Your place must be very similar to my native place. Can you see from your home, mountain peaks eternally covered by snow? If so, your place is like mine. . . .

December 19, 1926. *Charlestown Prison*

DEAR COMRADE DONOVAN:

With the fierce music of the cold and strong wind blowing through this bright morning, I am thinking how good it was of you to pay me a visit during this cold wave. As I told you to be expecting, Mr. Thompson came yesterday afternoon and brought me several weeklies from Europe and South America, and many letters. *The Authorized Life* of Eugene Debs and *What His Neighbors say of Him.* (Debs) So that I have much to read and much to write presently. . . .

You deserve indeed a better letter than this poor one that I am so willingly writing. Well, I am going to give you a tableau of our daily life routine. (1) At six o'clock in the morning, the wing's bells rings once: we can "get off" and light the pipe even before to begin to dress up. From 6 to 7, we can what we like in our room. (2) 7 A.M., a second ring; we must be ready to go and have breakfast at the kitchen window, and return to our room. From 7 to 8, we can do what we like in our room. (3) 8 A.M., a third ring; now we must have our room clean and orderly and be ready to leave it. One wing after another (the occupant) goes in line to empty the bucket at the dump situated against the wall that faces the freight yard. From there we line again, two by two this time, and go to the shops. (4) 11:45 A.M., a second whistle tells us to leave the shop, line in the yard side-walk, then go to the kitchen, take our dinner, and carry it to our room. (5) There we must stand at the door, clinging one of its bars, until the officer counts us and locks our doors. From then until 1 o'clock we are freely locked in our rooms. (6) At one o'clock another ring. The room must be in order, we go to the shops, as always, in line. (7) 3:20 P.M., a whistle tells us that the days work is finished; we are already dressed for the "yard," we go to the shop front, there to talk or play for a while. (8) 3:35 P.M., a whistle tells us to go to the yard—the general signal is given

by the yard bell, in which talking, playing and joking
is allowed. (9) 4:10 P.M., the yard bell rings; we
line, go to the kitchen, take our supper, and go to
our room. After that our doors are locked, we can
eat, or not, and until nine o'clock we can dispose of
our time to smoke, write, read and walk, think, swear,
and so on. We have evening schools, voluntary, not
obligatory. Some prisoners go two or three evenings
a week; some others don't go. It lasts an hour and
a half. (10) 8:55 P.M., the last ring of the day—
the lights go off, we must be in bed. This is our daily
routine. The "yard" time is changed several times
during the year, according to the length of the solar.
In the summer time, we stay longer in the yard; though
we quit working later than in the winter. Now, about
the Lord's day. At six o'clock the first ring; at seven,
the breakfast, then we can go to the first Catholic
service, then to the second, Protestant service, or we
can stay in our room. The last service ends after 11
o'clock, more or less after according to the length of
the two priests' bunk, and everybody goes to the yard,
from which we return to the kitchen and our rooms,
at 11:45 A.M. In the afternoon, we have either the
Christian nor Scientist service, except one Sunday
a month in which we have Methodist services. We
have also Hebrew services.

As you see the only thing of which the State does
not economize on us, is "religious dope"—and the
State is skumly wise. As a rule, we have a show or a
movie every other Sunday. . . .

December 21, 1926. *Charlestown Prison*

MY DEAR FRIEND MRS. EVANS:

This evening returning to my cell I found a little package on my little table: a glance to its address and I see your handwriting and realize a Christmas present from you. I like the necktie and more the beautiful *Emerson's Essays.*

Well, I will look less badly with the necktie on, and I will again delight myself at the lecture of Emerson's *Politics, Nature,* and *New England Reformers,* so exquisitely anarchist. In the latter, we can see poor Emerson sweats the proverbial seven shirts to dissipate the prejudices, mental fog, ignorance, and bigotry of people that pose as Saviour, and against their dreadful unconsciousness.

Yes, yes, you have sent me a great present, dear Mrs. Evans; I am glad and appreciative of it and I thank you very much.

Of course I wish you a happy Christmas and New Years—because they are days and I would be able to make each day an happy day for you.

I hope you are well and I wish you all that is good in life.

December 28, 1926. *Charlestown Prison*

DEAR FRIEND [MISS MARY DONOVAN]:

Just a few words in answer to your nice Christmas card and the good wishes thereby expressed. It reached me in due time and was most welcomed and appreciated.

I hope that everything goes with you, that you might

have passed the Yuletide at home and that all of yours are well.

I received many letters and cards this Christmas, but I realize that many of my good friends, most of them have just thought and wish good to me, and acted in my behalf, but not written. . . .

I would wish you a Happy New Year, but it seems idle to me, for I wish you that every day, not merely the first of the year, as the last fools do.

Mark Twain has said that "The only useful holiday that we have is April Fool, for it reminds us of what we are the other days of the year." Christmas, whereas, is a cheating holiday, for we pretend to be good then, which, when not a bad illusion is rank hypocracy—holy mackerel (is mackerel spelled correctly?)—I am sure of "holy," though I was a fish peddler. . . .

December 28, 1926. *Charlestown Prison*

DEAR FRIEND MRS. JACK:

Your two beautiful cards, that of your little home and that of my home's flowers, hills, and summits are here, to the gladness of my eyes and of my heart.

Thank you for the news of Nick, Rosi and the children, I am always pleased to hear of them and of you all. Poor Nick, and poor Rosi, their cross is heavy indeed. Even the children suffer.

But we must be brave, brave, brave. I am well and facing life fearlessly. . . .

I hope you are well, and I send you all the good wishes for the new year at the door. . . .

CHAPTER IV

IN January, 1927, final arguments on the Madeiros motion were made before the Supreme Court. On April 4, the Court again sustained Judge Thayer.

All legal steps for a new trial having failed, the men were brought again into court to receive sentence. Vanzetti was transferred from Charlestown prison to Dedham on April 9, and led into the court-room with Sacco.

On this occasion, when they were asked by the Court the conventional question whether they had anything to say before receiving sentence, Vanzetti spoke for three-quarters of an hour with an eloquence that stirred the court-room. In the midst of Judge Thayer's pronouncement, he interrupted to ask permission to add some remarks he had forgotten, but this permission was denied.

The ensuing three weeks were devoted to preparation of a petition to the Governor. Vanzetti joined Sacco in refusing to sign anything that might be interpreted as a request for pardon or mercy. Instead, with Mr. Thompson's help, he wrote his own petition, setting forth his and Sacco's anarchist views and summarizing the chief points of the case for the defense. Sacco remained steadfast in his refusal to sign any petition. It was therefore presented to the Governor, on May 3, with Vanzetti's signature alone.

The Governor immediately began his own investigation of the case. Petitions from all over the country, urging a thorough review of the case, were by this time beginning to pour in upon him. On June 1, the Governor announced the appointment of an advisory investigating committee composed of President Lowell of Harvard, President Stratton of the Massachusetts Institute of Technology, and Judge Grant, a former Probate Court judge.

During these weeks (after the petition was presented), Vanzetti viewed proceedings with a composure that drew comment from all who visited him. He redoubled his letter-writing, continued to read incessantly, and played an Italian bowling game with Sacco, in the daily hour allowed them together in the prison courtyard.

January 10, 1927. *Charlestown Prison*

DEAR COMRADE BLACKWELL:

I believe that I have answered to your good wishing card of Christmas. This year I received many presents and a lot of correspondence and money for Christmas and New Years. After, I received *The Life of Debs* and later, *Essays on Revolt* by Jack London. . . .

For the last six Christmases we have had moving pictures and a good dinner, after which we remained locked in our cells 'til the next morning. That was my sixth Hell-Christmas in prison. I look back; the past was bad enough, I thought, but the worst is yet to come. A bitter Christmas it was.

On the morning of the first day of the New Year, the Clives Company recited the comedy *A Pile of Money* here, for us. It has been very amusing. Mr. Clive [1] comes once yearly to entertain us. It is very good of him. After the comedy, we have had a full hour of yard. Then we got a good dinner with rice pudding, and were locked until the next morning. This, I thought, is my seven years of imprisonment, for the two crimes of which I am entirely innocent. How many other years will I have to drag in chain before the death will deliver me? A black self-query, I tell you.

I know perfectly well that within four months, Massachusetts will be ready to burn me. I know that the magistrature first, then the State, can do with me what they please and choose. Well, when I mentally put myself in their place and them in mine, I find myself embarrassed to choose of the two things; either give him life or electrocute him. Everything considered, there are many reasons pro and con to both of them. "To electrocute him" it may be unsafe, though it would free us of further troubles; to give him "life," that too has its inconveniences. That Massachusetts is predetermined to deny me the last right, and to kill me in one way or another, I am positive of it.

So every hope to get reparation and freedom has been killed in me by each and all the words and deeds

[1] E. E. Clive of England, head of the Copley Theatre of Boston.

of Massachusetts' black gowned, puritanic, cold-
blooded murderers. On the first day of the 1927, I
formulated the wish, that I may get out within this
year, no matter if alive or dead. And I hope with all
my force that this will come true. By it, I do not
mean suicide.

Very often I turn around my mind's eyes to see, contemplate and study the world even and mankind. The
spectacle is extremely repugnant and heart tearing.
At it, one does not know if to love or if to hate, if to
sympathize or if to despise humanity.

Things are going from bad to worse. War in China,
Nicaragua, revolution in Java, Mexico, Brazil; the
Balkans on foot of war; France and Italy mobilizing
one against the other; England, United States, France
and Japan in a crazy rivalry of armament; South
America and United States in danger of war; Italy
under the fascist dictatorship; Russia under the Bolsheviki one; scandals, corruption, crimes, diseases, degeneration, greed, hatred, unconsciousness, prejudices,
and insanity sweeping the earth. I wonder how it all
will end. There is but one system, one philosophy
through which I can explain to myself the causes of this
universal tragedy and the possible remedies, which of
course, should be prompted by the human voluntarism:
It is the *Philosophy of the Miseria* by Proudhon. I
have not yet read this book in whole, but only some
fragments of it here and there, now and then, in our
journals. But having translated selected pages of
The War and the Peace by Proudhon, I can understand
the former book because the latter is based on the

same criteria and theories as the first. Always and everywhere we find that pauperism is the first cause of war. The first of the rights is the right of the force, all other rights spring from it as branches from a sapling. That is the reason why, whenever and however is created a situation unresolvable by any or all the other rights, the single and the collectively recur to force. "Equality is the condition sine qua non of justice." The justice and the injustice have a common source; the man's respect of himself and of the dignity of the human person. If from these two loves and respects innate in man, follow plans and deeds of equalities in production and distribution, consideration and rights, that is justice. If we, because of these loves and respects are led to establish privileges for us and those whom we love more at the expense of other, that is injustice.

The destiny of man on earth, is poverty. To live little, to work hard, to always learn; the passion for the justice and the philosophy, to sustain and abstain,— such is our destiny. We have war because we are not sufficiently heroic for a life which does not need war.

Sublime, the Proudhon pictures of the consequences of pauperism and of wealth; both fatal. But I believe that the translation will not be published. I tell too much truth.

In the first 30 minutes of January 6th, the Massachusetts State killed three men in the electric chair. . . .

Coolidge, out of a false fame of a good strike breaker has formed his political "horse of Troy."

Fuller, to be president, will burn us all; all 7 of us.

I would like you to read his "Why I Believe in Capital Punishment" edited in *Success* of December 1926. You will see that he claims to have freed Massachusetts of criminality and that he believes to appear as a saviour in merit of the then-future executions.

On January 5th, I learned that the 3 men will be killed immediately after midnight. Because the participants and witnesses of the execution use to eat after it, at the warden's house, three hams had been cooked in our kitchen, and they were carried to the warden's house on January 5th. So we knew. I wished and tried to keep awake that night to attend to the execution from my cell. But, I fell asleep against my will, and at my awakening I was told of the triple murder. Three pair of eyes for one pair, three lives for one life. Massachusetts, Fuller that preaches to the children, the golden rule and the Sermon on the Mount, practiced a pre-Mosaic custom. What a chapter I could write—maybe I will write it—on this triple cold-blooded murder.

But one must be crazy or shameless to boast himself of having saved Massachusetts from criminality, when criminality has never been so wide spreaded, bold and terrible as it is now. Just after the execution, an orgy of crimes took place in Mass. Two days after in Quincy, Mass., two children, 13 and 15 year old girls, held up a woman. In Middleboro, a convict cut the head of a guard. Then came the battle of the hijackers. These are but few of the many crimes of every nature committed in this State after that triple execution—5 days.

Now, after that, everybody said that Sacco and Vanzetti will go. Most of my fellow prisoners were glad of it, and you should have seen how they looked at me the day after the execution. The friendly ones have not had the courage to look into my face. It is my belief that Fuller refused to commute the sentence of the Carbarn slayers and of the negro, previously burnt, in order to give no reasons or excuse to our friends, who would ask for his "grace." So, the negro, 1, went, the 3 boys went, Madieros will be the 5th, Jerry the Pole the sixth, then will be our turn: total 8 men burnt.

Jerry was convicted without evidences. Two days after, two young boys killed and robbed a grocery man. So we have another three candidates for the electric chair. Someone said that if Fuller will be convinced of our innocence, he will go to the limit in our behalf. I understand that Fuller does not want to be convinced, and who can convince a man who refuses to be convinced? They must kill us to save the dignity and honor of their Commonwealth. But out of love for himself, Fuller could "grace us" if he will deem it good for himself—if not, not.

These are my uncharitable opinions, beliefs and expectations. I am ready and willing to recognize my wrong—were I wrong, and to ammend for it.

Two weeks ago, Comrade Donovan was here, and told me that you wish me to write of my mother. Well, I know it. I am far from a proper condition to write of my mother, and I would never be satisfied of what

I may write of her, even if I could write it in the third rhyme with the ability of Dante. Yet, I have decided to write you of my mother, for you as a token of my affection and gratitude to you—it will be my present to you for the new year. Please accept it heartily.

I will try to be as brief as possible. But my mother has lived in an environment totally foreign to you and, fortunately, also, her life experiences have been very different from yours. Therefore, I shall write you very much of her, in order to give you a clear presentation of my mother.

January 18, 1927. *Charlestown Prison*

DEAR COMRADE ABBOTT:

You will have plenty to do for us. If the State Supreme Court will, as I expect, uphold again Thayer's decision, that will spell doom to us. Then you and all our friends will have plenty, plenty to do to save us—to try to save us from the flameless fire of the twentieth century.

February 15, 1927. *Charlestown Prison*

DEAR MRS. EVANS:

Well, that was a bad news. [1] But I am not going to display sorrow, because I know that you wish me to

---

[1] Mrs. Evans fell and broke her ankle early in the month Vanzetti wrote this letter.

not be afflicted and troubled, but free and confident.

Miss Bloom kindly told me that you said you are not suffering much pain, and I hope it is true and that you will soon recover.

She told me that you like your room from where you can see the dome of the State House which sight delights you. This is well, and it reminded me that I can see that dome from the chapel—when I go to the Christian Science Service—and I always think at its sight, "under that golden roof they have once murdered me"—and maybe, they are re-murdering me again.

But, Mrs. Evans, I would so much send you some flowers, if I could. I am glad to know that certainly you have flowers with you.

Please forgive my delay to write. I have expected Mr. Thompson day by day but have not seen him from before the discussion. Had I known this, I would have wrote you directly. Now, I hope he will be here to-morrow. And I'm working hard at the Italian translation of the later *Brief on Exceptions*. But my thought will be often to and with you, dear Mrs. Evans.

I am sure that you have read the wise men of India; their subtle and strange knowledge and phylosophy. Well, please just try them by taking this occasion of forced inactivity and convert it in a well deserved rest of mind, soul, and body.

I hope to hear soon good news from you, and in my expectations I send you an ocean of good wishes, greetings and affection.

March 23, 1927. *Charlestown Prison*

DEAR FRIEND MRS. CODMAN:[1]

I have received your most wellcome letter of March 10th. It was very good of you to write me such kind letter and inform me of our dear Mrs. Evans' conditions. Lately I received a letter from her—and she will received my answer at the same time in which you will receive this. I hope she is improving and patient. . . .

I am glad to have known you and Mrs. Winslow personally and that I did not disliked to both of you; and your visit will always be a joy for me.

Yes, Mrs. Codman, it would have been much better if Nick would have worked. As I told you, sometime I resent to work for profit of people who are giving me such a deal and for commodity of people who almost deserve more to be rided on by, than to ride in automobile. Yet I conform myself to the rules and to reasonable conduct because I realize that, after all, to work is better than idleness for my own little self.

You praise our patience and courage! Well, I like to be praised a little—maybe it is because I am so blamed—but, dear Mrs. Codman, to be is, to my understanding, a condition superior to my being. I exist, not for self choise or wish, but because I was put in existence by a power transcendental—no matter what it is.

To will? Well, to will, too is a condition—for I have been, and I have seen many other ones in such

---

[1] Mrs. E. A. Codman of Boston, Mass.

condition that their faculty to will was temporarily or definitely destroyed.

To do what one wills to do, also is a condition out of which I have often found myself and seen others.

The point that I wish to reach is that even if we really were patient and courageous—it would be far more a good luck than a merit.

Will you please express my gratitude to Mr. Codman for his ~ood care to Mrs. Evans.

March 24, 1927. *Charlestown Prison*

DEAR COMRADE ABBOTT:

. . . . I am told that in Europe and in South America, the agitation is general and intense. It also seems as if our American friends, or friends in America, are intentioned to exit from the world of mere words and pragmatical ceremonies to enter some practical action. And it is time indeed, that if half of what has been done in each of many other nations would have been done here, we would be freely working for the release of other prisoners and the victory of liberty.

You are more than right on this, friend Abbott, words, only words, too many words are often a ridiculous anachronism and a discredit and a shame. But what can one do against the wall which bricks are made of—well, think of a metaphor.

This, because in such contingence words are not the echo of the action—first motion, then thought—but symptoms of want of will. Then words are but empty voices to cloak a consciousness of nothingness, echoes, pretentions of want and of nothingness—and worse of course, to an aim or an object, than silence, might fall eloquent silence.

As for the appeal, I have always expected a refusal from the seven supreme just-ices of Massachusetts, and their protracted delay spells but evil to my understanding; but, of course, I could, and I would, be wrong.

Mr. Thompson has fought and is fighting bravely and splendidly in our defence—and so are his associates. They performed prodigies, won much favorableness, broken many icebergs of indifference or hostility.

But we know that in a case of such nature as ours, legality alone is not sufficient. Mr. Thompson has known to place the case in such perfect manner before the Supreme Court, that if the just-ices wish, they can give us justice now. . . . Therefore, if they are coming to a refusal, it would unmistakably prove that they have prostituted their conscience, their intellect, and will to a categoric order of an invisible and transcendental master or class; plutocracy. It would justify everything.

Anyhow, be of brave heart, comrade Abbott, *e, salute.*

March 29, 1927. *Charlestown Prison*
DEAR FRIEND BENTON:

Thank you for the beautiful booklet, *Flowers of Resurrection;* but yet more thank you for your good words, for the sympathy and remembrance. I look many times at the beautiful flowers, butterflies, buds, leaves and birds with a great extatic pleasure. The contemplation of the Nature's beauties, the meditation upon Nature's wonders and mysteries—from them I drink the highest joys of life.

The dearest manifestion of Nature to me is mankind with his miseries and proudness, his glories and his shames, his smallness and his grandeur. So you may understand what human solidarity means to me—especially now that I have lost all the material comforts—and how grateful I feel for those who cheer me with their goodness.

It is with pleasure that I learnt that you live in the open country, because I am fond of it. I love the solitude. I love the elements. To live free among the green and in the sunshine under an open sky, it was always my dream.

I love my comrades and there are many reasons for me to remember you. It is bitter not to be able to write more often and extensively. We work six days a week. I go to school three evenings a week. Remember that your words are always a welcomed blessing to me. My hearty regards to you and all the bread givers around you.

April 3, 1927. *Charlestown Prison*

DEAR MRS. WINSLOW: [1]

Your letter of April 1st, reached me yesterday evening and it was most welcomed.

[1] Mrs. Gertrude L. Winslow of Boston, Mass.

When you and Mrs. Codman called, I was perhaps more bitter than sad but I might have seemed more sad than bitter because they have already squashed out from me and crushed in me the best of my life so that I lack sufficient vital force to bring to the superfices what there is in my deepnesses. Another little bit of squashing and of crushing and I will become so sweet and suave to not even demonstrate at my autopsy. That is what will happen if the Massachusetts' Supreme Justices are going to refuse a new trial as I believe.

Then the next motion will take at least other six months before to be repelled—as all the previous ones —by the Supreme Justices. After that, you and other American friends will try to obtain from our murderors, by their good will, what they have failed to give us by reasons, evidences and justice. I would certainly never regret to have been wrong, or be sorry to recognize my actual mistake of judgement—my "temerary judgments," as the Catholic Church calls them.

Meanwhile I fear that they will succeed to kill Rosy before Nick and I—and, maybe, also my father.

It sounds as if Mrs. Codman and you are keeping me in a conceit of wise or learned man. I must confess that once I have believed to know a great deal and that even now, in spite of my humility I still think to understand certain primival, elemental truths so simple that they should be known by all—but are not.

Subjects of human nature or of a Revolution, such as those we happened to mention in our conversation, are indeed beyond human comprehension. What of objectiveness? Had I time and force for it, how I would like to write an essay on it to define the subject and disperse new errors about it.

It is a quarter century that I am struggling to dis-learn and re-learn; to disbelieve and re-believe; to deny and re-confirm. By little of school and very much experiences (well and rightly understood) I became a cosmopolite perambulating phylosopher of the main road,—crushing, burning a world within me and creating a new—better one. Meanwhile I am having the worst of the worst one. But if I stop to joke and begin to reason, I would scare not only you but myself.

Your visit and your letter were blisful. . . .

April 6, 1927. *Charlestown Prison*

DEAR MRS. WINSLOW:

My words came true [1]—and as for that I had not needed to be a profet or son of profets. Now I am confined in a cell of Cherry Hill wing, an antichamber of the death-house, waiting for my doom. Next Saturday we will be sentenced; then we will be executed as quickly as possible, for, as Mr. Wilbar [2] said publicly few months ago, "the sooner Sacco Vanzetti be brought to their ultimate justice the sooner the agitation we see will stop."

Will his words or the words of you in your later letter come true? I would but I cannot have any fur-

---

[1] On April 5, the Supreme Court found "no error" in Judge Thayer's denial of the motion for a new trial.

[2] W. M. Wilbar, District Attorney of Norfolk and Plymouth Counties, successor to Fred G. Katzmann.

ther illusions on the outcome of the case and the seal
of my fate. But in this black hour I like to express
you my and Nick's gratitude for your goodness to us.
Be brave and calm.

April 6, 1927. *Charlestown Prison*

DEAR COMRADE BLACKWELL:

. . . . Of late I have been absorbed in deemed-
urgent writings and so have had no time to finish "My
Mother Memories" for you. I had intended to do
something worthy of her and of you, useful to mankind. Things precipitated. Next Saturday, I will be
finally sentenced to death and I expect them to execute
us as soon as possible to stop the agitation,—as Wilbur
candidly and publicly declared, months ago. So, most
probably I will be unable to write of my mother, but
I will send you the "proofs" which I have. Be of
brave heart, dear Comrade Blackwell, and have all
my affection and many regards also to your cousin.

April 6, 1927. *Charlestown Prison*

DEAR MRS. EVANS:

Your good letter has reached me just now. Yes,
as far as our lives and freedom are concerned, all has
been vain. I am now confined in a cell of Cherry Hill
wing, antechamber of the death house, waiting for my
doom. As Wilbur has publicly said few month ago,
the sooner Sacco and Vanzetti be brought to their ulti-

mate justice (!??!!) the sooner the agitation will stop. And I have no illusions.

But yours and our comrades and friends' solidarity and generosity has written a wonderful paragraph in history. It helped us and it will safe other—it will never have been done in vain.

Be patient and of brave heart, Comrade Evans; and have all my good wishes and affection.

April 7, 1927. *Charlestown Prison*

DEAR COMRADE DONOVAN:

Please just be calm and of brave heart.   Don't let adversity overwhelm you.   I hope to see you soon.

April 7, 1927. *Charlestown Prison*

DEAR MRS. CODMAN:

The sad expectation has been fulfilled: once yet the State Supreme Court has decided negatively.   And it seems to seal our fate: *Consumatus est.*

I know that you and many other generous are hoping in the Governor—but I cannot entertain any further hope.   We are lost.   It will either be the chair or prison for life.   After seven years of struggle, of unspeakable pains, sorrows and anguish, I am now confined in an antichamber of the death house—in a cell of Cherry Hill.

I wish to express you all my gratitude for the good that you have done and are doing to us.   Please, extend my sentiments and regards to Mr. Codman.

April 11, 1927. *Dedham Jail*

DEAR COMRADE MARY [DONOVAN]:

Your letter has been read just before going to the court, and when I entered there, I looked around but have been unable to see you. No, I have not wondered for your absence, for I understood that admission must have been denied. . . .

Rosa and Mrs. Evans were here just a while ago, and they brought us a nice rose-bud, a plant of flowers, fruits and cakes. They were allowed ½ hour of conversation with each of us. Now, as you see, you may be admitted sooner than you expected. . . . And please, when you will come, do not bother yourself to carry anything. We have more than we need. . . .

Try to be brave and strong. I know that this is heavy and cruel beyond words to you, but you ought to be brave, to still your heart and your mind in order not to be overwhelmed by sorrow and despair, and keep fit to face the trial. We will see what we can do. Now just try to be calm, to still yourself and safeguard your health and vitality so to be fit for the test.

In a way, I am better here, there is more light and air here and we are allowed, Nick and I, a daily walk in the yard together. And I am quite well. You must not overtax yourself by thinking that I am suffering, for I am not suffering, and it would be greater to me if I knew that you are not despairing and suffering for me. For I know but too well that all this is far worse to you than to me. There is no doubt, that they determined to burn us, but we are still raw, and as you say "it is by no means through." So, dear Comrade, be brave, calm, do not despair and do your best to keep as well as possible under the circumstances, for I will know it, and it will help me greatly.

April 13, 1927. *Dedham Jail*

DEAR FRIEND MRS. WINSLOW:

Just a word to tell you that your letter of the 11th has been very good and dear to me.

Yes, yes, I had kept what I said last Saturday, [1] in my heart for a seemingly eternity. But that was only a fraction of the whole—I should have spoke for days.

Your words are wise and sensible—but our case is exceptional—and still I have no hope. The merit of what may happen, than what I expect, would be yours and of all our friends.

P.S. *April* 15, 1927.

Dear Mrs. Winslow, I pray you to tell Mrs. Codman that her good letter reached me this very morning. I ask the burning heaven and the enlighted earth to salute both of you, for me, in the glory of a bright morning.

April 14, 1927. *Dedham Jail*

DEAR COMRADE MARY [DONOVAN]:

Today I have written, written and written all the time. Now it is late and I am tired. Yet I cannot help to write to you. . . .

---

[1] April 9, 1927, the day Sacco and Vanzetti were sentenced to death in the Dedham Court House by Judge Thayer.

What I want to say to you is, again and ever, to be brave, calm and self restrained. Yes, just that and what I do not know to say. I knew that you lost your job.[1] Another of their nice things. Now you are working days and nights to save Nick and I. Remember, that you must rest, and rest at least for the necessity of it. Good-bye, and all my regards to you, also from Nick.

April 18, 1927. *Dedham Jail*

DEAR FRIEND MRS. CERISE JACK:

. . . . Of lately I received flowers and greeting from you and your dear Betty, and flowers and greetings are good and beautiful to me. I placed your flower in a glass of fresh water upon my window and they are still beautifully gladding. And I placed your living words into my living heart, nurrish them of its redest blood and of the whitest flowers of my soul.

P.S. I believe that you have tried and failed to be admitted here. But your merit remain and hoping in a better turn of things I again salute you.

April 19, 1927. *Dedham Jail*

DEAR MRS. EVANS:

I have thought very much of you and now will write few words. Your plants-flowers are just great; the

---

[1] Mary Donovan was removed from her position as industrial inspector in the Massachusetts Department of Labor and Industries in March, 1927.

Geranium is budding again and they are in full bloom. I noticed that the May flowers are absorbing a lot of water; when I sit, reading, at my window I am in a garden. Dear Mrs. Evans you are too good with us. I would not wonder if our enemy are mad for your benefacting us. Oh, while I remember, please don't bring us too much stuff, just some fruits—but less of it, if you please.

I salute you and greet you with all my heart.

April 19, 1927. *Dedham Jail*

DEAR MRS. WINSLOW:

Oh! Your mayflowers are dear and sweet and most heartly accepted. They remember me of Plymouth and of the woods; the woods which I love so much. They are the flowers of the woods. I thank you very much.

Was not that foolish and unjust to deny you admission? It seems impossible. I was sorry for me and for you. Let's hope that I may see you again before to die.

Meanwhile keep up a brave heart, dear Mrs. Winslow.

April 25, 1927. *Dedham Jail*

MY DEAR FRIEND [MRS. VIRGINIA MACMECHAN]:

I had realized from before my reading of your good later letter your utmost efforts to call on me—and their failure. And still before it, I had thought of asking

Mr. Thompson to bring you here with him. But I shall do it at its time, and beside, Mr. Thompson need to do other works to face life's necessities and he does not come here if not strictly necessary and generally brought some one else—either to acquaintanced them with us or to deal of defense. If you would come with him in such circumstance, it would be better than nothing, but I would hardly have time to look in your eyes, we would hardly have time to exchange a word. Rosy and Mrs. Evans are the only ones allowed alone. This week Mrs. Evans may not come and if Mr. the Sheriff pleases to admit one else in her place, alright, if he displease, nothing to do and less to say. But I will do my utmost to find a way for your admittance.

I am glad to know how you think of me about asking a pardon. At once we refused to sign a regular form of the paper for petitioning the pardon, just for the reason that you state. Since Mr. Thompson said that he could do nothing without our petition, we asked to carry it on a special, our petition. Few days ago it was stenographated, with the understanding that we will correct and modify it at our own will. Till now we have not yet received its proof, and I do not know what to think of the delay. However, it was explained us that "pardon" does not mean in this case "forgiveness of guiltness" because it may be asked and granted in all the possible grounds, "miscarriage of justice" and "innocence"—being a statutary power of the executive to correct judiciary errors or wrongs. Yet we insisted on a special plea. . . . Altogether, I do not know yet what we will do about it. But I'm convinced that to do or not to do it will not make the least bit of difference to the final outcome of the case. What the authorities will do pro or against us—they will do it without the least consideration to us—but in others and in their own consideration.

I am in a fit of self-boasting: Voltaire was brilliant and sharp, but I would be deeper in my petition.

Yes, dear friend, I am allowed to smoke and I smoke like a Turk. Fruits and candy are allowed and we have fruits. My window here is peopled of recipients, it is a riot of blissing colors and beauties forms: A giranium plant, a tulip and plant both from Mrs. Evans. White flowers, pink carnations, roseate peaches buds and flowers, bush-yellow flowers from Mrs. Jack, and a bouquet of May flowers from Mrs. Winslow. I know that you would like to send me something, and I like to receive from you. But I do not like candy; I can buy tobacco; please do not send us any fruits for we have plenty of it:—well, send me some flowers please, some mavflowers if you can afford. . . .

April 25, 1927. *Dedham Jail*

DEAR FRIEND MRS. WINSLOW:

Your dear letter is at hand. I am sorry of my incapacity to share your optimism. I have been disilluded and wronged too many times and too much: I can no longer trust the apparent conduct of men vested of authorities: I distrust them; I believe them deceitful, decided at heart to doom us for their hatred to my past and to my person. I distrust the executive as I distrusted, and rightly so, the judiciary.

Most of the people, of the good people, are with us —it is true; but the force of reaction are still and more than ever against us. As they have found me guilty two times of two crimes which I never committed, through two trials, cannot the executive act as the judiciary acted? In spite and through whatever formality? I believe that the Governor will never appoint an investigating commission. That would impose freedom; and the men of the judiciary and of the executive want save America by dooming us. Since they are potent but not omnipotent they of course will do what they can. I fear in life imprisonment. If you will be right—I will struck my chest in some Church and, making public ammend, ask forgiveness to you and the others. . . .

Bright Morning
April 27, 1927. Dedham Jail

DEAR COMRADE MARY DONOVAN:

I know that you are working out yourself in our behalf—yet, as it is quite a long time since I received your last letter, I fear that you may have written to me afterward, and that your missive might have gone —lost. . . .

We are allowed a *La Notizia* and a *Il Corriere* and receive daily, either the clippings on the case of the *Herald* or it in full. I follow the news eagerly, and most daily I see your name in it. It is harder to find a hall in Boston for us than it would be in the Sahara Desert! Don't you think so? That is eloquent.

Indeed the defending activities of the intellectuals and of the middle class and prominent persons and clergies is greater than I ever expected. It seems to me more active and energetic than the proletarian and unionist protest and defense.

I tell you nothing about our petition to the Governor, because you know all about it. . . . I am thoroughly convinced that to do or not to do it would not make the littlest difference to the outcome of the case. For the executive cares less than a rap of what we do or not. Yet, taking everything into consideration, I would sign it if it is as I would do it, a fine anarchist oration. But Nicola seems determined not to sign a petition, no matter how it may be. Many of his opinions for it are wrong, others are unilateral or narrow or intollerant. He said that if we sign a petition, the agitation would quail down at once; the executive would drive all of us from the nose, as the judiciary did, then refuse us everything, and then we will be asked again to sign some other appeal, and the case will never finish. It could be so, though this seems to be the last possible appeal. What I really believe that he really believes, is that once the case would be definitely closed, something will happen which will free us. It is a comfortable belief, but I cannot share it. He is in favor of a public declaration on the matter, by us, which is reasonable. But opinions and differences are all inhibalated by one positive; appeal or no appeal from us, the executive like the judiciary can do what it pleases.

Meanwhile it appears to come what I have expected. The Governor will not appoint the asked for commission to investigate. [1] Study the case himself. Well, that could mean much or nothing, or many different other things, and, in definitive, by that the Governor can do what he pleases and justify it as he pleases for that would not leave a tangible element of proof or of contradiction or objection. The report of a competent commission would be a very different thing. Therefore, we must do our utmost to obtain it, we will see. But after all, it all depends on the executive secret wishes and will—for it is in position to have them triumphing in whatever way. . . .

Here there is more air and sun than in Charlestown, and we have a daily walk together in the yard. I indeed am better now.

I wonder about you, hoping you are not forgetting yourself altogether and will at least have little of care and rest that the situation allows you to have. . . .

April 27, 1927. *Dedham Jail*

DEAR MRS. WINSLOW:

Your book came this morning. I have already perused it for I cannot help but peruse a book which first comes to my hand just as I must peruse a human being who comes under my sight.

[1] Governor Fuller had written the Defense Committee a short time before, stating that he would investigate alone.

Thank you for the dedication. The names of the high Authors from whose abstracts the book is made, make me bow in respect and my heart jump with joy. Franklin has already made me laugh and Emerson wonder. From sentences plucked in a random I already understood that if I will have the time to read the book which you have so wholeheartly sent me, I will have hours of blissing joy in company of this most congenial meeting of Great Ones—a sublime communication made even more sweet by the knowledge of your participation.

May 3, 1927. Dedham Jail

DEAR MARY [DONOVAN] :

This afternoon Aldino, Amleto, Milio and Rosa [1] were here with Messrs. Thompson and Ehrmann for the last correction and signatures of the petition to the Governor. It is to me legally splendid and passable as to principles. Yet Nick refused to sign it in spite of all the reasons and argumentations of all. Amleto went away alone, weeping silently. It is two weeks that I am hammering this matter with him [Sacco]. I got tired and hopeless. These seven years have told their tale on him, and it seems useless to reason with him. I am wholly disconcert of this plight, for I hate to disagree between us in this important and public matter. I hope his emotions will change his mind for to-morrow, and that some comrade from the

---

[1] Aldino Felicani, founder of the Defense Committee; Amleto Fabbri, secretary of the Defense Committee in 1925-26; Emilio Coda, Secretary of the Defense Committee in 1924, and Rosa Sacco, Nicola's wife.

Defense Committee will come back tomorrow for a last effort to obtain his signature. . . .

In a way, Nick is right, there are all the reasons for mistrust, pessimism, and scorn for further appeals after so many vain ones. Were the defense entitled to carry our case to the executive without our petition to the Governor, I too would have preferred to not appeal personally. But our signature to the petition being necessary; having after all, no right to scorn a man whose heart and bent towards the case we know not, and in consideration to those who wish our appeal to him, I toiled hard to edit the appeal and signed it, and I believe without incoherence or wrong. . . .

Meanwhile, be brave, steady, and have all the little care of yourself, as possible. We are beaten, yes; but not yet lost—we may still win. . . .

And now, I am going to close this long scribbling. It is after ten o'clock now. I would like you to be in deep and peaceful rest now, but I fear that you are still working for us at this moment. At any rate, I am going to bed. I am quite tired. I have written this after the light went out, in the penumbra, and it made me sleepy. May you receive it after a good rest. . . .

In the Bright Morning
May 7, 1927. Dedham Jail

DEAR FRIEND MRS. WINSLOW:

Your letter of May 5, reached me through men's hands, and the joy of your heart reached my heart through the universal aura. If you deem it good to us to publish extracts from my letters to Mrs. Evans and to you, my modesty has no objection to move at it, though my understanding perceives that they do not express my whole being but only a mood and one attitude: the mood and attitude of a crucify to those who have lightend his cross and assisted him along the Calvary.

I am glad that you like and are glad of my statement to the Governor. But it is not great and it was emasculated and disouled of its best, of its truer truths. After all Mr. Thompson wished it to save and free us; an address of libertarians to an authority man. Gag the truth; gag the right, gag the highest songs of your soul, the strongest note of your impulse, all your spontaneities, lest you offend others and harm yourself. So many things were left unsaid and others fogged or maimed or veiled. If time and chances will permit, sometime I will tell you the story of that statement. I was in earnest at it and I was sick, feeling heavily the earth gravitation, and my spirit bended upon itself. That work devoured my flesh.

I did it for conscience's sake. For I know that for us there is no sympathy nor consideration: we are liberty and right, which means equality and justice; they are authority and privilege, which means tyranny and injustice. Such is the truth in its complete nakedness. Is not there an eternal war to the last blood against the two? For this reason my prayer was a case of conscience. We will never accept life imprisonment any more than we accept death except as imposi-

tions from a stronger physical force and we consider
both as pure and simple murders committed by reaction against revolution: this is the ultimate essence of
our case, and being so we cannot depart, reccomending
pardon. To do so we should love and estimate more
tyranny than liberty, priviledge than justice, our enemies than our parents, women, brothers, comrades
and children. Who is [it] that has said beware from
the wrath of the patient and of the meek? I know
that one of our poets, Gori, said: Alas! to him upon
whose head are gathering the women's and especially
the mothers' maledictions. He was talking of the
Czar. The ruffians laughed at him. Let them laugh
now, if they can.

From the news-papers of to-day I see that they left
the most important and strong of the petition out of
publication. This is a striking, unescapable example
of how the great doctrines are maimed, deformed and
falsify by conservatism. If they do so with a trifle
as my writing, think of what has happened to the great
doctrines of the geniuses of the past. I know that had
Socrates spoke as the Harvard classics make him speak
—he would never have known the taste of hemlock
but would have been placed indeed in the Parthenon,
as "the living voice of reason," as his smiling audacity
dared to say, by the very ones who dispatched him
because a dead man tell no story.

From the same papers it seems that the Governor
has decided to order a public investigation on the whole
case. Let us hope that it will not be one more mockery
as the two trial and seven appeals have been. At any

rate, the merit would be yours. And here I must add that Messrs. Thompson and Ehrmann and others have more merit for the statement than I. My earnest and difficulty have put their patience to the fire's proof and exasperated the poor stenographer. . . .

May 12, 1927. *Dedham Jail*

DEAR MRS. HENDERSON: [1]

Your letter to me and the one to my sister and the fruits, cheese and other goods that you sent me were received yesterday when I translated at once your letter to my sister, happy at the thought of the cheer and confidence it will give to my family. I also wrote a reply to you. But I was still sleeping early this morning when I felt unsatisfied of my answer, remembered to have forgotten a thing, and decided to write you this one—and here I am.

I had just thought that your silence might be due to the bad blow upon you by the Supreme Court refusal and consequent Thayer's sentencing—which might have made you sick—and I have been, so much so, right.

Those two happenings had been too well foreseen and expected to me—so that I was neither surprised nor shaken by them.

Now, dear Mrs. Henderson, I am going to be truthful and sincere—that is to say fanatic, rough and seemingly wrong and unfair. We have already hoped

---

[1] Mrs. Jessica Henderson of Wayland, Mass.

in seven appeals, all of them repulsed. Of course we hoped in Just-ices. What did they? Now that we are compelled to hope no longer in them, of course, we begin to hope in Gov. Fuller. Victor Hugo was almost right in saying that hope would be the last goddess were not for desperation; for true, after desperation there is only more anasthetism and unconsciousness before death.

Do you remember your confidence in the just-ices? Well, you say to have hope and confidence in Gov. Fuller. Of course you must believe to have reasons for it, and most probably you know him well. Whereas I only know his name and the appearances of some of his public acts and utterances. And yet I differ with your opinion of his attitude toward our case. I believe that he has been so much against us that he doomed the three young bandits and veterans of the car-barn, just to avoid excuse or reasons to commute our death sentence in life imprisonment. Of course he felt sure that we would have been doomed. It takes so little to understand that we are murdered in conservation of the Capitalist regime, by the Capitalist Just-ices who are before and after all servants of it.

Every one who think to know the Gov. says that he is a courageous man, honest and straight, aiming energically to what he deems right. Very well. But the people who know him and like him are all like or similar to him. I know him better than them because I have been just as they are now: believed in the same things; liking or disliking the same things; having the same opinions, reactions, beliefs and morale they have now. Now I have changed entirely and only for that I can know now what I was then.

I have been for seven years in the hell of Massachusetts State Prison. There are virtues, understanding, intelligence, unspeakable experiences within the lost ones that populate that hell. And there I and my companions of doom have read Fuller's words: "Why I believe in Capital Punishment," published in the *Success* magazine of last December. And we understood: that was not incidental (the interview). It was planned and predisposed with clear and definite aims by at least one of the parties, (Fuller or the journalist) and allowed by both of them. It foretold and preassured the executions of Madeiros, Jerry, and the three car-barn bandits and of Sacco and Vanzetti. The same Boston journals took pain to make it understood that the publication of that interview just before the Governor's going to Europe intended to be as a declaration of what his attitude to all and our case is, to the European people. And we, the lost, said: Lo! a man who says to be going to Europe with his good wife, as in a "second honeymoon trip"—and begins it by crushing three old mother's hearts, foretelling their young sons' doom. Could not he have his good time without increasing the agonies of those three old mothers?

His words do not specify the case of which he spoke so that his opinions, judgments and affirmations, innuendo and inferences are always withdrawful at his pleasure and will, uncontrollable and unconfutable.

For example, he says: what we have to look after is, if they (the condemned) were guilty. Now, if the reader believes that the Governor has said that with our case in his mind, well, the reader understand that the Governor says that such is our case. But suppose that one says or proves that such a thing has not been done in our case, then the Governor can answer: I did not speak of their case. . . .

But enough of this. Let us hope that you are right and I am wrong about his feelings and intention. He may be 100 times better than I—but I would not trust a feather of an anarchist sparrow to the *bon plesir* of him.

We owe our life to you, our friends, comrades and people of the world who have fought for seven years for us—and to you and them we will owe our freedom if we ever will be free, Mrs. Evans, you, the Committee, Mr. Thompson. If it were not for you we would from long time have been buried, dead, in a grave, or alive in a prison.

I pray you to not let my above words to harm your feelings. I have been positive that the supreme judges would have murdered us. They did it. Had I told you of my opinion of them it would have seemed monstrous to you; I would have harmed and upsetted you. Yet I was positive of it. From a man like Fuller, in a case between reaction and revolution as our case has been from its very beginning, and to two anarchists— well I am positive of it.

He may give us justice—I expect nothing. . . .

And now I am not going to try to express you our gratitude for what you are doing to our families and ourselves. We cannot. . . .

May 12, 1927. Dedham Jail

DEAR COMRADE BLACKWELL:

I wonder of your unusually long silence. It is since Easter that I have heard from you. Are you unwell? Have you received my answer to your Easter message to me?

Here I am closed in a cell all the time, except an hour a day, walking in the yard. This enclosure affects my mind a great deal. I feel dizzy and I am never in a good discreet mood to write. I want to write letters on the case to a comrade in France who would publish them in his weekly in Paris, translate them in French for your French journals, and send to other periodicals in Italian language.

Well, I have scribbled for over a week without succeeding to produce a single satisfactory line. I have now ready some 32 pages—but it is what we call a "ugly copy." Yet, I hope to accomplish it soon and, next, to fulfill my promise to you.

May 15, 1927. Dedham Jail

DEAR BIGELOW:

Well, your good letter of April 17th was handed to me yesterday afternoon, and it was good to hear from you again. I do not know if the sentence will be execution for us, or commutation of life imprisonment, or what the outcome will be. I only know that we are quite reduced in extremes.

Dear Bigelow, subjectively it is nothing to me, our world-wide notoriety, except my love to the race is highly gratified—, for that love is all what I care for and not a fig for fame, honors, etc. But objectively, to me, this universal insurgence against a wrong, in behalf of two humblest men, is an apotheosy. Do you remember what I wrote to all: "You have done for us, what once was only done for Saints and kings." This is a real progress. It should cheer everyone of good-will.

Alas! China and Russia are thriving poorly and unhappily, to my understanding. Yet there is good to them in their chances and travail. I refrain from entering into a discussion on these two subjects, because it is beyond the realm and possibilities of a poor letter. But I tell you to provide yourself with the Pier John Proudhon's books (possibly two volumes or one). *The War and the Peace.* . . . Try hard to get it, and, if you succeed, read it carefully, patiently, with all your might, it will enlighten your mind upon the very actual situation of mankind, and on the real problems of each individual, nation, and of the race. It will also help your morale against the brutures of life and cheer your heart. But, if you fail to find it, and care to have my thoughts, we will chat longer by and by. . . .

Your offering to us is most appreciated by us. Here we can receive food, flowers and books, but we pray you to not disturb yourself in that, for we received already more than we need. Just keep the flame of friendship and solidariety as vigorously burning as presently.

Nick joins me in sending you our cheers and regards.

May 22, 1927. Dedham Jail

DEAR MARY [DONOVAN]:

. . . . You are pessimist on account of your case.[1] Strange enough, these last few days I often thought of it in your same way. The laws are the codified will of the dominating classes; the laws are made to legalize the State organization of violence; the laws and the courts are therefore the tools of the bosses as the judges, police, hangers and spies are their servants. Then an inferior is always wrong, in the courts which [are] made to uphold the superior will and command. Then a rebel or a novator is always guilty before the laws made for conservation. This is why each new idea, religion, regime, truth, has been compelled to smash by violence the resisting violence of the pre-established and resisting ideas, religion or regime. So, turning from the general to your particular, you are an inferior and a known novator,—a great disadvantage because the judges are there to buttress the superior; and a guilt very much worse than that which your bosses may pretend. As we before the judges are

---

[1] Mary Donovan had a public hearing on her dismissal from the State Department of Labor and Industries. Subsequently she had a court hearing on the charges on which her dismissal was based.

guilty of a worse guilt than that of an alleged murder
—you are guilty of a worse guilt than the alleged
fault.   This is why you have been thinking on the outcome of your case.   Yet, because each rule has its exception, you may win the case and such is my wish. . . .
What I wish to recommend to you is that, if you lose,
do not let it bother you.   I understand the reasons why
one is apt to be hurt by such things as these.   I am
not one of those who claim that things are nothing,
except what our mind and feelings make them to be.
On the contrary, I deem that things are what they are
in themselves no matter what we think of them or how
we feel toward them.   But, it is wise not to let them
boss us—master, we must oil our swivels and keep
calm and undisturbed, at least, as much as possible.
Take for example, the matter of the *Herald* clippings
and subscription which you sent and made for me.   You
already know what the keepers did about it, and I
know also the sneaky, mean way they did it—they are
not men enough to admit that they barred those papers
and hid it under the lie "nothing has come," finally
when forced to speak, they say that the "papers is
against the rule, but we will give you the clippings"—
which they did not.   I felt like to jump at their
throat. . . . But, do you want me to spoil my blood
and my kidneys in useless wrath?   No, no, some day if
I can, I will tell it to the world. . . . But to spoil myself by allowing these things to over-work me—no, it
is not wise.   You should do just the same.   And never
mind about the clippings; I have enough of them to

prove my subject. From now send all through the Defense.

. . . . Sometime I get impatient or harsh or resented from Nick. Then I think that I might be worse had I been seven years segregated as he is. And then I consider everything and get ashamed of my conduct with him and regret it. All depends on one's idiosincrazy. Now I put myself in this mood, he does not intend to offend or even if he intends so, you must be man enough to understand it all and be just. Then nothing disturbs me. Whereas, if I do not consider well and take things as they are not and let myself rule, I suffer and react. You see, I just handle well the swivels of my being—and everything is O.K. . . .

There is a guy in New York who directs *Il Proletario*, the weekly of the Italian I.W.W. Like me, he likes to boast his own and keeps calling his paper "the oldest revolutionary journal of the U.S. of America and Canada." He printed it on a circular letter for fund, a copy of which was sent to me—to me that I know the story. So I wrote him: "Say, Mangano, your paper is the youngest revolutionary paper in U.S. of American and Canada. It was found by the Italian socialist, who you call 'reformist,' and it was their unrevolutionary organ until 1911 when, at the Utica Congress came the scission between 'syndicalists' and 'socialists.' The former get the *Proletario* and turned it into 'revolutionary syndicalism' from 'reformist socialism' as it had been 'til then. The socialist issued another weekly which they boast as the oldest in U.S.

and Canada. He who hears both, and does not know the facts, wonder which one is wrong. But the socialist are right and yours is the youngest revolutionary paper in this country, because it became so when the two anarchists ones have been published for decades." And I sent him a couple of dollars, saying that this is a trifle and that I would be glad to renounce the elderness of our own papers were I able to begin anew something better.

You know what Comrade M. answered me? "Well, the next time I will call it the oldest worker's paper. Is it alright?" Maybe, and I care a rap. I just laugh at that "fixed idea of elderness." But he also explains that he cannot call it "the oldest socialist paper" for all of us are socialists, even you. He seems to have discovered America in saying so. But I like his general way of editing his paper, and to be sure, he sticks with us.

Of all this, I am only sorry because a great Cause needs great men to triumph—while, alas! these letters do not testimony it—for all the rest I just turn the swivels close.

This is Sunday morning, and mine seems a sermon on "the swivels." It was suggested by my consciousness of your being in trying circumstance and by my wish to lend you a hand. If you would be compelled to delay your call, let this help a little.

But when you write "arrivaderci" instead of "arrivederci," I let every swivel open and laugh well. That is unreasonable and ungenerous, don't you think? Well, *arrivederci* dear comrade.

May 24, 1927. *Dedham Jail*

DEAR FRIEND MRS. EVANS:

Miss Bloom was very carefully in sending me a copy of the *Unity* issue of May 16, containing your story article on the case: "Shall Massachusetts Commit a Judicial Murder?"

That is just what they have labored for seven long years to do. It seems positive that they will do it. When the Justices gave me the later stab, I said to you: "the case is lost and ended!" You answered: "Your case just really begin now." You hoped so because you had faith in Fuller. I knew that we were dead because I am sure that Fuller cannot even help to be against us two libertarian, on the side of money and tyranny.

I said to you: Fuller has outspoke himself in his "Why I believe in Capital Punishment."

You answered: "That was a case of sure guilt—your case is different."

Yes, our case is different; not even a sheep-killing dog would have been found guilty by an American Jury on the evidences produced against us. The Massachusetts Supreme Court would have granted a new trial to a leprous dog on the motions that are presented; professional, conservative criminals (they are all conservative) would have been freed at once. But they convicted us because we are Italian, against war, and anarchist: to succeed they were compelled to the most vile, criminal conduct: and now, to save their faces and uphold their institution they must kill us—also to quench their fears. We dead, they think they will have rest, peace, retributions, and honors. How transparently it appears that the gods deprive of wisdom those who they want to lose. The insanity of our murderers—who kill us for worldly honors and conservations of injustice—does not consist in lack of wit, suttleness, or what not, but in being invaded by a sort of obsession which lead them into an abyss—to innihilation. It has been so at the even of all the revolutions. . . .

Why do Fuller refuses to appoint the investigation commission? For two reasons or three at least: 1st. Because it would be as an admittion of doubt that either the trial or the Courts were unfair. To seems to admit it is a thing which must be avoided at every cost for conservation and reaction aims, in a time so revolutionary and critical as our times. Besides, the cost is very cheap: our lives.

2nd. Fuller and those to whom he really sticks know very well that an open, full investigation of the case would freed us and expose to the world the unfairness, cruelty, and ferocity of our blood-thirsty persecutors.

So Fuller is conducting this review of the case in the only possible way that can inable him to despose as he please of us and seem right. No trial, no confrontations of the two party; not openly but beyond closed doors; no presence of the defence, no records of interview, testimony, opinions, etc. etc.; he is assisted solely by persons who are dependents, friends of the same clique of him. At the last he will give the decision on the case that he has carried in his heart from years

and claim that it is the result of his recent study of
the case.   The reasons with which he will justify his
decisions as well as his conduct, at the investigation
shall be taken for granted—for they, by the secrecy of
his inquiry will be uncontrollable, unanalysable and un-
answerable.

To expect that Fuller will stand against the judiciary, the middle class, the big money of Massachusetts
in behalf of two damned dagos and anarchists—seems
absurd to me.   Fuller's actual (seemingly) conduct is
proving that he had us in mind when he give his "Why
I Believe in Capital Punishment"—as the whole Boston press said at the time.

Why then, he did not made it clear and definite so
that we could have defended ourselves?   If he was
decided to repel everything in our behalf and convinced to be right, brave, and just before his God and
men in so doing, why do not say it?   Why few days
after its publication, did he told to the delegation of
the foreign radical-papers of New York which interviewed him at his sailing to Europe that he do know
nothing of the case, which is in Court and therefore not
of his pertinance, but that he will give full and careful
consideration to it if it will come before him.   Why did
he say the same thing in France? . . .

Why did he repeat the same thing when he returned
from France?   Why even now do he ask but: are Sacco
and Vanzetti guilty? not if the trial was fair but if
they are guilty or not?

Except if one saw himself the convicted person to
commit the crime or that one see another person than

the convicted to commit the crime for which the latter was convicted, except in one of these two cases, the only way one can try to learn if a convicted is guilty or innocent is to study the case. To study the case does not means at all to only read the records and questioning secretly some witnesses. To study a case means to determine the conduct of the Judge, the prosecution, and the defence; the characters of both parties' witnesses; the conduct and psychology of the jurors; the characteristics of the place in which and of the time in which the trial took place; the indirect influences, interests and elements which played pro and con the convicted; and a thoroughly study of the exhibits by experts made in the presence of both parties.

It seems to me that the governor is not doing these things at all. It seems to me that he is acting like Thayer and the Supreme Judges did—in the same spirit, with the same manner and predetermined aim and decision. It seems that he is proving my opinions by his actual conduct, and dooming us. . . .

May 25, 1927. Dedham Jail

DEAR FRIEND [MRS. SARAH ROOT ADAMS] : [1]

Nick and I are now at Dedham Jail where we will be kept until ten days before the execution when we will be taken to the death house of the State Prison in Charlestown. So I have received your letter of May 1 and also read the one which you sent to Nick.

[1] Mrs. Sarah Root Adams of Norfolk, Va.

Since your letters breathe sincerity, love and earnest good will toward us and show that you, your sister, and some of your friends have been in our behalf from the beginning of the case—your deeds and sentiments are too high to be recompensed by mere words so that I will not try to express you my sentiments and gratitude but will strife to answer you with utmost clearness and integrity. I will only deal with the three capital points of your letters, namely, your hope, yours and our beliefs, radicalism, about our conduct to win freedom.

You hope to see us walking free in the Boston streets this summer, and you base your hope chiefly on the help and petitions of so many who ask for our freedom. That a friend shall hope for a friend in danger, in sorrow or in trial is as much natural as for a friend to sympathize for a friend in suffering, sorrow and misfortune. When one is friend, one love; and loving, he wishes good to the loved; and wishing good to the loved he hopes that good will prevail upon evil upon his friend; and thus he become optimistic which means just to expect a good outcome of whatever thing; and a good outcome is the victory of the forces good to us over the forces bad to us. To my ultimate analysis, it seems to me that the forces of good and of evil are of a same nature and that all the forces are essentially good inasmuch they create life, preserves life, are life themselves. Their good or bad influence upon us are determine by the quantities, conditions, circumstances and forms in which they exercise themselves. You understand that I relate here to the elemental forces of

nature, such as fires, waters, winds, etc., and not of the
forces which manifest themselves in forms of conscious
lives—for in this latter case the thing are more complicated. Fire give life and destroy it; water, just the
same, and so does wind. One of the noblest woman,
friend of mine, broke her arms some months ago.
She wrote me: My arm's bone refused to heal again
for quite long time; then the doctor recurred to electricity applying it to my fracture and I recuperated
quickly and well. *How sorry I am to think that this
same force which healed me may be applied to kill you.*

Now let us return to hope and optimism. If one
loves another and this other is sick, one hopes that
the loved will recuperate. If one hate a sick person,
one hopes that the hated will die. So is my case in
respect to my friends and my enemy.

I have understood from the beginning that Judge
Thayer wanted to kill us because we were hated and
feared by the ragged and the golden rabbles so that
he will be recompensed by them by being appointed
judge of the Massachusetts Supreme Court—this vanity has been the obsession of his live. Yet, for a while,
I hoped that I would have won by showing my innocence. But since I have been found guilty at the
Plymouth trial, I understood that I was lost except if
my friends would become physically stronger than my
enemies. Were not the first Christians believed to be
blood-drinkers? Yes, they were believed so and insulted, tortured, martyrized by the ragged and golden
mobs of their time. Even the so sage Marcus Aurelius
feared, hated, insulted, and killed them. Of course

the first Christians were outlaws [because] they were against the laws who legalize slavery; against the powerful Roman Empire oppressing mankind and masters of the Courts and laws; they were gods-destroyers but destroyers of false gods. In this was their right, greatness, sanctity; for this they were put to death. What chance of fair deal and acquital those not only innocent first Christians could have had in being tried by pagans to whom the fact of one being Christian was all the crimes and all the guilts at once and in one? From those times, I could come down through the centuries showing you that the same dealings has been imposed by the golden and the ragged mobs to all those who have discovered, wished, and labored for a little more of truth, justice, freedom, triumph and sublimization of the men, women and of the life— down, down to this very date. . . .

"Radicalism" is a very general term, applicable to several parties and doctrine each of which differs from the other ones. Both Nick and I are anarchists—the radical of the radical—the black cats, the terrors of many, of all the bigots, exploitators, charlatans, fakers and oppressors. Consequently we are also the more slandered, misrepresented, misunderstood and persecuted of all. After all we are socialists as the social-democrats, the socialists, the communists, and the I.W.W. are all Socialists. The difference—the fundamental one—between us and all the other is that they are authoritarian while we are libertarian; they believe in a State or Government of their own; we believe in no State or Government. But enough of this—and

I have said nothing. You have read my talk in Court and my petition to the Governor; in both of them I have spoke on this matter. If you care, read "Anarchy" in the *Encyclopedia Brittannica*—the explanation is O.K. Here, I will simply add that there are several schools of anarchy: there are communists anarchists, individualist anarchists, religious ones, and gnostic and atheistic ones. As for me, I have my own taken from what seems to be the better that is in each and all of the schools.

I have been born of a Catholic family and believed in Roman Church until my 18 [year]. But actually, as far as religion goes, I believe in no religion, though I try to learn and practice all that to me seems to be of truth and good in each and all of them. Just for this reason I am for the utmost liberty of conscience, and I make no difference and therefore I neither fear nor hate any sincere believer, be he a Christian, a Jew, a Maomettan, a Buddhist, or what not. My bases, measures and relation from man to man, is as man to man—and nothing else. If I am at odds with churches and religions, it is surely not for conscience's freedom—but for historical, economical, moral reasons.

Now, few words on the statement which you suggested us to send out because it would help our freedom. We cannot make it because it is a thing against our understanding and conscience. You think and believe differently than us and to your understanding to do what you suggested would be not only an helpful deed, but would also voice the most honest behavior that all should act. I cannot explain you why it is not so to our understanding. It would be too long to explain it. But we too have a faith, a dignity, a sincerity. Our faith is cursed, as all the old ones were at their beginning. But we stick to it as long as we honestly believe we are right. Both I and Nick would have followed our old beliefs, practiced the old moral and life sanctioned by laws and churches—we could have grown rich on the poor, have women, horses, wealth, honors, children, all rests, boundnesses and pleasures and joys of life. We have renounced voluntarily to almost all of even the most honest joys of life when we were at our twenties. Lately we have sacrificed all to our faith. And now that we are old, sick, crushed, near death: should we now after having endured three deaths and lost all, should we now quack, recant, renegate, be vile for the love of our pitiable carcasses? Never, never, never, dear friend Adams. We are ready to suffer as much as we have suffered, to die, but be men to the last. On the contrary, if I am shown to be wrong—then I would change. This is the only thing which could change me.

Well, this is almost all for now.

Not all the American people are desirous of doing us justice. In our side are the high-class professional together with the labor unions, the humble, the Italians, and almost all the other immigrants, and of course, the radicals. Against us are business, money and power: business-men, small property owners, salesmen, butchers, bakers, storekeepers, the candle-stick makers, the members of the newest country club, the broker, the courts, etc. (Taken from the N. Y. *World*.)

Our friends must speak loudly to be heard by our murderers, our enemies have only to whisper and even be silent to be understood. If one does not detect this fact, he is liable to be misleaded by the appearances and sounds of things. The Governor has refused to appoint a commission for a full, public and recorded investigation on all the facts of the case—it would have been the only thing capable to impose my vindication and freedom—and it was rejected. So, it will be either electric chair or life imprisonment to us. If this is wrong, so much the better; the apologizer would be happier than the apologized. But I see clearly into the future.

I learnt last night that the Governor is going to have a public hearing of the case. What he intends it to be, I do not know yet. But whatever it will be it cannot fail to help us. So, I am glad of it.

May 31, 1927. *Dedham Jail*

DEAR COMRADE BLACKWELL:

Your letter of May 19th was received yesterday. Good. I am glad to hear that you have been (as I hope you are now) fairly well; but not so glad I am to hear that you are desperately busy (most on our account and behalf) because that is too much. One who as I boast to be a follower of Pythagoras cannot approve it.

Yes, I have had many letters during the past few days, (a queer one from a little out of mind person), some of which requires a rather long answer, but I wished to hear of you. I suppose your arm is quite well now.

Two things are paramount to me in this case: First, that that whole prosecution has been so evidently dishonest to compel the most illuminated and normal part of the conservatives to require reparation for the very purpose of conservation; second, that what has been done for us by the people of the world, the laborers, (I mean workers) and the greatest minds and hearts proves beyond any possible doubt that a new conception of justice is plowing its way in the soul of mankind; a justice that centered on man as man. For as I have already said, you, they are doing for us what once could only have been done for saints and kings. This is real progress.

I too, am surprised by such protest from the students and the Intelligentia. Well, you have done a great thing in saying to the Governor that he shall either give us freedom or death, but I refrained for the only reason that I judged it a little too imposing on him. I managed to say so by—I mean that he should have had to understand it by inference—but also the directions of this was weakened. Yet, in spite of all I hope that that is clearly readable between the lines and beyond the words of the petition. Your letter to the Governor is certainly a great writing that I would like to read. . . .

I am dissatisfied that the Governor does not appoint

a commission. For it is true that he can do also alone
what he could do with a commission—but I counted
on a public investigation and a tangible report which
would have been unrefutable and undeniable. But,
like this—in secret, who can know what is passing on,
it is not a trial and if he will answer negatively, the
reasons that he will give are unanalizable, uncontrollable. . . .

My point is that Fuller did not order a public investigation on all the facts of the double case, because it
would have revealed a judiciary scandal, and so he
chose to save the face of Thayer and the other Justices
rather than vindicate us. And I further doubt that he
may be interested to give us life imprisonment and
knows that only without a public inquiry on the case
is it possible. For nothing yet has changed my mind.
The State of Mass. wants to kill us and it will give us
just that. . . .

June 10, 1927. *Dedham Jail*

Dear Friend Mrs. Winslow:

Well, I have just finished my morning exercise (I
began to do it since my sickness) and my hand is still
trembling for its recent efforts but my heart is steady
and glad in answering to your good letter of June 3.
Do you know that when the doctor visited me he wonder again and again at the strength of my heart.

It was good to me to see you last Wednesday. This
age finds a refuge for its uncertainties, disillusions, and
going from bad to worse, in a semi-philosophical meta-

physic voiced by most ancient believes, dressed and presented in another ways by new and florid religious groups thriving fat and well on human credulity, unhappyness, misfortune and longings. As one of my friends of the West tells me: "The farmers and small middle-men has an hard time here with a worst propect before them and they look for cheerfulness to Christian Science!" Which, I say, tells you how to change a bad thing in a good one by cheating yourself in believing it good in spite of its bad effect upon you; in spite of your senses, reason and understanding which, though poor things in us all, are never-the-less the only means to judge given us by the All.

It works well for awhile, just as long as your autosuggestion lasts and the troubles do not get worse. But it is a wonderful means of stagnation which means regress. It appear most clearly and unrefutably so when you think of the poor farmers induced by it to believe that by thinking that everything will be O.K. it will be so—while the banks, the trusts, the Railroad Corp. and the greedy variety of parassites living off the farmers' sweat and the consumers' need are sharping their teeth and their robbery; and the Government, by other force of things becomes always more costly and tyrannical. . . .

This long sermon was inspired by your letter, not by my friend of the West who laughs at Christian Scientist and believes in other quite merry things— merry things to me but very serious for her. For since I began to exercise a little in my room and to play balls in the yard I am another man: it was better to me than hundreds of sermons and of speculation. So that yesterday I was able to write seven passable letters and, the day before, to talk with you.

You say that I have no reason to despair. Victor Hugo said that hope would be the last goddess were not for despair. When one has reason to despair and he despairs not, he may be more abnormal than if he would despair. At any rate, when one can help himself not even desperately, it is better to save the trouble of it. I am overwhelmed by the physical superior force of the State, so—! . . .

It is not that I distrust the men appointed to investigate the case or the Governor himself nor because I believe that the master classes are deprived of the sense of justice that I am pessimist on the outcome of the case. No indeed, for I do not know those four men [1] and I know that nature breaths the same instincts and sentiments in the breast of each born of woman— though they are perverted by bad environment, exercise of authority, ruling, privileges, extreme wants and plenties, idleness and overwork etc etc. But I have my opinions and previsions on different and more sure facts and dates than the above mentioned. Thayer has did his best to murder us for class hatred, for personal career and honors, to be appointed Judge of the State Supreme Court. The supreme justices have sticked with him terribly and they are presently mov-

---

[1] Joseph A. Wiggin, Governor Fuller's personal attorney, who was at the Governor's elbow throughout the investigation, and the Governor's committee composed of President Lowell of Harvard, President Stratton of the Massachusetts Institute of Technology, and Judge Grant.

ing third persons to urge our killing. No doubt that
both the judiciary and the legislative of Massachusetts
would like to kill us by their own hands. (See the
State Congress behavior at the Rep. Sawyer resolution.) Now, the records of the case would impose a
tardy liberation of us if we were scorpions instead of
men; but do you believe that the four men have nerves
and will enough for it? That they will free us? I
would like you to be right, but I cannot see any reason,
any precedent, any factor authorizing me to believe it.
Almost seven years ago I clearly perceived that the
State of Massachusetts would have done its best to
kill us and that if it would have become too shameful
and dangerous, the State will bury us alive in Charlestown, as the State of California did with Mooney
whose case is like ours as two drops of water are alike.
That case is a terrible precedent and it must be striken
off from the judiciary record by those who have the
right and the might to do it—and the duty.

Then, once burried in Charlestown Prison, we will
come out when we will come out; either two dead
bodies or two shadows of men—but men no more.
I like to look truth and reality in their face, eyes into
eyes—and give me one man out of every ten males,
and you would see what a job the world over I would
do!

But, let go this raveing. You are good to me and
you are doing very much to us—and I like to believe,
as it seems so (because it seems so) that you together
with all our friends have won an half victory already. . . .

June 20, 1927. *Dedham Jail*

DEAR FRIEND MRS. WINSLOW:

In the hope to see you to-morrow, I have just finished my letter presentation for you and my family.

Now, just few words on your trip. I really believe that your plan to go first to see my family and then to go to see the one of Nick—by the Adriatic line —is the better one were not for the reason that you will avoid to be brought suddenly from a cold to a hot clime.

From here to Paris, you are more acknowledged than I, in traveling. If there is a direct [train] from Paris to Turin that would be O.K. If not, you should take a ticket from Paris to Modane; then from Modane to Torino. From Turin you will take a ticket to my famous mocropolis—known by the whole universe and other places as well, under the name of Villafalletto. (For this I will provide you of a written request.)

Now, when you will reach my native home—just think to be at your own. You will be tired by the long trip and that is a good place for rest and restor. To went and left in a day, would be a senseless fatigue and there would not be time enough to explain things to my people. Besides that, the interpreter could be out of home or busy—while if you can stay there longer, all of you will have time to understand and explain one another. My sisters will be happy to have you there—they love all who help us and are proud of them. So, please, just think to be at home and don't leave the place untill you feel well.

If when you arrive in Turin (you will have to take the train to Villafalletto at the same station) you have time to go to the American Express office there and get informations on the times and lines to go to Nick's home, so much the better—if not, you will find out it at your return to Turin. Try to avoid a night in Turin, but if you will be compelled to it, just remember what I said to you about it.

Well, I wish you a good trip and I will accompany you in thought and good wishes.

I am not too optimist in the case outcome—and I see the possibility to be unable to see you and greet you on your return home. Though it seem to be sure that the Governor will postpone the date of the execution to next September—I don't see neither justice or good ahead; the force of darkness and tyranny are rapidly strifing to our doom.

But be of brave heart—and please, tell to my one all what you have in your heart.

June 22, 1927. *Dedham Jail*

Mrs. Sarah Root Adams:

Thank you for your good reply of June 17—and for *Words of Truth*. I believe with you that the Judges can be good men, maybe some are, but not the ones who murdered me so directly and cold-bloodly. The judges as judges are, were, and will always be bad as long as mankind will be divided in fools and knaves and will have judges, police, spies, informers, hangers, prisons and prison's guards, prosecutors, soldiers, prostitutes, thieves, oppressed and oppressors, exploited and exploiters—which is why we have judges and vice-versa.

As a man who I really love and admire as a good and great man, Malatesta, has said—"every new idea, in history, that menaces established interests and disturbs the mental laziness, ignorance and false pride of the more, has always arised three bad enemies against it; the calumny, the ignorance, and the falsehood." I rather believe to be in prison because I fought to eliminate the exploitation and oppression of man by the man, than on account of my past thought.

Well, dear Mrs. Adams, I will try to broadcast as many and big, and as far and high as I can, great message of love to everybody, since I cannot prevent and stop "evil acts in action."

Governor Fuller has not yet said to postpone our execution, and if he will keep quiet other eight days, we will be brought to the death house of the State Prison, and soon burnt to death, or, or—who can tell—Yet, things seem very tough, anyway.

We will remember you with love.

June 22, 1927. *Dedham Jail*

DEAR, DEAR FRIEND MRS. EVANS:

It was good of you to write me such a good and beautiful letter as yours of last, amid the troubles and botherings of a begining at a summer house.

Oh! that sea, that sky, those freed and full of life winds of Cape Cod!   Maybe I will never see, never breath, never be at one with them again. . . .

The two volumes of *The Rise of American Civilization* came with your letter. . . .   Well, I reached page 136, first volume, reading almost exclusively at bedtime after 9 oclock, when the nearest of the two electric lamps is extinted.   Then I sit on the end of my bed, place a pillow against the wall, a blanket on my shoulder, and, in the corner of my room beside the window, I enjoy that history at the light of one lamp, managing to avoid the window's bars shadows.

I like the style and temper of the authors—and quite well their criterions.   Of course, for people of my little education, and not helped by a long past of researchs and meditations, not enlighten by a Proudhon, a Michelet, Marx, Malatesta and other, these books will make the effect like the effect that a man ignorant in arithmetic would receive in seeing a foreigner-speaking man in an ununderstood language and resolving an algebraic problem on a black board.   Those lines and letters and number, riductions and operations would explain nothing to the unlearned foreigner.   This history as far as I reached it, would tell plenty of cronicles and of contrasting interests, almost exclusively between a ruling class and another semy-ruling class inspiring to the liberty of a full and sovereign ruling—and thus it would left, at the end of its reading, a bourgeaus worker or little fellow as bourgeaus as at the beginning.

Nothing, I found in it till now of the instinctive and

intuitive aspirations of the poor, of the hardly articulated but incommensurable souls of the humbles—except if I must believe that they are like the master—which, at least now day, it does not seems so to me.

Maybe I am wrong and unjust in my judgment of this work, because I know just its begining now. And my criticism, it may be acid, does not mean that I am not greatly enjoying and learning from the book. I read it in the light of Proudhon; and to my mind, contrary but learned doctrines are salutary. The only great trouble is that Massachusetts' hanger may not give me time to finish the lecture. All the rest is O.K.

I noticed that, in the begining, the authors affirm that though the economical factor is very dominant it is not alone in history; but they fail badly in showing the other historical factor, while they show that politics, religion, legislature and magistrature, are historically subservient to all for economic aim (power and rule) of master classes or classes aspiring to mastering. I have something on this matter in my phylosophycal sack, and some day I am going to send you a sample of it.

Humily and humble I belong to those anty-marxist socialist who affirm that though economy be a base of life it is not the only, and maybe neither the greatest of the historical factor. Proudhon declare that the cause prima of all war, strife and revolution is pauperism—which is not poverty—that poverty, work, sobriety, study and the steadfast passion of phylosophy (search of the truth) is the destiny of men in earth. Whereas we seek dominion, idleness, materialism, and hence our misery; the war will destroy mankind if we will not be heroic enough to destroy war in its causes and in ourselves.   And what pages he wrote—pages that make you think of a titanic—of a forehead large as the State Prison cursed dome.   I think that it is by drinking at that genius' source that Malatesta, a wondrous synthesist, if your intelligence caught the spirit of his simple sentences, says "that after all the life's problem is a moral problem." . . .

Well, when my traduction of Proudhon *Peace & War* will be published by Vanguard, I send you a copy if—if—if Fuller will give me his *beneplacido* instead of its contrary. . . .

Is this double investigation going to be another mockery? spitting on our faces? sponge of vinager and bitterness on the top of a lance? the last stubbing between our ribles?   Alas I have been treated by all so meaningly and bestially, that I can trust no one of the other side of the barricade—though knowing to be wrong.

The light is gone, I am closing this letter to go to prepare my corner for the reading of your American History.   Good night, dear Mrs. Evans, and be well.

June 25, 1927. Dedham Jail

DEAR ABBOTT:

Good as all of your letters are, the one of June 22nd reached me on the next day.   Though you had been silent for a while, I often thought of you as one of our best friends—for I know your heart and your good will. . . .

My keepers kept for themselves the hand-bill and the circular which you enclosed in your letter, and I am going to ask them if they are sending them to the District Attorney, as they did with one of my writings sent to Nick; or else to make an affidavit, as they did with the "General Account of the Sacco-Vanzetti Committee."

Oh yes! Mr. Bruce Bliven is a nice youth. He was here and promised to send us a copy of the *New Republic* containing the interview; he sent it to my keepers who kept it for themselves. They are so fine and so interested in our—doom! . . .

The Defense and the Committee have asked a reprieve to be given before the 1st of July, on two grounds: 1. To give sufficient time to the appointed commission; 2. To avoid our being carried to the death-house of the State Prison on July 1st. Two good reasons, these.

The commission appointed by the Governor has just begun its reading of the case some days ago, and except a reprieve, we shall be executed on the second or third week of next month. Is it humanly possible to study, duly, thoroughly and complete in three weeks, a case which two trials have lasted ten weeks, and which five appeals and two motions for a new trial are very voluminous, and which participant are over 100 persons?

Now, if the respite is ordered before July 1st, we would be kept here until the Governor's decision announcement, or until ten days before the ending of the time fixed by the reprieve. And here we have at least some air, light, a slice of land and of sky to contemplate, and a daily bliss of an hour of sunshine and free air in the yard, and also some weekly visitors. But if the respite is not given before July 1st, on that day we would be brought to the death-house in Charlestown Prison. The death-house is a bad place in all seasons, but windowless, airless, lightless as it is, it is a terrible place in hot weather.

One summer, I remember, a doomed waiting for his doom was kept there—and we heard that some guards fainted from the heat and suffocation of the place. If we remain here, we will not suffer so much until ten days before our execution, if the Governor will finally doom us. But if we will be carried there on July 1st, we will agonize at once from the heat and want of air. Then, if a reprieve would be given, we would be removed in Cherry Hill Wing where we would be kept in solitary confinement until the Governor will have decided our fate.

As you see, I am not concerned in a reprieve, but in the date of it. If before July 1st, alright; if after, I prefer no reprieve at all;—for if I have to be executed, better in July than in September, after two months more of torture. It seems sure that the Governor will order a reprieve. He will discuss this matter on the 28th with his Council of lawyers. But if he will refuse it, or keep silent until after we will be taken in the death-house—this would mean to me that he is now decided to send us to the electric chair, or to bury us alive and forever in the malebolgic of the State Prison, and for this reason he wants to have us safe and sound in the death-house before to announce his decision.

I hate to advance doubts, suspicions and temerity judgement on things and persons—but my atrocious experiences, the way I was dealt by Massachusetts State, my phylosophy itself authorizes and justifies my pessimism and the blackest hypothesis.

Yet, I am confident, my heart is steady and I will and hope—in spite of all.

Friend Abbott, Sacco and I pray you to extend our greetings and regards to all our friends whom you will meet, and hoping to find you in good health, we send you all that is good in our heart.

CHAPTER V

SACCO and Vanzetti were originally sentenced by Judge Thayer to be executed on July 10, 1927. Shortly after the appointment of the advisory committee, Governor Fuller respited the men (including Madeiros) to August 10. It is the custom to transfer convicts to the Cherry Hill section of Charlestown prison two weeks before the date set for their execution. The midnight removal of Sacco and Vanzetti from Dedham to Charlestown on July 1 was therefore unexpected.

The change disturbed Vanzetti especially, because he was not given time to gather together his books and papers. The transfer was made in two automobiles, one containing the men shackled to the sheriffs, and the other following, with armed guards.

On July 8, the Lowell advisory committee interviewed Sacco and Vanzetti in prison. Soon thereafter, in protest against the attitude of the Governor towards defense witnesses, as conveyed to him by Mrs. Sacco and other visitors, Vanzetti joined Sacco in a hunger strike. It lasted fifteen days, until the threat of forcible feeding made him stop.

On July 22, in the midst of Vanzetti's hunger strike, Governor Fuller interviewed him at Charlestown for more than an hour. A few days later, when all the prisoners had retired for the night, the Governor again interviewed Vanzetti at length. Vanzetti did not finish what he wanted to say at this time, and secured the Governor's permission to dictate the remainder in a letter. This he did a few days before the date of the Governor's decision, August 3.

Vanzetti was temporarily much disturbed by the decision, but soon began a calm preparation for the end. He wrote farewell letters to dispose of his books and belongings to friends, and to make his last gifts of pens, necklaces and cigarette cases carved by the prisoners, which he had done continuously during his long imprisonment.

The last-minute respite of twelve days which came half an hour before the official midnight execution set for August 10, gave Vanzetti the opportunity to see his sister, Luigia, who had just arrived from Italy after a separation of nineteen years. All visitors were now denied him except his lawyers, Mrs. Sacco and his sister.

He watched with close attention the final legal steps which followed in quick succession, and their outcome. At the end, he asked to be allowed to see Mr. Thompson, who had been succeeded by Mr. Arthur D. Hill after the Governor's decision. Mr. Thompson arrived at the death house in the early evening of August 22, a few hours before the time of execution. He found Vanzetti tranquil and alert. They talked first of details of the case. The conversation turned to Vanzetti's philosophy of the reorganization of society. "At parting," wrote Mr. Thompson afterwards, "he gave me a firm clasp of the hand and a steady glance, which revealed unmistakably the depth of his feeling and the firmness of his self-control."

July 8, 1927. *Charlestown Prison*

DEAR FRIEND MRS. WINSLOW:

You certainly know at this time that the' Sheriff has dragged us here at the midnight of July 1—as a kidnapper—and that our execution was postponed to August 10.

Mr. Thompson was here yesterday, and from what he said I got the impression that both the Governor and the Commission are going to give a decision before that date—so that it will be a contrary one, we will be despatched that night.

Though the authorities of this institution are generous in allowing me many letters, here I cannot write so much as I did while at Dedham, and I do not know when and if I will be able to write to you again, and the chances and my believe are that I may not see you again. This would make your mission to our families extremely sorrowful. [1]

I will not try to thank you and to express you my gratitude for all the great good that you have done and are doing to us. But I have it all in my heart.

In the hope to find you well, wishing you a good permanence in Europe and a better return home, and saluting you also for Nick, I remain sincerely yours.

P.S. Rose and Mrs. Codman visited us on the twen-

---

[1] Mrs. Winslow went to Italy in the summer of 1927 and visited the families of Sacco and Vanzetti.

ty-eighth. Mrs. C. brought us roses of her garden, and Rose, the ones you sent us. I have never seen so beautiful roses, buds of roses, before then, than those ones. They glads the heart and all who saw them wondered at their beauty. And so far, they were the latest flower to us. Good bye.

July 14, 1927. *Charlestown Prison*

DEAR MRS. CODMAN:

Just in the evening of June 30 I had written you a short note of thanks for your goodness, of congratulation for having seen you so well looking and for an hearty regard to Dr. Codman and your little, brave nephew. Then, suddenly, it happened what it happened and my note to you went lost and my hope of other 30 days of a little of fresh-air and vital sun-light. Our god-fearing law-abitting enemies are not satisfy to kill us, they want to inflict upon us more pain that they can. If I have to die on August 11, that makes little difference anyhow. . . .

Here we are not hated and despised as by the bigots of Dedham, and it help a good deal; but of course, the very nature of the place impose strickter rules than there and considerations and kindness cannot obliterate completely this fact. I would like to have those who wrote that Medeiros has prolonged his life of a years, by his confession, to believe that they are condemned to death, that there is no escape from it, then to keep them for a month where I am, and see if at the end of it they would not invoke their execution to end it all, as Medeiros himself is doing from long time.

As for us, they said the Governor is honest, indipendent and couragious; I do not know of the contrary, and I wish it to be true.

But I have too much experience of things chances and persons to permit me optimism. My heart presenses nothing good for the future. . . .

July 14, 1927. *Charlestown Prison*

DEAR FRIEND MUSMANNO:[1]

I am so eager to send my best friends a word, that I made four notes out of a folio of letter paper, confident that the warden will be kind enough to accede to my natural and honest wish, and you may receive these few words as symbols of my affection and gratitude. I cannot say much, as you know the proceedings and the prospect of the case better than I. There is little hope in my heart, but the certitude of a valiant defence of us from you.

July 14, 1927. *Charlestown Prison*

DEAR, DEAR MRS. EVANS:

By courtesy of Mr. Hogsett's [2] I received yesterday your two letters and sent you an hurried note. . . .

---

[1] Michael A. Musmanno, Italian lawyer of Pittsburgh, Pa., sent to present a petition to the Governor by the Sons of Italy of Pittsburgh. Mr. Musmanno remained in Boston and contributed his services to the defense till the execution.

[2] Deputy Warden of the State Prison.

Thank you, also, for the branch of little roses,—it is a special bless here. I am sorry that you were not admitted, for I would like to see you—but you know the circumstance and though the authorities here are generous and considerated—yet, it is hard, very, very difficult. But if I have to be executed, I will do all the little I can to see you again. I am positive that to order our execution in spite of all the facts and evidence of our innocence, is a plain cold-blood murder—but if it will be, let it be. I have brought my pebble to the altar of freedom and life and even if the great all will disintegrate my body and soul into its immence bosom, it will infuse my faculties and attributes in the new borns of women and, safe, the race will abjure life to death; my banner, falled from my hand is allready plucked up and uphold by stronger hands and will be in the highest whenever the ideal triumphs.

I feel rather to think than to read, and I have much to write. I wrote you something on the *American Civilization*;[1] surely the letter went lost somehow. Well, I only read about 1/3 of the 1st volume and some 100 pages of the second. (Rose did not found the first volume in Dedham; it is lost for now with 3 others my books) so that I cannot have an ultimate idea of it. But it seems to me well written, serene, quite impartial and I learnt and delighted in its pages. Certainly it is not Proudonian—that is, it gives no place to invert processes and subtle, preponderant factors of history—and therefore it close with an obtiniest

---

[1] *The Rise of American Civilization*, by Mary and Charles A. Beard.

that may be right but is based on facts evil-promising. Yet, the hail to its author, it is a good and nice work. If I will finish and survive its lecture I will write more of it.

July 17, 1927. *Charlestown Prison*

DEAR MRS. EVANS:

Your good letters are received. I have no more time to discuss of other than the case. Am writing a booklet to France comrades, dealing with the situation. As long as I can hold a pen, I must write on my assassination. I am a revolutionist and each my words are intended to be a blow. I dont forgive any murderors. It would be to betray my beloved ones, my ideas, my comrades, the best of mankind, all the future generation and myself.

As for theosophy I cannot believe in it. It is not to face the unknown, that I fear. And if there is something beyond the grave, I will learn it when the midnight of August 10, 1927—will have struck—maybe before. I do not want escape the reallities or the truth —but change them in good by destroying the evils in them.

Be of brave heart, dear friend and comrade, Mrs. Evans. I hold you in my heart; and I bless you. . . .

P.S. Dear Mrs. Evans:
Rose told us you were here today. . . .
Yes, I am in hungry strike this time—a real anty-

agitation. [1] I am convinced to never be able to finish the lecture of *The History of American Civilization.* I have no more time to read. But the title of "American Barbarism" fills of water my intellectual mouth— so much so because I am fasting from Thursday evening—and it appeal to me tremendously. For, you see, I believe that the only way to do well is to discover and eliminated the evils of the truths. Because men can transform the truths from evil ones to good ones & vice versa. It is the doctrine of my volontarism. . . .

But my hungry strike is progressing because I know that both the Governor and the commission have ill-treated our witnesses, wrongly, and that they believe nothing of what our witnesses say. They believe, and treat well those handful of criminals, harlots, and degenereted who perjured against us.

I know that Mr. Wiggin [2] is false with Mr. Thompson and that the Governor does not want to understand anything favorable to us because that is the only honest way to murder us and quiet his christian conscience. He is relatively straight relatively to a crook world.

He cannot understand me but I can understand him —because I have been like him before to become what I am. To murder us is to his friend's and class's criterions and feelings the only way to save the face of Thayer and of the other black-gownd vallets of

---

[1] Vanzetti, in the middle of July, began a hunger strike that lasted fifteen days.

[2] Governor Fuller's personal counsel.

the plutocracy; the reputation of the dear, old Commonwealth of Massachusetts; to check revolution and save America.

The Czars and all the tyrants have paid for it—none of them will escape what they deserve, except it to be paid by their children or grand children, but it must be paid.

I stop now because I am bitter.

Afternoon of July 20, 1927. *Charlestown Prison*

DEAR MRS. HENDERSON:

Not knowing what to think of your long silence, I wondered of it and thought many things: that you may have been unwell, or too busy, or abroad or travelling or—or that you might have been sorry for what I had said to you of the Governor. . . .

I too would like to see you and have a good conversation with you—but, but it cannot be for now, and maybe, for nevermore.

The day before yesterday I asked my friend Aldino to send a telegram for my family to Giacomo Caldera, your interpreter at my home. I told him to tell my sister Luigina, if she can, to come here for I wish to see her before to die—since from all I can understand the Gov. is decided to execute us. I begged Giacomo to prepare my Ones to the bad news before to give it to them. Maybe I did wrongly, but I wish too much to see and talk at least with Luigina, before I die.

I see, dear Mrs. Henderson, that you are still optimist and hopeful, greatly trusting in Governor Fuller. Maybe you are right and will be right—but for all that I am told and I can understand both the Governor and the Commission distrusts all our witnesses; trusts all the Government's perjurors; cannot or want not understand or both of that.

Gov. Fuller told Rosa that my lawyers at the Plymouth trial wanted me to take the stand; that I refused to take it and sent a boy of 12 years to talk for me by reciting a lesson learnt by heart. A greatest wrong than this was never done to truth and to an innocent man as I am. How can the Governor not believe in Beltrando and all my truthful witnesses? How can he believe that a 12 year old boy could have perjured and resist a three hours of cross-examination by Katzmann?—and Katzmann put him on the stand again, for more than an hour, next day, and without warning. If the Governor does not believe Beltrando, he neither believes all the other of my witnesses. How can he believe that a boy, as Beltrando is now, would insist in a perjury? Is capable of perjury? Why then, Beltrando tells now of his positiveness of my innocence everywhere? always? to all? How can the Governor believe in the States' perjurors against us, he who knows or should know that they changed three times their dispositions, in order to fit them to me and convict me?

And what of the Commission? Judge Grant is against us to death as he has always been since our arrest and without knowing the case. We know now positively that all he wants is to execute us.

Also the attitude of the other two members is against us. Few days ago they abuse three Italian men because they witnessed the truth. Lately it was found out that the three men had told the truth—but as an indication of feeling the fact remains.

These are the reasons why we began our hungry strike. If after seven years and three months of agony, during which we proved our innocence and the iniquity of our trial and trialers, we have to be murdered in such way as this for crimes of which we are innocent—we prefer to die of starvation rather than die without a protest. I wonder if our enemies can believe that we are wrong.

Well, tomorrow after having read your letter sent by Rosa, I will write something more. But while I have it in mind: If you are not sure of anything, try, yes, if you please, to encourage my people with words of fortitude, but don't be too optimist with them, because if I am not wrong and things are turning to the worst, is better to prepare them from now to bear my loss, rather than give them hopes which would make more terrible a fatal news.

July 21, 1927. Charlestown Prison

DEAR MRS. HENDERSON:

Rosa was just here now and gave us your promised and waited-for letters.

No, Mrs. Henderson, I did not know that you have been in Dedham to see us and were not admitted.

From the Commission interview of us I got the impression that President Lowell and President Stratton are honestly intentioned and not hostile to us by predetermination. Yet it seemed to me that in spite of their great scholarship, they had not understood certain most vicious actions of the prosecution and the iniquity of Thayer's conduct. As for Judge Grant he is but another Thayer.

These things I explain and will explain in our Statement why we are in hungry strike.

Since then, all what I was told and can understand of both the Governor and the Commission's words and attitude, convinced me that they are against us, inclined and prejudiced against us, disbelieve all our witnesses and believe the Government perjurors: in short, that either they cannot or want not understand, or both, but are without doubt against us.

You know what the Governor told Rosa of Beltrando Brini. After that he grilled again Beltrando who said the same things; and after that the Governor told someone that Beltrando must have come at my house at 9 A.M. (so that I have had time to come back from Bridgewater).

Well, after that Beltrando went to him and told him that he had never told him so and all the Governor seemed to care for was to learn who had told Beltrando that he had said so. So you can see that his attitude is one of a man who honestly and hardly tries to convince himself that he is right to send S and V to the chair, and not at all the attitude of a man impartial and unpreconcetted.

It is all this that gave us the certitude that we are going to be murdered and this investigation will be the extreme insult. And for this we are fasting; we want, at least, protest. Being so, it does not matter if the forced nutrition will hurt us, because we will soon be killed.

Nevertheless we appreciate your warning us of the hurtfulness nutrition and your advice to stop our fast, because we understand that, given your believe that we will have justice—which we cannot share—you are advicing us for our own good, proving to the last your good will and generous friendship to us.

I wish to thank you Mrs. Henderson, for all that so very much that you have done and are doing for us and our poor families.

And if we cannot meet anymore, I assure you that I will carry in my grave my appreciation, gratitude and affection to you. You could not do more than you are doing for us.

July 21, 1927. *Charlestown Prison*

DEAR MRS. EVANS:

Well, I will try to drop few words to you this morning, before to begin to finish the long letter on the case to some French Comrades in Paris, and my statement of the reasons of my hungry strike.

But my belly is very empty and as Mirbean put it:

"But I was hungry, and it seems impossible and yet it is true that when there is nothing in the belly there is nothing in the heart—" and nothing in the head, I like to add. . . .

As for my idea of heroism, it is not to let me [be] murdered in the foulest way without even a protest. I have indured my predicament the best I could—for it was the only thing better to be done. But now it is the time that I must do my better to concurr with the little that I can to the fastening of the palingenesis.

Of Jesus, the only thing worth of reading, except the Bible, which I read, was *The Life of J. Christ,* by Ernest Renan, and *J. Christ has never Existed,* by an Italian author. All the rest, included Papini's *Story of J. Christ,* only make me sick. Your book may be very good, and I thank you very much of your promptness to have us delight in its lecture, but I have no more time to read. Yet if you please send it to us that Nick will read it.

Try to be calm and steady as much as possible. . . .

All in Dedham should believe we innocent had they been so eager to observe and study the trial and the case as they were and are eager to burn us. But they were and are too much against us to be willing to reason or observe the things and actually they ignore the facts just as they did before the trial. If it is Curtis or Barrett [1] who told you he believe Nick innocent, tell him that we know that they told to everybody else except those who they know positively to be our friends that we are guilty and must be executed. . . .

[1] Deputy sheriffs at the Dedham Jail.

July 22, 1927. Charlestown Prison

DEAR COMRADE DRAGAN: [1]

Your letter of the 14th reached me yesterday, and I thank you for it. I don't think that the fight between communists and reformists at the later meeting in Union Square, N. Y. on July 7th, help us in any way, and it offered a wished for opportunity for the police to beat all. My policy has always been of free speech to all; but if others do not want me to speak at meetings of their own, especially if the meetings are for prisoners, I always did what I could have with my own comrades.

As long as the several schools of socialism will look for power to themselves, be fatalist and authoritarian, and the workers follow their leaders, there will always be brotherly strife and hatred among them, instead of brothers and harmony. This was clearly seen at the beginning of the Socialist movement, by men who had eyes to see.

Power and abuse of power are synonims. The working class shall smash all the powers against it, not create a power for itself, except for self defense.

Before the last denial of the Massachusetts Supreme Court, I was under the common rule for all the prisoners of this prison. But afterward, I was placed in solitary confinement, under the rule for the sentenced to death, and deprived of all kinds of journals. I can receive letters and I receive quite many of them, more than I can answer to. We, Nick and I, are in two

[1] Harry Dragan of N. Tonawanda, N. Y.

contiguous cells, subjected to the same rules and can only see and talk to one another when Rosa visits us, or the lawyer, or when we walk daily, in the balcony of our floor. From all I can understand, we are doomed. Maybe I am wrong; I would be wrong, but things look like that.

This morning the Governor was here. He interviewed Madeiros, Sacco and then me. He stayed but a short time with the two former ones, but with me he stayed an hour and a half, and he will come back again. Anyhow, even if they will kill us, they cannot kill all of us; all the working class; all the good men and women, and still less, kill ideas, rights, necessities, aspirations and ideals. So the cause of freedom and justice, of class and of human emancipation will not be destroyed nor stopped by the bodies, burnt, of two more victims of our foes.

So have heart, be cheerful, victory is ahead, and do your share with glad heart.

July 23, 1927. Charlestown Prison

DEAR LITTLE COMRADE [LI PEI KAN] : [1]

Your letter dated July 11th was given to me a few days ago, and it gives me joy each time I read it. I will not try to find words with which to thank you for your little picture you sent me. Youth is the hope of

[1] Li Pei Kan of Shanghai, China, a student at the Collège de Chateau Thierry, Aisne, France, during the last years of the Sacco-Vanzetti case. He wrote several pamphlets on the case in Chinese, the principal one being *On the Scaffold*.

mankind, and my heart exults when I look at your photograph and say to myself "Lo! one of those who will pluck and uphold, highly, the flag of freedom, the flag of our supremely beautiful anarchy, which is now slowly falling down from our weakening hands,"— and a good one, as for that. You need to live for many others years, and hard ones, before to realize and understand what comfort and joy such a thought is to your old and dying Bartolo.

I have read of that—say, incident, and I thought it happened to you. It is less bad if it happened to an elderly one, because the elders are more worried and hardened by the vicissitude and adversities of life, so that they can bear better the hard blows of fate, while the young ones are more tender, and could be bent and split by black adversities. You will surely resist to all, and separate all, I am sure of it.

In regards to what you said of our Ideal in your letter, I fundamentally agree with all of it. My words on this subject, of my antecedent letter, were principally intended to fortify your spirit to better face the tremendous struggle for freedom and prevent future delusions by weakening fatalism and fortify voluntarism in you, as I do with all our young ones and neophites.

Perhaps you know Proudhon better than I, but if not, I advise you to study him. Read his *Peace and War*. I think he approached truth in many subjects nearer than other more recent great ones.

To my understanding, we are actually certainly

dragged, with the rest of mankind, toward tyranny and darkness. Where will we land?

The relatively known history testifies, it is true, that mankind has continuously progressed, slowly, insteadily, with advances and retrocessions, yet, steadily progressed.

But the dead civilizations tell their tale as well and what came and passed before the dawn of our historical knowledge, we cannot know. History, like evolution, as we know of it now, fails far from explaining the request of a deep thinker. Then, what will follow to this age of reversion and tyranny? A false democracy again, which in its turn would inevitably yield to another tide of tyranny? As it is happening from thousands of years?

Anarchy, the anarchists alone, we only can break these deadly circles and set life in such a way that by a natural synchronism, produced by the very nature of the things which create the new order, more exactly, which constitute the new order, history will be streamed toward the infinite sea of freedom, instead to turn in the above said dead, close circle, as, it seems, it did 'til now.

It is a titanic task—but humanly possible, and if we know, we will create the happy kingdom of Freedom when the traviated, misled tralignated working class, and people of all classes will, most instinctively, join us for the greatest emancipation of the history. But even then we will have to be at the brightness of our task, or else, only a new tyranny will be substitute to the present one as corollary of the immense holocaust.

These are the reasons why I tell you, young Comrade, heavy and hard words, just as your juvenile ardor, enthusiasm and faith bliss me, I hope my old experience will complete and fortify you.

My friends must have forgotten to send you *A Proletarian Life*,[1] or they are running short of the copies. But I hope to provide you with a copy in the near future. It is a poor thing, but you will take it for what it is. It was modified without my knowledge of it, to fit it to the Americans, to whom you can tell everything, and they like everything, except the pure, naked truth. In general, of course, but the exceptions to the rule are desperately few. . . .

And now, dear Li, I embrace you with brotherly and glad heart.

July 27, 1927. Charlestown Prison

DEAR COMRADE BLACKWELL:

Your good letter of the 24th reached me yesterday evening. You understand things and situations; your letters never make me mad, (as many others do) but always help me. You really feel and understand the great Cause and you love its humble militants.

You certainly know that last Saturday Gov. Fuller interviewed me—it was that he received me humanly and I spoke to him for 96 minutes, and he left promis-

---

[1] *The Story of a Proletarian Life,* an account of his own life written in Italian by Vanzetti during the first years of his imprisonment and published in a translation by Eugene Lyons in 1924 by the Defense Committee.

ing to return at that evening, which he did not. He had had to go to receive Lindbergh. Mr. Thompson came instead. He prayed me to drink some coffee, so as to be able to stand and speak to the Governor when he would have returned next Monday. So, last Saturday evening I drank half a cup of sugarless tea; Sunday morning a cup of sugarless coffee and milk, and half cup of coffee at noon, then I stopped, and I wrote all the day long a memorandum of what I should have said to the Governor. Well, that little milk came near killing me. I felt poisoned for two days, yesterday I succeeded in vomiting it. Then last night at 9:15, I was called in the guard room and brought in the Warden office, the Governor having come to see me. Again I spoke with him 'til after 11 o'clock. If I live to see you again, I will tell you what I told him; but now I will only say that he gives me the impression of being just as you say of him; an honest man, as I understand it, an sincere, courageous, stubborn man, but well intentioned at the bottom of it, and in a way, clever. And I like to tell you that he gave me a good heartfelt hand shake before he left. I may be wrong, but I don't believe that a man like that is going to burn us on a case like ours. Life imprisonment, for innocents as we are, after seven years of unspeakable suffering, would be a monstrosity. This I fear—but while we live, we can fight for justice and freedom to us and to all. And if we will live, we will fight to the last. And with all the reasons, evidences, people and comrades in our behalf we can hope in a late victory.

Since I have had no time to say half of what I
wished, I told the Governor that I would write him the
rest. Today I sent for Mr. Thompson to bring here
a stenographer to whom I will dictate my thoughts,
for I am too weak to write them down well.

Meanwhile, this morning, I feel much, very much
better. The doctor wondered of the vigor of my pulse.
Sacco is quite well too.

Returning to the Governor, my fear is that he conducts his inquiry with wrong criterions which may mislead him and wrong us supremely, from what he told
me. He considered much what Vahey, Graham and
Katzmann[1] told him. He gave great importance to
the cocksureness of both the juries. If the jurors pluck
the chance to kill us for their hatred and prejudice
against us, they will never tell it to the Governor. If
they were honestly convinced of our guilt (and I cannot see how this can have been possible) of course they
say so to him. I felt positive that they never followed
or studied the case after their murderous verdict: not
only that, but they resented and mad as dogs of our
desperate resistence and struggle. . . .

And now, dear Comrade Blackwell, I will stop. Eat
your bread with glad and satisfying heart that you
have all the right to it. Have my most hearty regards
and please share them with your old and brave cousin.

---

[1] John Vahey of Plymouth, Vanzetti's counsel at the Plymouth
trial and later Katzmann's partner; James H. Graham, Sacco's
first counsel and associated with Vahey in the defense of Vanzetti at Plymouth; Fred G. Katzmann, prosecutor of Vanzetti
at the Plymouth and Dedham trials in his capacity as district
attorney of Norfolk and Plymouth Counties.

July 27, 1927. Charlestown Prison

DEAR MRS. EVANS:

Last night from 9:30 to 11:10, I was again interviewed by the Governor. We have had a good talk, and he gave me a good and hearty handshake at the parting.

As long as I had been able, I wrote on the case in a desperate defence, to comrades and people that love us and are ready to all to defend us to the last.

Put down thoughts? Write a moral or political testament? An impossibility to men in our condition. I have wrote all of that with 15 years of militancy; Sacco did better than I. Babblers count nought.

I stop, dear Mrs. Evans, for, it is too hard to me to write more (having wrote already another letter and corrected our statement on our fastings). . . .

August 4, 1927. From the Death House

TO THE DEFENSE COMMITTEE: [1]

Governor Alvan T. Fuller is a murderer as Thayer, Katzmann, the State perjurors and all the other. He shake hand with me like a brother, make me believe he was honestly intentioned and that he had not sent the three carbarn-boy to have no escuse to save us.

[1] This note passed through the hands of Warden Hendry of State Prison to counsel for Sacco and Vanzetti who conveyed it to the Defense Committee. The handwriting in it is exceedingly jagged and irregular, unlike Vanzetti's usual handwriting, and the spelling is unusually imperfect. It was written immediately after Vanzetti learned of the Governor's decision, which was issued the night of August 3, 1927.

Now ignoring and denia all the proofs of our innocence and insult us and murder us. We are innocent.

This is a war of plutocracy against liberty, against the people.

We die for Anarcy. Long life Anarcy.

August 4, 1927. *Charlestown Prison*

DEAR MRS. EVANS:

Last night, after 9:00 P.M. Medieros, Nick and I were brought from our cells in Cherry Hill into the three cells of the deathhouse. In coming, I got a glance to the nighty, starry sky,—it was so long I did seen it before—and thought it was my last glance to the stars.

This morning Rose came to us and have had to stay beyond the bars of our cells. That is a thing for a wife.

Rose brought us your letters which I read both; your article on the actual phase of our case; and the poem of Brent Dow Allinson.

You ask for the Governor interviews with Nick and I. As for Nick, he spoke alone with the Governor and I didn't heard their conversation. Nick told me something of it,—but I prefer to let him say what he wish about it. I know that he stayed for very short time with the Governor.

As you know, I spoke with the Governor for about 90 minutes at both his interviews with me.

The impression he gave me at the first interview, he repeated at his second one. It is as I told to Mrs.

Codman. Only it seemed to me he inclined to see things in a contrary way to us—in fact he should assert a tremendous effort against himself to overwhelm that which, for thousands reasons, feelings and facts is to him a natural hostile tendency toward us, our persons, our case, our ideas, our environment. We are his opposite all at all and all in all, while our enemies are officers to him in all most everything. Consciously, subconsciously and unconsciously he cannot escape to be tremendously influenced and predisposed against us. But he gave me the impression to be sincere; had made great efforts to know the truth and was not settled, at least deliberately, against us, before to begin his inquiry.

Of course I may be wrong, but this seems to be the truth to me.

We spoke of allmost all the matters of the case. The Governor was man to tell me what troubles his mind against us. Unfortunately, given to the fact that at both time I have believed to be able to told him all my reasons and thoughts, it happened that I spoke to him more of other matters than the ones he mentioned having in mind to tell him of them at the last. Yet I wrote and dictated on these matters to the Governor.

If he is sending us to death, it does not matter how honestly the Governor can be convinced of our guiltiness, his conviction will not make us guilty—we are and will remain innocent, our execution would be the same as murder, our blood will call for revenge. It is for these reasons, for my duty toward my father, brother, sisters, friends, comrades and all at large and toward myself that I opened my heart to the Governor and talk to him as clear and forceful as I was able. Then even when agonizing, I wrote and dictate to him everything I can remember. I did all I can.

Not a dog, not a snake, not even a scorpion would have been dealed and be dealed as we have and as it seems we will be—in case like our,—by sane or good men.

Dear Mrs. Evans, you have been most good with us. I bless you for all that you have done to our own and to us.

Be of brave heart.

August 6, 1927. Charlestown Prison

MY DEAR COMRADE MARY [DONOVAN]:

Thank you very much for your good letter of this morning, for your great solidariety and friendship, and also for the good spirit you prove to have that comforts me.

Forgive if I write seldom. I know you know what I have in my heart and mind. Be brave. My love to all your family and to you. Always your comrade.

August 10, 1927. Charlestown Prison

DEAR COMRADE MRS. EVANS:

This is just to tell you good bye and bless you for all you have done for us. Please give our most hearty regards to all our friends.

With great heart yours.

P.S. *on August* 12, 1927

Dear Mrs. Evans:

I can salute you, once again, today, because of the bravery of all those who are fighting for us.

How I like their active resistence to evil in action. They that are O.K.

Always yours.

August 10, 1927. *Charlestown Prison*

DEAR MRS. WINSLOW:

Since I can no more see you, I write you this few words to testimony to you my immence gratitude for all that you have done for us and our family.

I bless you and I bid you with great heart my last good bye.

August 12, 1927. *Charlestown Prison*

DEAR MRS. WINSLOW:

Being still alive I renew to you my best regards and good wishes.

August 10, 1927. *Charlestown Prison*

DEAR MRS. CODMAN:

I thank you with all my heart for all you and Dr. Codman have done for us and for Rose.

I wish you all the good you deserve. I wish you to ask one of my book in English language for your little and brave nephew, as for my remembrance.

With all my heart yours.

August 12, 1927. *Charlestown Prison*

DEAR MRS. CODMAN:

Well, I am glad to salute you again on the day I had supposed to be the one after that of my execution, when I wrote the above note of good-bye.

August 10, 1927. *Charlestown Prison*

DEAR MRS. HENDERSON:

I bless you for all the great good you have done for us and for our family.

Wishing you all the good you deserve,

I am yours.

P.S. *on August* 12, 1927

Dear Mrs. Henderson:

When I wrote the above letter I never dreamt of being able to salute you again today.

Always yours.

August 17, 1927. *Charlestown Prison*

DEAR MRS. HENDERSON:

I cannot remember of any one who knows or is known personally by my sister—except a certain Mrs. M——, a town-woman, but I am not even sure if she lives in New York.

I had thought that some my comrades in New York would have received my sister in New York and brought her here in Boston.

I would be most glad and obliged if you will go to receive my sister in New York.

As for the rest, better to say nothing more. With most hearty greetings.

August 21, 1927. *Charlestown Prison*

DEAR MRS. HENDERSON:

I wish to thank you most heartfully for your care for my poor sister Luigia. In a way it was a great consolation to me to see her again after 19 years of separation. But since I saw her my heart lost a little of its steadyness. The thought that she will have to take my death to our mother's grave, it is horrible to me—to think of what she will soon have to stand and to bear revolts all my being and upsets my mind. Please, Mrs. Henderson you have already been so good with my sister and family, I pray you to assist her in this crucial hours. I wish to thank also your daughter and all those who helped me and my sister and family, and Nick and his family. This may be my last good by to you. . . .

I send you all the regards, good wishes and goodness of and in my heart.

August 21, 1927. *From the Death House*
of Massachusetts State Prison

DEAR FRIENDS AND COMRADES OF THE
SACCO-VANZETTI DEFENSE COMMITTEE:

After tomorrow mid-night, we will be executed, save
a new staying of the execution by either the United
States Supreme Court or by Governor Alvan T. Fuller.

We have no hope. This morning, our brave defender and friend Michael Angelo Musmanno was here
from his return from Washington, and told us he
would come back this afternoon if he would have time
for it. Also Rosa and Luigi were here this morning,
and they too, promised us to return this afternoon.
But now it is 5:30 P.M. and no one returned yet.
This tells us that there is no good news for us, for, if
so, some of you would have hurried to bring them to us.
It almost tells us that all your efforts have failed and
that you are spending these remaining few hours in
desperate and hopeless efforts to evitate our execution.
In a word, we feel lost! Therefore, we decided to
write this letter to you to express our gratitude and
admiration for all what you have done in our defense
during these seven years, four months, and eleven days
of struggle.

That we lost and have to die does not diminish our
appreciation and gratitude for your great solidarity
with us and our families.

Friends and Comrades, now that the tragedy of this
trial is at an end, be all as of one heart. Only two
of us will die. Our ideal, you our comrades, will live

by millions; we have won, but not vanquished. Just treasure our suffering, our sorrow, our mistakes, our defeats, our passion for future battles and for the great emancipation.

Be all as of one heart in this blackest hour of our tragedy. And have heart.

Salute for us all the friends and comrades of the earth.

We embrace you all, and bid you all our extreme good-bye with our hearts filled with love and affection. Now and ever, long life to you all, long life to Liberty. Yours in life and death,

BARTOLOMEO VANZETTI
NICOLA SACCO

August 21, 1927. *From the Death House of Massachusetts State Prison*

MY DEAR DANTE:

I still hope, and we will fight until the last moment, to revindicate our right to live and to be free, but all the forces of the State and of the money and reaction are deadly against us because we are libertarians or anarchists.

I write little of this because you are now and yet too young to understand these things and other things of which I would like to reason with you.

But, if you do well, you will grow and understand your father's and my case and your father's and my principles, for which we will soon be put to death.

I tell you now that all that I know of your father,

he is not a criminal, but one of the bravest men I ever knew. Some day you will understand what I am about to tell you. That your father has sacrificed everything dear and sacred to the human heart and soul for his fate in liberty and justice for all. That day you will be proud of your father, and if you come brave enough, you will take his place in the struggle between tyranny and liberty and you will vindicate his (our) names and our blood.

If we have to die now, you shall know, when you will be able to understand this tragedy in its fullest, how good and brave your father has been with you, your father and I, during these eight years of struggle, sorrow, passion, anguish and agony.

Even from now you shall be good, brave with your mother, with Ines, and with Susie—brave, good Susie [1] —and do all you can to console and help them.

I would like you to also remember me as a comrade and friend to your father, your mother and Ines, Susie and you, and I assure you that neither have I been a criminal, that I have committed no robbery and no murder, but only fought modestly to abolish crimes from among mankind and for the liberty of all.

Remember Dante, each one who will say otherwise of your father and I, is a liar, insulting innocent dead men who have been brave in their life. Remember and know also, Dante, that if your father and I would have been cowards and hypocrits and rinnegetors of our faith, we would not have been put to death. They

---

[1] Faithful friend of Mrs. Sacco, with whom she and her children lived during the last years of the case.

would not even have convicted a lebbrous dog; not even executed a deadly poisoned scorpion on such evidence as that they framed against us. They would have given a new trial to a matricide and abitual felon on the evidence we presented for a new trial.

Remember, Dante, remember always these things; we are not criminals; they convicted us on a frame-up; they denied us a new trial; and if we will be executed after seven years, four months and seventeen days of unspeakable tortures and wrong, it is for what I have already told you; because we were for the poor and against the exploitation and oppression of the man by the man.

The documents of our case, which you and other ones will collect and preserve, will prove to you that your father, your mother, Ines, my family and I have sacrificed by and to a State Reason of the American Plutocratic reaction.

The day will come when you will understand the atrocious cause of the above written words, in all its fullness. Then you will honor us.

Now Dante, be brave and good always. I embrace you.

P.S. I left the copy of *An American Bible* to your mother now, for she will like to read it, and she will give it to you when you will be bigger and able to understand it. Keep it for remembrance. It will also testify to you how good and generous Mrs. Gertrude Winslow has been with us all. Good-bye Dante.

BARTOLOMEO

August 22, 1927. From the Death House of Massachusetts State Prison

DEAR FRIEND DANA: [1]

Rosa and my sister Liugi paid us a visit just now and told us of your letter to us, which they had forgotten home. They will bring it to us this afternoon, if they will come back. But they told us the contents of your letter, and I am writing now because it seems that nothing and no one is going to stop our execution after this midnight; so we may have no chance to see your letter.

Judge Holmes repelled our appeal on the ground that the State Supreme Court had passed on the case and he does not want to invade the State Court ground.

Yesterday, Judge Brandeis repelled our appeal on the ground of personal reasons; to wit, because he or members of his family are favorably interested in our case, as demonstrated by the facts that after our arrest Rosa and her children went to live for a month in an empty house of Justice Brandeis in Dedham, Mass.

These two justices are the symbols of liberalism in the Federal Supreme Court and they turned us their shoulders.

Now our lawyers are presenting the appeal to Justice Stone. Since the other Federal Supreme Justices are reactionary, well, that will be a good ground on which to repel our appeal. So that it is coming to pass

[1] H. W. L. Dana of Cambridge, Mass., formerly of the Harvard faculty, now lecturer at the New School for Social Research, New York City.

that some justices repel our appeal because they are friendly with us and the other justices repel our appeal because they are hostile to us, and through this elegant Forche Caudine, we are led straight to the electric chair.

My poor sister and Rosa are really living on a cross. My sister was optimistic as all the world seemed to have been in our case that is not yet well understood not even by our most intelligent and experienced friends and comrades. But since she arrived here, on the place, and faced the real facts, her optimism withered away by degrees and this morning she was suffering terribly.

The Defense Committee, the Defense, our friends here, Rosa and Luigia are working frantically day and night in a desperate effort to avoid our execution, and they fail second by second and our execution appears always nearer and unavoidable. There are barely 12 hours to its moment, and we are lost—if we refuse to hope against reason.

And in our coffin will lay our friends' optimism and our pessimism. What I wish more than all in this last hour of agony is that our case and our fate may be understood in their real being and serve as a tremendous lesson to the forces of freedom—so that our suffering and death will not have been in vain.

I do not enter into particulars because I know you will learn of them before receiving this letter. But the situation appears to be in this moment as follows: All the Federal Justices will repel our appeal and from hence the other few hours our fate will be completely

in the hands of Governor Fuller. To me this means—
death. So much the better if I will be wrong.

So, dear friend and comrade Dana, I wish to thank
you for all that you have done for Nicola, I, and for
our families. My sister brought me your regards and
informs me of your going to Italy and to our families.
Please salute for us all the friends and comrades you
will meet in Europe, and express to them what you
know that we have in our hearts. And to you we send
our extreme good-bye and brotherly embrace. Be
brave and of good cheer, brother Dana.

Also for Nicola, we are yours,

NICOLA AND BARTOLOMEO

P.S. . . . I wish and hope you will lend your faculties in inserting our tragedy in the history under its real
aspect and being.

APPENDICES

APPENDIX I

The Story of the Case

A complete record of the numerous proceedings which constitute the case of Sacco and Vanzetti has now been made available through the publication of the entire documentation of the case by Henry Holt & Company, in six volumes, entitled *The Sacco-Vanzetti Case*. What follows is a summary of these long-drawn-out proceedings based upon Felix Frankfurter's book, *The Case of Sacco and Vanzetti*, supplemented by a statement of events which followed the publication of Mr. Frankfurter's book. We are indebted to the publishers, Messrs. Little, Brown & Company, for permission to make use of the book.

At about three o'clock in the afternoon of April 15, 1920, Parmenter, a paymaster, and Berardelli, his guard, were fired upon and killed by two men armed with pistols, as they were carrying two boxes containing the pay roll of the shoe factory of Slater and Morrill, amounting to $15,776.51, from the company's office building to the factory through the main street of South Braintree, Massachusetts. As the murder was being committed a car containing several other men drew up to the spot. The murderers threw the two boxes into the car, jumped in themselves, and were driven away at high speed across some nearby railroad tracks. Two days later this car was found abandoned in woods at a distance from the scene of the crime. Leading away from this spot were the tracks of a smaller car. At the time of the Braintree hold-up the police were investigating an earlier, unsuccessful hold-up in the neighboring town of Bridgewater. In each case a gang was involved. In each they made off in a car. In each eyewitnesses believed the criminals to be Italians. In the Bridgewater hold-up the car had left the scene in the direction of Cochesett. Chief Stewart of Bridgewater was therefore, at the time of the Braintree murders, on the trail of an Italian owning or driving a car in Cochesett. He thought he found his man in one Boda, whose car was then in a garage awaiting repairs. Stewart instructed the garage proprietor, Johnson, to telephone to the police when anyone came to fetch it. Pursuing his theory, Stewart found that Boda had been living in Cochesett with a radical named Coacci.

Now on April 16, 1920, which was the day after the Braintree murders, but before the discovery of any clue to their perpetrators, Stewart, at the instance of the Department of Justice, then engaged in the rounding-up of Reds, had been to the house of one Coacci to see why he had failed to appear at a hearing regarding his deportation. He found Coacci packing a trunk and apparently very anxious to get back to Italy as soon as possible. At the time (April 16), Coacci's trunk and his haste to depart for Italy were not connected in Chief Stewart's mind with the Braintree affair. After he discovered what he believed to be tracks of Boda's car near the so-called murder car and that Boda had once been living with Coacci, he connected Coacci's packing, his eagerness to depart, his actual departure, with the Braintree murders, and assumed that the trunk contained the booty. In the light of later discoveries Stewart jumped to the conclusion that Coacci, Boda's pal, had "skipped with the swag." As a matter of fact, the contents of the trunk, when it was intercepted by the Italian police on arrival, revealed nothing. In the meantime, however, Stewart continued to work on his theory, which centred around Boda: that whosoever called for Boda's car at Johnson's garage would be suspect of the Braintree crime. On the night of May 5, Boda and three other Italians did in fact call.

To explain how they came to do so let us recall here the proceedings for the wholesale deportation of Reds under Attorney-General Palmer in the spring of 1920. In particular the case of one Salsedo must be borne in mind—a radical who was held incommunicado in a room in the New York offices of the Department of Justice on the fourteenth floor of a Park Row building. Boda and his companions were friends of Salsedo. On May 4 they learned that Salsedo had been found dead on the sidewalk outside the Park Row building, and, already frightened by the Red raids, bestirred themselves to "hide the literature and notify the friends against the federal police." For this purpose an automobile was needed and they turned to Boda. Such were the circumstances under which the four Italians appeared on the evening of May 5 at the Johnson garage. Two of them were Sacco and Vanzetti. Mrs. Johnson telephoned the police. The car was not available and the Italians left, Sacco and Vanzetti to board a street car for Brockton, Boda and the fourth member, Orciani, on a motorcycle. Sacco and Vanzetti were arrested on the street car, Orciani was arrested the next day, and Boda was never heard of again.

Stewart at once sought to apply his theory of the commission of the two "jobs" by one gang. The theory, however, broke down. Orciani had been at work on the days of both crimes, so he was let go. Sacco, in continuous employment [1] at a shoe factory in Stoughton, had taken a day off (about which more later) on April 15. Hence, while he could not be charged with the Bridgewater crime, he was charged with the Braintree murders; Vanzetti, as a fish peddler at Plymouth and his own employer, could not give the same kind of alibi for either day, and so he was held for both crimes. [2] Stewart's theory that the crime

---

[1] At the trial Sacco's employer testified as follows about him: ". . . he was a very steady worker. He worked very steady from seven in the morning until quitting time at night and was on the job every day that you could expect any healthy man to work. There was times when he was two or three hours late on account of sickness, but outside of his getting through and talking of going to the old country, he was absolutely on the job every day."

[2] In an account of the joint trial of Sacco and Vanzetti the details of Vanzetti's separate trial cannot find a place, but Vanzetti's prosecution for the Bridgewater job grew out of his arrest for, and was merely a phase of, the Braintree affair. The evidence of identification of Vanzetti in the Bridgewater case bordered on the frivolous, reaching its climax in the testimony of a little newsboy who, from behind the telegraph pole to which he had run for refuge during the shooting, had caught

was committed by these Italian radicals was not shared by the head of the state police, who always maintained that it was the work of professionals.

Charged with the crime of murder on May 5, Sacco and Vanzetti were indicted on September 14, 1920, and put on trial May 31, 1921, at Dedham, Norfolk County. The setting of the trial, in the courthouse opposite the site of the old home of Fisher Ames, furnished a striking contrast to the background and antecedents of the prisoners. Dedham is a quiet residential suburb, inhabited by well-to-do Bostonians with a surviving element of New England small farmers. Part of the jury was specially selected by the sheriff's deputies from persons whom they deemed "representative citizens," "substantial" and "intelligent." The presiding

a glimpse of the criminal and "knew by the way he ran he was a foreigner." Vanzetti was a foreigner, so of course it was Vanzetti! There were also found on Vanzetti's person, four months after the Bridgewater attempt, several shells, one of which was claimed to be of a type similar to a shell found at the scene of the Bridgewater crime. The innocent possession of these shells was accounted for at the Dedham trial. More than twenty people swore to having seen Vanzetti in Plymouth on December 24, among them those who remembered buying eels from him for the Christmas Eve feasts. Of course all these witnesses were Italians. But the fact that Vanzetti bought eels for his Christmas sales was subsequently established by incontestable documentary evidence. The circumstances of the trial are sufficiently revealed by the fact that Vanzetti, protesting innocence, was warned by his counsel against taking the witness stand for fear his radical opinions would be brought out and tell against him disastrously. From a verdict of conviction counsel took no appeal. The judge and district attorney were Judge Webster Thayer and Mr. Katzmann, as also in the Braintree trial. The Bridgewater conviction was played up with the most lurid publicity when Vanzetti faced his trial for the Braintree crime.

judge was Webster Thayer of Worcester. The chief counsel for these Italians, Fred H. Moore, was a Westerner, himself a radical and a professional defender of radicals. In opinion, as well as in fact, he was an "outsider." Unfamiliar with the traditions of the Massachusetts bench, not even a member of the Massachusetts bar, the characteristics of Judge Thayer unknown to him, Moore found neither professional nor personal sympathies between himself and the Judge. So far as the relations between court and counsel seriously, even if unconsciously, affect the temper of a trial, Moore was a factor of irritation and not of appeasement. Sacco and Vanzetti spoke very broken English, and their testimony shows how often they misunderstood the questions put to them. A court interpreter was used, but his conduct raised such doubts [1] that the defendants brought their own interpreter to check his questions and answers.

At the trial the killing of Parmenter and Berardelli was undisputed. The only issue was the identity of the murderers. Were Sacco and Vanzetti two of the assailants of Parmenter and Berardelli, or were they not? This was the beginning and the end of the inquiry at the trial.

On that issue there was at the trial a mass of conflicting evidence. Fifty-nine witnesses testified for the Commonwealth and ninety-nine for the defendants. The evidence offered by the Commonwealth was not the same against both defendants. The theory

[1] Some time after the trial this interpreter was convicted of larceny.

of the Commonwealth was that Sacco did the actual shooting and that Vanzetti sat in the car as one of the collaborators in a conspiracy to murder. Witnesses for the Commonwealth testified to having seen both defendants in South Braintree on the morning of April 15; they claimed to recognize Sacco as the man who shot the guard Berardelli and to have seen him subsequently escape in the car. Expert testimony (the character of which, in the light of subsequent events, constitutes one of the most important features of the case) was offered seeking to connect one of four bullets removed from Berardelli's body with the Colt pistol found on Sacco at the time of his arrest. As to Vanzetti, the Commonwealth adduced evidence placing him in the murder car. Moreover, the Commonwealth introduced the conduct of the defendants, as evinced by pistols found on their persons and lies admittedly told by them when arrested, as further proof of identification in that such conduct revealed "consciousness of guilt."

The defense met the Commonwealth's eyewitnesses by other eyewitnesses, slightly more numerous than those called by the Commonwealth and at least as well circumstanced to observe the assailants, who testified that the defendants were not the men they saw. Their testimony was confirmed by witnesses who swore to the presence of Sacco and Vanzetti elsewhere at the time of the murder. Other witnesses supported Sacco's testimony that on April 15—the day that he was away from work—he was in Boston seeing about a passport to Italy, whither he was planning shortly to return to visit his recently bereaved father. The truth of his statement was supported by an official of the Italian consulate in Boston who deposed that Sacco visited his consulate at 2:15 P.M. If this were true, it was conceded that Sacco could not have been a party to this murder.

The alibi for Vanzetti was overwhelming. Thirty-one eyewitnesses testified positively that no one of the men that they saw in the murder car was Vanzetti. Thirteen witnesses either testified directly that Vanzetti was in Plymouth selling fish on the day of the murder, or furnished corroboration of such testimony.

At a later stage of the proceedings, Judge Thayer stated that the conviction of the men did not rest upon the identification of Sacco and Vanzetti by eyewitnesses to the crime. According to him, "the evidence that convicted these defendants was . . . consciousness of guilt."

By "consciousness of guilt" Judge Thayer meant that the conduct of Sacco and Vanzetti after April 15 was the conduct of murderers. This inference of guilt was drawn from their behavior on the night of May 5, before and after arrest, and also from their possession of firearms. It is vital to keep in mind the exact data on which, according to Judge Thayer, these two men were sentenced to death. There was no claim whatever at the trial, and none has ever been suggested since, that Sacco and Vanzetti had any prior experience in hold-ups or any previous association with bandits; no claim that the sixteen thousand dollars taken from the victims ever found its way into their pockets;

no claim that their financial condition, or that of Sacco's family (he had a wife and child, and another child was soon to be born), was in any way changed after April 15; no claim that after the murder either Sacco or Vanzetti changed his manner of living or employment. Neither of these men had ever been accused of crime before their arrest. Nor, during the three weeks between the murder and their arrest, did they behave like men who were concealing the crime of murder. They did not go into hiding; they did not abscond with the spoils; they did not live under assumed names. They maintained their old lodgings; they pursued openly their callings, within a few miles of the town where they were supposed to have committed murders in broad daylight; and when arrested Sacco was found to have in his pocket an announcement of a forthcoming meeting at which Vanzetti was to speak. [1]

What, then, was the evidence against them?

1. Sacco and Vanzetti, as we have seen, were two of four Italians who called for Boda's car at Johnson's garage on the evening of May 5. It will be remembered that in pursuance of a prearranged plan Mrs.

---

[1] The manifesto ran as follows:

"You have fought all the wars. You have worked for all the capitalists. You have wandered over all the countries. Have you harvested the fruits of your labors, the price of your victories? Does the past comfort you? Does the present smile on you? Does the future promise you anything? Have you found a piece of land where you can live like a human being and die like a human being? On these questions, on this argument, and on this theme, the struggle for existence, Bartolomeo Vanzetti will speak. Hour —— day —— hall ——. Admission free. Freedom of discussion to all. Take the ladies with you."

Johnson, under pretext of having to fetch some milk, went to a neighbor's house to telephone the police. Mrs. Johnson testified that the two defendants followed her to the house on the opposite side of the street and when, after telephoning, she reappeared they followed her back. Thereafter the men, having been advised by Mr. Johnson not to run the car without the current year's number plate, left without it:

Q. Now, Boda came there to get his car, didn't he? *A*. Yes.

Q. There were no 1920 number plates on it? *A*. No.

Q. You advised him not to take the car and run it without the 1920 number plates, didn't you? *A*. Yes.

Q. And he accepted your view? *A*. He seemed to.

Q. He seemed to. And after some conversation went away? *A*. Yes.

This was the whole of the testimony on the strength of which Judge Thayer put the following question to the jury:

Did the defendants, in company with Orciani and Boda, leave the Johnson house because the automobile had no 1920 number plate on it, or because they were conscious of or became suspicious of what Mrs. Johnson did in the Bartlett house? If they left because they had no 1920 number plates on the automobile, then you may say there was no consciousness of guilt in consequence of their sudden departure, but if they left because they were consciously guilty of what was being done by Mrs. Johnson in the Bartlett house, then you may say that is evidence tending to prove consciousness of guilt on their part.

2. Following their departure from the Johnson house, Sacco and Vanzetti were arrested by a police-

man who boarded their street car as it was coming into Brockton. Three policemen testified as to their behavior after being taken into custody:

[As to Vanzetti] He went down through the car and when he got opposite to the seat he stopped and he asked them where they were from. "They said 'Bridgewater.' I said, 'What was you doing in Bridgewater?' They said 'We went down to see a friend of mine.' I said, 'Who is your friend?' He said, 'A man by the—they call him "Poppy."' 'Well,' I said, 'I want you, you are under arrest.' Vanzetti was sitting on the inside of the seat."

Q. When you say "on the inside," you mean toward the aisle or toward the window? *A.* Toward the window. The inside of the car; and he went, put his hand in his hip pocket and I says, "Keep your hands out on your lap, or you will be sorry."

The Defendant Vanzetti: You are a liar!

[As to Sacco] I told them when we started that the first false move I would put a bullet in them. On the way up to the Station Sacco reached his hand to put under his overcoat and I told him to keep his hands outside of his clothes and on his lap.

Q. Will you illustrate to the jury how he placed his hand? *A.* He was sitting down with his hands that way (indicating), and he moved his hand up to put it in under his overcoat.

Q. At what point? *A.* Just about the stomach there, across his waistband, and I says to him, "Have you got a gun there?" He says "No." He says, "I ain't got no gun." "Well," I says, "Keep your hands outside of your clothes." We went along a little further and he done the same thing. I gets up on my knees on the front seat and I reaches over and I puts my hand under his coat but I did not see any gun. "Now," I says, "Mister, if you put your hand in there again, you are going to get into trouble." He says, "I don't want no trouble."

3. In statements made to the District Attorney and to the Chief of Police, at the police station after their arrest, both Sacco and Vanzetti lied. By misstatements they tried to conceal their movements on the day of their arrest, the friends they had been to see, the places they had visited. For instance, Vanzetti denied that he knew Boda.

What of this evidence of "consciousness of guilt"? The testimony of the police that Sacco and Vanzetti were about to draw pistols was emphatically denied by them. These denials, it was urged, were confirmed by the inherent probabilities of the situation. Did Sacco and Vanzetti upon arrest reveal the qualities of the perpetrators of the Braintree murders? Those crimes were committed by desperadoes—men whose profession it was to take life if necessary and who freely used guns to hold bystanders at bay in order to make their "get-away." Is there the slightest likeness between the behavior of the Braintree bandits and the behavior of Sacco and Vanzetti, when the two were arrested by one policeman? Would the ready and ruthless gunmen at Braintree so quietly have surrendered themselves into custody on a capital charge of which they knew themselves to be guilty? If Sacco and Vanzetti were the hold-up men of Braintree, why did they not draw upon their expert skill and attempt to make their escape by scattering shots? But, if not "gunmen," why should Sacco and Vanzetti have carried guns? The possession of firearms in this country has not at all the significance that it would have, say, in England. The extensive carrying of guns by people who are not "gunmen" is a matter of common knowledge. The widespread advertisement of fire-arms indicates that we may not unfairly be described as a gun-carrying people. The practice is unfortunately rife for a variety of reasons. Sacco and Vanzetti had credible reasons, wholly unrelated to professional banditry. Sacco acquired the habit of carrying a pistol while a night watchman because, as his employer tes-tified, "night watchmen protecting property do have guns." Vanzetti carried a revolver, "because it was a very bad time, and I like to have a revolver for self-defense":

Q. How much money did you use to carry around with you? *A.* When I went to Boston for fish, I can carry eighty, one hundred dollars, one hundred and twenty dollars.

There were many crimes, many hold-ups, many robberies at that time.

The other evidence from which "consciousness of guilt" was drawn, the two Italians admitted. Sacco and Vanzetti acknowledged that they behaved in the way described by Mrs. Johnson, and freely conceded that when questioned at the police station they told lies. What was their explanation of this conduct? To exculpate themselves of the crime of murder they had to disclose elaborately their guilt of radicalism. In order to meet the significance which the prosecu-tion attached to the incidents at the Johnson house and those following, it became necessary for the de-fendants to advertise to the jury their offensive views, and thereby to excite the deepest prejudices of a Norfolk County jury, picked for its respectability and sitting in judgment upon two men of alien blood and abhorrent philosophy.

Innocent men, it is said, do not lie when picked up by the police. But Sacco and Vanzetti knew they were not innocent of the charge on which they *supposed* themselves arrested, and about which the police interrogated them. For when apprehended they were not confronted with the charge of murder; they were not accused of banditry; they were not given the remotest intimation that the murders of Parmenter and Berardelli were laid at their door. They were told they were arrested as "suspicious characters," and the meaning which that carried to their minds was rendered concrete by the questions that were put to them:

[As to Vanzetti] Did you tell Mr. Katzmann the truth about Pappi and why you— *A*. About Pappi, yes, but I don't say that I was there to take the automobile and I don't speak about the literature . . . I don't tell him about the meeting on next Sunday. Yes, I told them, I explained to them the meeting, I think.

Q. Tell us all you recall that Stewart, the chief, asked of you? *A*. He asked me why we were in Bridgewater, how long I know Sacco, if I am a Radical, if I am an anarchist or Communist, and he asked me if I believe in the government of the United States.

Q. Did either Chief Stewart at the Brockton police station or Mr. Katzmann tell you that you were suspected of robberies and murder? *A*. No.

Q. Was there any question asked of you or any statement made to you to indicate to you that you were charged with that crime on April 15th? *A*. No.

Q. What did you understand, in view of the questions asked of you, what did you understand you were being detained for at the Brockton police station? *A*. I understand they arrested me for a political matter. . . .

Q. . . . Why did you feel you were being detained for political opinions? *A*. Because I was asked if I was a Socialist. I said, "Well,—"

Q. You mean by reason of the questions asked of you? *A*. Because I was asked if I am a Socialist, if I am I.W.W., if I am a Communist, if I am a Radical, if I am a Blackhand.

[As to Sacco] What did you think was the time when the crime that you were arrested for had been committed? *A*. I never think anything else than Radical.

Q. What? *A*. To the Radical arrest, you know, the way they do in New York, the way they arrest so many people there.

Q. What made you think that? *A*. Because I was not registered, and I was working for the movement for the working class, for the laboring class.

Q. What occurred with Mr. Stewart [Chief of Police] that made you think you were being held for Radical activities? *A*. Well, because the first thing they asked me if I was an anarchist, a communist or socialist.

Plainly their arrest meant to Sacco and Vanzetti arrest for radicalism. That being so, why should they evade police inquiries; what fear governed them in making lies to escape that charge?

The early winter of 1919–20 saw the beginning of an elaborately planned campaign by the Department of Justice under Attorney-General Mitchell Palmer for the wholesale arrest and deportation of "Reds"— aliens under suspicion of sympathy with the Communist régime. The details of these raids, their brutality and their lawlessness, are set forth authoritatively in decisions of United States courts condemning the misconduct of the Department of Justice. These findings the Attorney-General never ventured to have reviewed by the higher courts.

Boston was one of the worst centres of this lawlessness and hysteria. Sacco and Vanzetti were notorious Reds. They were associates of leading radicals. They had for some time been on the list of suspects of the Department of Justice, and were especially obnoxious because they were draft-dodgers.

The press made them daily anxious for their safety. The newspapers, it will be recalled, were filled with lurid accounts of what the Reds had done and were planning, and equally lurid accounts of the methods of the Government in dealing with the Reds. Not only were Sacco and Vanzetti living in this enveloping atmosphere of apprehension; the terrorizing methods of the Government had very specific meaning for them. Two of their friends had already been deported. Deportation, they knew, meant not merely expulsion and uprooting from home. Among Vanzetti's radical group in Boston the arrest of the New York radical Salsedo, and his detention incommunicado by the Department of Justice, had been for some weeks a source of great concern. Vanzetti was sent to New York by this group to confer with the Italian Defense Committee having charge of the case of Salsedo and all other Italian political prisoners. On his return, May 2, he reported to his Boston friends the advice which had been given to the Italian Defense Committee by their New York lawyer: to dispose of their radical literature and thus eliminate the most damaging evidence in the deportation proceedings they feared.

The urgency of acting on this advice was intensified by the tragic news of Salsedo's death after Vanzetti's return from New York. It was to carry out this advice that Vanzetti and his friends were trying to get Boda's car from Johnson's garage on May 5. The day before had come the news of Salsedo's death.

Though Salsedo's death was unexplained, to Sacco and Vanzetti it conveyed only one explanation. It was a symbol of their fears and perhaps an omen of their own fate.

Let us now resume the story of the trial. The witnesses for the Commonwealth had dealt with identification of men and of bullets, and the suspicious conduct of Sacco and Vanzetti at the time of arrest. On the witness stand Sacco and Vanzetti accounted for their movements on April 15. They also accounted for their ambiguous behavior on May 5. Up to the time that Sacco and Vanzetti testified to their radical activities, their pacifism and their flight to Mexico to escape the draft, the trial was a trial for murder and banditry; with the cross-examination of Sacco and Vanzetti patriotism and radicalism became the dominant emotional issues. Of course, these were not the technical issues which were left to the jury. But, as Mr. Justice Holmes has admonished us, "in spite of forms [juries] are extremely likely to be impregnated by the environing atmosphere." Outside the court-room the Red hysteria was rampant; it was allowed to dominate within. The prosecutor systematically played on the feelings of the jury by exploiting the unpatriotic and despised beliefs of Sacco and Vanzetti, and the judge allowed him thus to divert and pervert the jury's mind. Only a detailed knowledge of the conduct of the prosecutor, sanctioned by the Court, can give an adequate realization of the extent to which prejudice, instead of being rigorously excluded, was systematically fostered.

After a trial lasting nearly seven weeks, on July 14, 1921, Sacco and Vanzetti were found guilty of murder in the first degree.

To various rulings made by Judge Thayer during the trial, exceptions were taken which were made the basis of an application for a new trial, which Judge Thayer refused. Subsequently a mass of new evidence was unearthed by the defense, which was made the subject of other motions for a new trial, all heard before Judge Thayer and all denied by him. The hearings on these later motions, in October and November, 1923, brought into the case Mr. William G. Thompson, a distinguished Boston lawyer.

The facts underlying one of these motions may be indicated briefly. One of the vital parts of the proof that Sacco and Vanzetti were the murderers, was a demonstration that one of the fatal bullets came from Sacco's pistol. The five other bullets found in the dead bodies admittedly were not fired either by Sacco or Vanzetti. When Judge Thayer placed the case in the jury's hands, he told them that the Commonwealth had introduced the testimony of two experts, Proctor and Van Amburgh, to the effect that it was Sacco's pistol

"that fired the bullet that caused the death of Berardelli." After their conviction, Proctor made disclosures which remained uncontradicted by the District
Attorney, that Proctor did *not* believe that the fatal
bullet in Berardelli came out of Sacco's pistol, for he
was unable to find evidence for such belief; that he
refused to accede to the view that the mortal bullet
came out of Sacco's pistol and that the District Attorney knew that such was not intended to be his testimony. By prearrangement Proctor testified at the
trial as follows:

Q. Have you an opinion as to whether bullet No. 3 (Ex-
hibit 18) was fired from the Colt automatic, which is in evidence (Sacco's pistol)? *A.* I have.
Q. And what is your opinion? *A.* My opinion is that it is
consistent with being fired from that pistol.

Proctor, at the time of his testimony, was head of the
Massachusetts State Police and was qualified by the
Commonwealth as an expert who for twenty years had
made examinations of firearms and bullets and had
testified in over a hundred capital cases. The prosecution thus brought before the jury, on a vital issue, a
piece of evidence apparently most damaging to the
defendants, when, in fact, the full truth concerning this
evidence was most favorable to them. Nevertheless,
Judge Thayer found no warrant in this Proctor dis-
closure for granting a new trial.

Hitherto the defense had maintained that the circumstances of the case all pointed away from Sacco
and Vanzetti. But the deaths of Parmenter and Berar-

delli remained unexplained. Now the defense adduced new proof, not only that Sacco and Vanzetti did *not* commit the murders, but also, positively, that a well-known gang of professional criminals *did* commit them.

Celestino F. Madeiros, a young Portuguese with a bad criminal record, was in 1925 confined in the same prison with Sacco. On November 18, while his appeal from a conviction of murder committed in an attempt at bank robbery was pending in the Supreme Court, he sent to Sacco through a jail messenger the following note:

I hear by confess to being in the South Braintree shoe company crime and Sacco and Vanzetti was not in said crime.

CELESTINO F. MADEIROS

As soon as Sacco's counsel was apprised of this note, he began a searching investigation of Madeiros's claim. It then appeared that Madeiros had tried several times previously to tell Sacco that he knew the real perpetrators of the Braintree job, but Sacco, fearing he was a spy who was trying to ensnare him, as Sacco well might, had disregarded what he said. An interview with Madeiros revealed such circumstantiality of detail that his examination, both by the defense and the Commonwealth, was plainly called for. Several affidavits given by Madeiros and a deposition of one hundred pages, in which he was cross-examined by the District Attorney, tell the following story.

In 1920 Madeiros, then eighteen years old, was living in Providence. He already had a criminal record and was associated with a gang of Italians engaged in robbing freight cars. One evening, when they were talking together in a saloon in Providence, some members of the gang invited him to join them in a payroll robbery at South Braintree. A hold-up was a new form of criminal enterprise for him, but they told him "they had done lots of jobs of this kind" and persuaded him to come along. As an eighteen-year-old novice he was to be given only a subordinate part. He was to sit in the back of a car with a revolver and "help hold back the crowd in case they made a rush." Accordingly a few days later, on April 15, 1920, the plan was carried into execution. In the party, besides Madeiros, were three Italians and a "kind of a slim fellow with light hair," who drove the car. In order to prevent identification they adopted the familiar device of using two cars. They started out in a Hudson, driving to some woods near Randolph. They then exchanged the Hudson for a Buick brought them by another member of the gang. In the Buick they proceeded to South Braintree, arriving there about noon. When the time came the actual shooting was done by the oldest of the Italians, a man about forty, and one other. The rest of the party remained near by in the automobile. As the crime was being committed they drove up, took aboard the murderers and the money, and made off. They drove back to the Randolph woods, exchanged the Buick again for the Hudson, and returned to Providence. The arrangement was that Madeiros should meet the others in a saloon at Providence the following night to divide the spoils. Whether this arrangement was kept and whether he got any of the Braintree loot Madeiros persistently refused to say.

This refusal was in pursuance of Madeiros's avowed policy. From the outset he announced his determination not to reveal the identity of his associates in the Braintree job, while holding nothing back which seemed to implicate himself alone. To shield them he obstinately declined to answer questions and, if necessary, frankly resorted to lies. Thus, examination could not extort from him the surnames of the gang, and he further sought to cover up their identity by giving some of them false Christian names. He showed considerable astuteness in evading what he wanted to conceal. But in undertaking to tell the story of the crime without revealing the criminals he set himself an impossible task. In spite of his efforts, a lawyer as resourceful as Mr. Thompson was able to elicit facts which, when followed up, established the identity of the gang and also strongly corroborated the story of Madeiros.

Madeiros said that the gang "had been engaged in robbing freight cars in Providence." Was there such a gang whose composition and activities verified Madeiros's story and at the same time explained the facts of the Braintree crime? There was the Morelli gang, well known to the police of Providence and New Bedford as professional criminals, several of whom at the time of the Braintree murders were actually under indictment in the United States District Court of Rhode Island for stealing from freight cars. Five out of nine indictments charging shoe thefts were for stealing consignments from *Slater and Morrill at South Braintree* and from Rice and Hutchins, the factory next door. In view of their method of operations, the gang must have had a confederate at Braintree to spot shipments for them. The Slater and Morrill factory was about one hundred yards from the South Braintree railroad station and an accomplice spotting shipments would be passed by the paymaster on his weekly trip. It will be recalled that the payroll was that of the Slater and Morrill factory and that the murders and the robbery occurred in front of the Slater and Morrill and Rice and Hutchins factories. The Morellis under indictment were out of jail awaiting trial. They needed money for their defense; their only source of income was crime. They were at large until May 25, when they were convicted and sent to Atlanta.

Madeiros did not name the gang, but described the men who were with him at Braintree. How did his descriptions fit the Morelli gang? The leader of the gang was Joe, aged thirty-nine. His brothers were Mike, Patsy, Butsy, and Fred. Other members were Bibba Barone, Gyp the Blood, Mancini, and Steve the Pole. Bibba Barone and Fred Morelli were in jail on April 15, 1920. According to Madeiros there were five, including himself, in the murder car, three of whom were Italians, and the driver "Polish or Finland or something northern Europe." The shooting was done by the oldest of the Italians, a man of about forty and another called Bill. A fourth Italian brought up the Buick car for exchange at Randolph. As far as his descriptions carry, Madeiros's party fits the members of the Morelli gang. But the testimony of independent witnesses corroborates Madeiros and makes the identification decisive. One of the gravest difficulties of the prosecution's case against Sacco and Vanzetti was the collapse of the Government's attempt to identify the driver of the murder car as Vanzetti. The District Attorney told the jury that "they must be overwhelmed with the testimony that when the car started it was driven by a light-haired man, who gave every appearance of being sickly." Steve the Pole satisfies Madeiros's description of the driver as well as the testimony at the trial. To set the matter beyond a doubt two women who were working in the Slater and Morrill factory identified Steve the Pole as the man they saw standing for half an hour by a car outside their window on that day. Two witnesses who testified at the trial identified Joe Morelli as one of the men who did the shooting and another identified Mancini. The Morellis were American-born, which explains the testimony at the trial that one of the bandits spoke clear and unmistakable English, a thing impossible to Sacco and Vanzetti.

The personnel of the Morelli gang fits the Braintree crime. What of other details? The mortal bullet came out of a 32 Colt; Joe Morelli had a 32 Colt at this time; Mancini's pistol was of a type and calibre to account for the other five bullets found in the victims. The "murder car" at the trial was a Buick. Madeiros said a Buick was used; and Mike Morelli, according to the New Bedford police, at this time was driving a Buick, which disappeared immediately after April 15, 1920. In fact, the police of New Bedford, where the Morelli gang had been operating, suspected them of the Braintree crime, but dropped the matter after the arrest of Sacco and Vanzetti. Shortly after the Braintree job, Madeiros was sent away for five months for larceny of an amount less than $100. But immediately after his release, he had about $2800 in bank, which enabled him to go on a pleasure trip to the West and Mexico. The $2800 is adequately accounted for only as his share of the Braintree booty: the loot was $15,776.51, and according to his story there were six men in the job. Joe Morelli, we know, was sent to Atlanta for his share in the robbery of the Slater and Morrill shoes. While confined he made an arrangement with a fellow prisoner whereby the latter was to furnish him with an alibi if he ever needed it, placing Morelli in New York on April 15, 1920.

Even so compressed a précis of the evidence of many witnesses will have made it clear that the defense had built up a powerful case, without the resources at the command of the State in criminal investigations. The witnesses other than Madeiros of themselves afforded strong probability of the guilt of the Morellis. What of the intrinsic credibility of Madeiros's confession, which, if believed, settles the matter? A man who seeks to relieve another of guilt while himself about to undergo the penalty of death does not carry conviction. The circumstances of Madeiros's confession, however, free it from the usual suspicion and furnish assurances of its trustworthiness. Far from having nothing to lose by making the confession, Madeiros stood to jeopardize his life. For while, to be sure, at the time of his confession he was under sentence for another murder, an appeal from this conviction was pending, which was in fact successful in getting him a new trial. Could anything be more prejudicial to an effort to reverse his conviction for one crime than to admit guilt for another? So clearly prejudicial in fact was his confession that by arrangement with the District Attorney it was kept secret until after the outcome of his appeal and the new trial which followed it. Moreover, the note of confession sent by Madeiros to Sacco on November 18 was not, as we have seen, his first communication to Sacco. Nor was it his first explicit confession. The murder for which he had been convicted, together with a man named Weeks—the Wrentham bank crime—was a hold-up like the Braintree job. Weeks, under life sentence in another jail, when questioned, revealed that in planning the Wrentham job Madeiros drew on his experience at Braintree. During their partnership Madeiros, he said, frequently referred to the Braintree job, saying it was arranged by the Morelli gang (whom Weeks knew), and at one time identifying a speak-easy in which they found themselves as the one the gang visited before the Braintree hold-up. In planning the Wrentham job Madeiros further told Weeks that he "had had enough of the Buick in the South Braintree job." Before the Wrentham crime he had talked to the couple who kept the roadhouse where for a time he was a "bouncer" of his part in the Braintree crime, and said "that he would like to save Sacco and Vanzetti because he knew they were perfectly innocent."

These earlier disclosures by Madeiros refute the theory that he was led to make his latest confession by the hope of money. It is suggested that in November 1925, he had seen the financial statement of the Sacco-Vanzetti Defense Committee. But the State conceded that there was no evidence that "aid of any description had been promised to Madeiros" on behalf of the defendants. Secondly, he could not have had knowledge of this statement before he talked to Weeks and the others, and when he attempted the prior communications to Sacco, because it was not then in existence. It is incredible that a man fighting for his life on a charge for one murder would, in the hope of getting money, falsely accuse himself of another murder. He knew the danger of a confession, for his conviction in the Wrentham case largely rested upon confessions made by him. Why should he be believed and suffer death when he confesses one crime and not be believed when he confesses another of the same character? Is not his own statement in accordance with the motives even of a murderer?

I seen Sacco's wife come up here [jail] with the kids and I felt sorry for the kids.

In the light of all the information now available, which is the more probable truth: that Sacco and Vanzetti or the Morelli gang were the perpetrators of the Braintree murders? The Morelli theory accounts for all members of the Braintree murder gang; the Sacco-Vanzetti theory for only two, for it is conceded that if Madeiros was there, Sacco and Vanzetti were not. The Morelli theory accounts for all the bullets found in the dead men; the Sacco-Vanzetti theory for only one out of six. The Morelli explanation settles the motive, for the Morelli gang were criminals desperately in need of money for legal expenses pending their trial for felonies, whereas the Sacco-Vanzetti theory is unsupported by any motive. Moreover Madeiros's possession of $2800 accounts for his share of the booty, whereas not a penny has ever been traced to anybody or accounted for on the Sacco-Vanzetti theory. The Morelli story is not subject to the absurd premise that professional hold-up men who stole automobiles at will and who had recently made a haul of nearly $16,000 would devote an evening, as did Sacco and Vanzetti the night of their arrest, to riding around on suburban street cars to borrow a friend's six-year-old Overland. The character of the Morelli gang fits the opinion of police investigators and the inherent facts, of the situation, which tended to prove that the crime was the work of professionals, whereas the past character and record of Sacco and Vanzetti have always made it incredible that they should spontaneously become perpetrators of a bold murder, executed with the utmost expertness. A good worker regularly employed at his trade but away on a particular day which is clearly accounted for, and a dreamy fish peddler, openly engaged in political propaganda, neither do nor can suddenly commit an isolated job of highly professional banditry.

Upon the entire body of new evidence Judge Thayer in September, 1926, was asked to grant the two Italians a new trial. The issue before him was not to determine the guilt of the Morellis or the innocence of Sacco and Vanzetti. It was not to weigh the new evidence as though he were a jury, but merely to decide whether there was new material fit for a new jury's judgment. On October 31, 1926, Judge Thayer, in an opinion of some 25,000 words, ruled that the verdict of guilt must stand, that the new evidence did not call for submission to a new jury.

On all these rulings the Supreme Court of Massachusetts found no ground as a matter of law for reversing Judge Thayer. According to Massachusetts law only matters of law are open on review by the Supreme Court even in capital cases. "Matters of law" do include what is called an "abuse" of discretion, that is to say if "no conscientious judge acting intelligently could have honestly taken the view expressed by the trial judge." Such limited scope of review makes the reviewing power practically illusory. For "it is needless to say" reports the Judicial Council of Massachusetts, "that such an abuse will so rarely be found by the Supreme Court to have existed that there is no real appeal from that judicial act."

By the decision of the Supreme Court on April 5, 1927, finding "no error" in the legal exceptions in Judge Thayer's rulings the end had apparently been reached for resort to the courts. Accordingly on

Saturday, April 9, 1927, sentence of death was pronounced upon the men by Judge Thayer. This was the occasion of Vanzetti's famous address to Judge Thayer.

Vigorous effort was now bent towards securing relief through executive clemency. Vanzetti himself set forth his case as well as a statement of his political faith, in a petition to the Governor. Sacco refused to make even formal application for an exercise of the pardoning power. Governor Fuller undertook a private investigation, both of the Plymouth and the Dedham trials, and an independent inquiry into the guilt of the men. He saw witnesses whom the defense suggested and he heard argument on behalf of the men by Mr. Thompson and his associate, Mr. Herbert B. Ehrmann. But he declined to hear witnesses against the men in the presence of their counsel or to let the defense know the identity of witnesses he did hear or to disclose what information they gave him. On June 1, 1927, Governor Fuller announced the appointment of Judge Robert Grant, President Abbott Lawrence Lowell of Harvard University and President Samuel W. Stratton of the Massachusetts Institute of Technology "as an advisory committee in connection with the Governor's investigation of the Sacco-Vanzetti case." This committee denied the request of Messrs. Thompson and Ehrmann for public hearings. They did permit defendants' counsel to be present and to examine the witnesses before them. But they interviewed privately Chief Justice Hall of the Superior Court of Massachusetts, Judge Webster Thayer, eleven of the jurors at the Dedham trial and, in part, Frederick G. Katzmann who as District Attorney had charge of the prosecution against Sacco and Vanzetti. The committee also withheld from the counsel for the defense whatever these private interviews disclosed.

On August 3, 1927, the Governor announced his adverse decision, and on August 7 the report of his advisory committee was made public, likewise finding against the men. Having exhausted his professional resources, Mr. Thompson felt that any further legal efforts should be pursued by new counsel. But as a citizen he continued unabatedly his devotion to the men and their cause.

After the men were sentenced, a number of influential citizens submitted to the Governor evidence of Judge Thayer's prejudice against Sacco and Vanzetti because of their anarchistic views, and of his consequent inability to accord them impartiality in the various rulings he was called upon to make on the motions for a new trial subsequent to the jury's verdict and after the jury was discharged. This proof of Judge Thayer's prejudice was now made the basis of further legal efforts to save the men, undertaken by Mr. Arthur D. Hill of the Boston Bar. He invoked both the state and Federal courts. By direction of Chief Justice Hall of the Superior Court, the issue of Judge Thayer's prejudice was brought before Judge Thayer himself. Judge Thayer found that he had been without prejudice. Equally unavailing were other efforts in the state courts. The claim of Judge Thayer's prejudice was then made the basis of application to Mr. Justice

Holmes and Mr. Justice Stone of the United States Supreme Court and to Judges Anderson and Morton of the lower Federal Court.

All efforts were unavailing. The men were doomed by the Governor's decision. Shortly after midnight of August 22, 1927, they went to their death.

APPENDIX II

Speeches to the Court

The speeches of Sacco and Vanzetti to Judge Webster Thayer in the Dedham Court House on April 9, 1927 were taken down by court stenographers. The difference between the spelling and punctuation in them and the spelling and punctuation in the letters of the two men is thereby explained.

CLERK WORTHINGTON: *Nicola Sacco*, have you anything to say why sentence of death should not be passed upon you?

NICOLA SACCO: Yes, sir. I am no orator. It is not very familiar with me the English language, and as I know, as my friend has told me, my comrade Vanzetti will speak more long, so I thought to give him the chance.

I never knew, never heard, even read in history anything so cruel as this Court. After seven years prosecuting they still consider us guilty. And these gentle people here are arrayed with us in this court today.

I know the sentence will be between two classes, the oppressed class and the rich class, and there will be always collision between one and the other. We fraternize the people with the books, with the literature. You persecute the people, tyrannize them and kill them. We try the education of people always. You try to put a path between us and some other nationality that hates each other. That is why I am here today on this bench, for having been of the oppressed class. Well, you are the oppressor.

You know it, Judge Thayer—you know all my life, you know why I have been here, and after seven years that you have been persecuting me and my poor wife, and you still today sentence us to death. I would like to tell all my life, but what is the use? You know all about what I say before, that is, my comrade, will be talking, because he is more familiar with the language, and I will give him a chance. My comrade, the kind man to all the children, you sentenced him two times, in the Bridgewater case and the Dedham case, connected with me, and you know he is innocent.

You forget all this population that has been with us for seven years, to sympathize and give us all their energy and all their kindness. You do not care for them. Among that peoples and the comrades and the working class there is a big legion of intellectual people which have been with us for seven years, to not commit the iniquitous sentence, but still the Court goes ahead. And I want to thank you all, you peoples, my comrades who have been with me for seven years, with the Sacco-Vanzetti case, and I will give my friend a chance.

I forget one thing which my comrade remember me. As I said before, Judge Thayer know all my life, and he know that I am never guilty, never—not yesterday, nor today, nor forever.

CLERK WORTHINGTON: *Bartolomeo Vanzetti*, have you anything to say why sentence of death should not be passed upon you?

BARTOLOMEO VANZETTI: Yes. What I say is that I am innocent, not only of the Braintree crime, but also of the Bridgewater crime. That I am not only innocent of these two crimes, but in all my life I have never stolen and I have never killed and I have never spilled blood. That is what I want to say. And it is not all. Not only am I innocent of these two crimes, not only in all my life I have never stolen, never killed, never spilled blood, but I have struggled all my life, since I began to reason, to eliminate crime from the earth.

Everybody that knows these two arms knows very well that I did not need to go into the streets and kill a man or try to take money. I can live by my two hands and live well. But besides that, I can live even without work with my hands for other people. I have had plenty of chance to live independently and to live what the world conceives to be a higher life than to gain our bread with the sweat of our brow.

My father in Italy is in a good condition. I could have come back in Italy and he would have welcomed me every time with open arms. Even if I come back there with not a cent in my pocket, my father could have give me a position, not to work but to make business, or to oversee upon the land that he owns. He has wrote me many letters in that sense, and as another well-to-do relative has wrote me letters in that sense that I can produce.

Well, it may be said to be a boast. My father and my aunt can boast themselves and say things that people may not be compelled to believe. People may say they may be poor when I say that they are in good condition to give me a position any time that I want to settle down and form a family and start a settled life. Well, but there are people maybe in this same court that could testify to what I have said and that what my father and my aunt have said to me is not a lie, that really they have the means to give me a position any time that I want.

Well, I want to reach a little point farther, and it is this, that not only have I not been trying to steal in Bridgewater, not only have I not been in Braintree to steal and kill and have never stolen or killed or spilt blood in all my life, not only have I struggled hard against crimes, but I have refused myself of what are considered the commodity and glories of life, the prides of a life of a good position, because in my consideration it is not right to exploit man. I have refused to go in business because I understand that business is a speculation on profit upon certain people that must depend upon the business man, and I do not consider that that is right and therefore I refuse to do that.

Now, I should say that I am not only innocent of all these things, not only have I never committed a real crime in my life—though some sins but not crimes—not only have I struggled all my life to eliminate crimes, the crimes that the official law and the moral law condemns, but also the crime that the moral law and the official law sanction and sanctify,—the exploitation and the oppression of the man by the man, and if there is a reason why I am here as a guilty man, if there is a reason why you in a few minutes can doom me, it is this reason and none else.

There is the best man I ever cast my eyes upon since I lived, a man that will last and will grow always more near to and more dear to the heart of the people, so long as admiration for goodness, for virtues, and for sacrifice will last. I mean Eugene Victor Debs.

He has said that not even a dog that kills chickens would have found an American jury disposed to convict it with the proof that the Commonwealth has produced against us. That man was not with me in Plymouth or with Sacco where he was on the day of the crime. You can say that it is arbitrary, what we are saying from him, that he is good and he applied to the other his goodness, that he is incapable of crime, and he believed that everybody is incapable of crime.

Well, it may be like that but it is not, it could be like that but it is not, and that man had a real experience of court, of prison and of jury. Just because he wanted the world a little better he was persecuted and slandered from his boyhood youthness to his old age, and indeed he was murdered by the prison.

He knew, and not only he knew, but every man of understanding in the world, not only in this country but also in other countries, men to whom we have provided a certain amount of the records of the case at times, they all know and still stick with us, the flower of mankind of Europe, the better writers, the greatest thinkers of Europe, have pleaded in our favor. The scientists, the greatest scientists, the greatest statesmen of Europe, have pleaded in our favor.

Is it possible that only a few, a handful of men of the jury, only two or three other men, who would shame their mother for worldly honor and for earthly fortune; is it possible that they are right against what the world, for the whole world has said that it is wrong and I know that it is wrong? If there is one that should know it, if it is right or if it is wrong, it is I and this man. You see it is seven years that we are in jail. What we have suffered during these seven years no human tongue can say, and yet you see me before you, not trembling, you see me looking you in your eyes straight, not blushing, not changing color, not ashamed or in fear.

Eugene Debs said that not even a dog—something like that—not even a dog that kill the chickens would have been found guilty by an American jury with the evidence that the Commonwealth have produced against us. I say that not even a leprous dog would have had his appeals refused two times by the Supreme Court of Massachusetts—not even a leprous dog.

They have given a new trial to Madeiros for the reason that the Judge had either forgot or omitted to tell the jury that they should consider the man innocent until found guilty in the court, or something of that sort. That man has confessed. The man was tried on his confession and was found guilty, and the Supreme Court gave him another trial. We have proved that there could not have been another Judge on the face of the earth more prejudiced, more cruel and more hostile than you have been against us. We have proven that. Still they refuse the new trial. We know, and you know in your heart, that you have been against us from the very beginning, before you see us. Before you see us you already know that we were radicals, that we were underdogs, that we were the enemy of the institutions that you can believe in good faith in their goodness—I don't want to discuss that—and that it was easy at the time of the first trial to get a verdict of guiltiness.

We know that you have spoken yourself, and have spoke your hostility against us, and your despisement against us with friends of yours on the train, at the University Club of Boston, at the Golf Club of Worcester. I am sure that if the people who know all what you say against us have the civil courage to take the stand, maybe your Honor—I am sorry to say this because you are an old man, and I have an old father—but maybe you would be beside us in good justice at this time.

When you sentenced me at the Plymouth trial you say, to the best of my memory, of my good faith, that crimes were in accordance with my principle—something of that sort—and you took off one charge, if I remember it exactly, from the jury. The jury was so violent against me that they found me guilty of both charges, because there were only two. But they would have found me guilty of a dozen of charges against your Honor's instructions. Of course I remember that you told them that there was no reason to believe that if I were the bandit I have intention to kill somebody, so that they should take off the indictment of attempt to murder. Well, they found me guilty of what?

Also of an attempt to murder. And if I am right, you take out that and sentence me only for attempt to rob with arms,—something like that. But, Judge Thayer, you give more to me for that attempt of robbery than all the 448 men that were in Charlestown, all of those that attempted to rob, all those that have robbed, they have not such a sentence as you gave to me for an attempt at robbery.

I am willing that everybody that does or does not believe me that they can make commission, they can go over there, and I am very willing that the people should go over there and see whether it is true or not. There are people in Charlestown who are professional robbers, who have been in half the prisons of the United States, that have stolen, or injured men or shot them. Most of them guilty without doubt, by self-confession, and by confession of their own partners, and they got eight to ten, eight to twelve, ten to fifteen. None of them has twelve to fifteen, as you gave me for an attempt at robbery. And besides that, you know that I was not guilty; that I had not been in Bridge-water attempting to steal. You know that my life, my private and public life in Plymouth, and wherever I have been, was so exemplary that one of the worst fears of our prosecutor Katzmann was to introduce proof of our life and of our conduct. He has opposed it with all his might and he has succeeded.

You know that if we would have had Mr. Thompson, or even the brothers McAnarney, in the first trial in Plymouth, you know that no jury would have found me guilty. My first lawyer has been a partner of Mr.

Katzmann, as he is still now. The first lawyer of the defense, Mr. Vahey, has not defended me, has sold me for thirty golden money like Judas sold Jesus Christ. If that man has not told to you or to Mr. Katzmann that he knew that I was guilty, it is because he cannot, it is because he knew that I was not guilty. That man has done everything indirectly to hurt us. He has made a long speech to the jury about things that do matter nothing, and on the point of essence to the trial he has passed over with few words or with complete silence. This was a premeditation in order to give to the jury the impression that my own defender has nothing good to urge in defense of myself, and therefore is compelled to go around the bush on little things that amount to nothing and let pass the essential points either in silence or with a very weakly resistance.

We were tried during a time whose character has now passed into history. I mean by that, a time when there was a hysteria of resentment and hate against the people of our principles, against the foreigner, against slackers, and it seems to me—rather, I am positive of it, that both you and Mr. Katzmann have done all what it were in your power in order to work out, in order to agitate still more the passion of the juror, the prejudice of the juror, against us.

I remember that Mr. Katzmann has introduced a witness against us, a certain Ricci. Well, I have heard that witness. It seems that he has nothing to say. It seemed that it was a foolishness to produce a witness that has nothing to say. And it seemed as if he were called by the Commonwealth to tell to the jury that he was the foreman of those laborers who were near the scene of the crime and who claimed, and who testified in our behalf, that we were not the men, and that this man, the witness Ricci, was their foreman, and he has tried to keep the men on the job instead of going to see what was happening so as to give the impression that it was not true that the men went towards the street to see what happened. But that was not very important. The real importance is what that man said and that was not true, that a certain witness who was the water boy of the gang of the laborers testified that he took a pail and went to a certain spring, a water spring, to take water for the gang—Ricci testified it was not true that that man went to that spring, and therefore it was not true that he saw the bandit, and therefore it was not true that he can tell that neither I nor Sacco were the men. But Ricci was introduced to show that it was not true that that man went to that spring, because he knew that the Germans had poisoned the water in that spring. That is what he, Ricci, said on that stand over there. Now, in the world chronicle of the time there is not a single happening of that nature. Nobody in America—we have read plenty things bad that the Germans have done in Europe during the war, but nobody can prove and nobody will say that the Germans are bad enough to poison the spring water in this country during the war.

Now, this, it seems, has nothing to do with us directly. It seems to be a thing said by incident on the stand between the other things; why, whereas, that is the essence here. Because the jury were hating us because we were against the war, and the jury don't know that it makes any difference between a man that is against the war because he believes that the war is unjust, because he hate no country, because he is a cosmopolitan, and a man that is against the war because he is in favor of the other country that fights against the country in which he is, and therefore a spy, an enemy, and he commits any crime in the country in which he is in behalf of the other country in order to serve the other country. We are not men of that kind. Nobody can say that we are German spies or spies of any kind. Katzmann knows very well that. Katzmann knows that we were against the war because we did not believe in the purpose for which they say that the war was fought. We believed that the war is wrong, and we believe this more now after ten years that we studied and observed and understood it day by day,—the consequences and the result of the after war. We believe more now than ever that the war was wrong, and we are against war more now than ever, and I am glad to be on the doomed scaffold if I can say to mankind, "Look out; you are in a catacomb of the flower of mankind. For what? All that they say to you, all that they have promised to you—it was a lie, it was an illusion, it was a cheat, it was a fraud, it was a crime. They promised you liberty. Where is liberty? They promised you prosperity. Where is prosperity? They have promised you elevation. Where is the elevation?"

From the day that I went in Charlestown, the misfortunate, the population of Charlestown, has doubled

in number. Where is the moral good that the war has
given to the world? Where is the spiritual progress
that we have achieved from the war? Where are the
security of life, the security of the things that we possess for our necessity? Where are the respect for
human life? Where are the respect and the admiration for the good characteristics and the good of the
human nature? Never before the war as now have
there been so many crimes, so much corruption, so
much degeneration as there is now.

In the best of my recollection and of my good faith,
during the trial Katzmann has told to the jury that a
certain Coacci has brought in Italy the money that,
according to the State theory, I and Sacco have stolen
in Braintree. We never stole that money. But Katzmann, when he told that to the jury, he knew already
that that was not true. He knew already that that
man was deported in Italy by the federal police soon
after our arrest. I remember well that I was told that
the federal policeman had him in their possession—
that the federal policeman had taken away the trunks
from the very ship where he was, and brought the
trunks back over here and look them over and found
not a single money.

Now, I call that murder, to tell to the jury that a
friend or comrade or a relative or acquaintance of the
charged man, of the indicted man, has carried the
money to Italy, when he knows it was not true. I can
call that nothing else but murder, a plain murder.

But Katzmann has told something else also against
us that was not true. If I understand well, there have

been agreement of counsel during the trial in which the counsel of defense shall not produce any evidence of my good conduct in Plymouth and the counsel of the prosecution would not have let the jury know that I was tried and convicted another time before in Plymouth. Well, it was masterly called "a one-sided agreement" by someone very competent. In fact, even the telephone poles knew at the time of this trial at Dedham that I was tried and convicted in Plymouth; the jurymen knew that even when they slept. On the other side the jury have never seen I or Sacco and I think we have the right to incline to believe that the jury have never approached before the trial anyone that was sufficiently intimate with me and Sacco to be able to give them a description of our personal conduct. The jury don't know anything about us. They have never seen us. The only thing that they know is the bad things that the newspaper have said on the Plymouth trial.

I don't know why the defense counsel have made such an agreement but I know very well why Katzmann had made such agreement; because he know that half of the population of Plymouth would have been willing to come over here and say that in seven years that I was living amongst them that I was never seen drunk, that I was known as the most strong and steadfast worker of the community. As a matter of fact I was called a mule and the people that know a little better the condition of my father and that I was a single man, much wondered at me and say, "Why you work like a mad man in that way when you have no children and no wife to care about?"

Well, Katzmann should have been satisfied on that agreement. He could have thanked his God and estimate himself a lucky man. But he was not satisfied with that. He broke his word and he told to the jury that I was tried before; he told it to this very court. I don't know if that is right in the record, if that was taken off or not, but I heard with my ears. When two or three women from Plymouth come to take the stand, the woman reached that point where this gentleman sits over there, the jury were seated in their place, and Katzmann asked these women if they have not testified before for Vanzetti, and they say, yes, and he tell to them, "You cannot testify." They left the room. After that they testified just the same. But in the meanwhile he told the jury that I have been tried before. That I think is not giving justice to the man from one who is looking after the truth, and it is with such insuperable frameups with which he has split my life and doomed me.

It was also said that the defense has put every obstacle to the handling of this case in order to delay the case. That sounds weak for us, and I think it is injurious because it is not true. If we consider that the prosecution, the State, has employed one entire year to prosecute us, that is, one of the five years that the case has lasted was taken by the prosecution to begin our trial, our first trial. Then the defense makes an appeal to you and you waited, for I think that you were resolute, that you had the resolution in your heart from even when the trial finished that you will have refused every appeal that we will put up to you. You waited a month or a month and a half and just lay down your decision on the eve of Christmas—just on the eve of Christmas, eve of Christmas. We do not believe in Christmas, neither in the historical way nor in the church way. But, you know, some of our folks still believe in that, and because we do not believe in that, it don't mean that we are not human. We are human, and Christmas is sweet to the heart of every man. I think that you have done that, to hand down your decision on the eve of Christmas, to poison the heart of our family and of our beloved. I am sorry to be compelled to say this, but everything that was said or done on your side since then has confirmed my suspicion time after time until that suspicion has changed to certitude.

Then the defense, in presenting the new appeal, has not taken more time than you have taken in answer to that. Then there came the second appeal, and now I am not sure whether it is the second appeal or the third appeal where you waited eleven months or one year without an answer to us, and I am sure that you had decided to refuse us a new trial before the hearing for the new appeal began. You took one year to answer it, or eleven months,—something like that. So that you see that out of the five years, two were taken by the State from the day of our arrest to the trial, and then one year to wait for your answer on the second or the third appeal.

Then on another occasion that I don't remember

exactly now, Mr. Williams was sick and the things were delayed not for fault of the defense but on account of the prosecution. So that I am positive that if a man take a pencil in his hand and compute the time taken by the prosecution in prosecuting the case, and the time that was taken by the defense to defend this case, the prosecution has taken more time than the defense, and there is a great consideration that must be taken in this point, and it is that my first lawyer betrayed us,—the whole American population were against us.

We have the misfortune to take a man from California, and he came here, and he was ostracized by you and by every authority, even by the jury, and is so much so that not even Massachusetts is immune from what I could call a universal prejudice,—the belief that each people in each place of the world, they believe to be the better of the world, and they believe that all the other people of the other places of the world are not so good as they. So of course the man that came from California into Massachusetts to defend two of us, he must be licked if it is possible, and he was licked all right. And we have our part, too.

What I want to say is this: Everybody ought to understand that the first beginning of our defense has been terrible. My first lawyer did not try to defend us. He has made no attempt to collect witnesses and evidence in our favor. The record in the Plymouth court is a pity. I am told that they are part or almost one-half lost. So that later on the defense have had a tremendous work to do in order to collect some evidence, to collect some testimony to offset and to learn what the testimony of the State had been. And in this consideration it must be said that even if the defense take double time of the State about delays, double time than they (the State) delayed the case, it would have been reasonable just the same, whereas it took less than the State.

Well, I have already say that I not only am not guilty of these two crimes, but I never committed a crime in my life,—I have never stolen and I have never killed and I have never spilt blood, and I have fought against crime, and I have fought and I have sacrificed myself even to eliminate the crimes that the law and the church legitimate and sanctify.

This is what I say: I would not wish to a dog or to a snake, to the most low and misfortunate creature of the earth—I would not wish to any of them what I have had to suffer for things that I am not guilty of. I am suffering because I am a radical and indeed I am a radical; I have suffered because I was an Italian, and indeed I am an Italian; I have suffered more for my family and for my beloved than for myself; but I am so convinced to be right that you can only kill me once but if you could execute me two times, and if I could be reborn two other times, I would live again to do what I have done already.

I have finished. Thank you.

THE COURT: Under the law of Massachusetts the jury says whether a defendant is guilty or innocent. The Court has absolutely nothing to do with that question. The law of Massachusetts provides that a Judge cannot deal in any way with the facts. As far as he can go under our law is to state the evidence.

During the trial many exceptions were taken. Those exceptions were taken to the Supreme Judicial Court. That Court, after examining the entire record, after examining all the exceptions,—that Court in its final words said, "The verdicts of the jury should stand; exceptions overruled." That being true, there is only one thing that this Court can do. It is not a matter of discretion. It is a matter of statutory requirement, and that being true there is only one duty that now devolves upon this Court, and that is to pronounce the sentence.

First the Court pronounces sentence upon Nicola Sacco:

It is considered and ordered by the Court that you, Nicola Sacco, suffer the punishment of death by the passage of a current of electricity through your body within the week beginning on Sunday, the tenth day of July, in the Year of our Lord One Thousand Nine Hundred and Twenty-seven. This is the sentence of the law.

Then upon Vanzetti:

It is considered and ordered by the Court that you, Bartolomeo Vanzetti . . .

VANZETTI: Wait a minute, please, your Honor. May I speak for a minute with my lawyer, Mr. Thompson?

THOMPSON: I do not know what he has to say.

THE COURT: I think I should pronounce the sentence. . . . *Bartolomeo Vanzetti, suffer the punishment of death . . . .*

SACCO: You know I am innocent. Those are the same words I pronounced seven years ago. You condemn two innocent men.

THE COURT: . . . *by the passage of a current of electricity through your body within the week beginning on Sunday, the tenth day of July, in the year of our Lord, One Thousand Nine Hundred and Twenty-seven. This is the sentence of the law.*

The next day Vanzetti handed to friends the notes of what he had wished to say further to Judge Thayer when he interrupted the pronouncement of sentence. Included in those notes was this estimate of Sacco:

I have talk a great deal of myself but I even forgot to name Sacco. Sacco too is a worker from his boyhood, a skilled worker lover of work, with a good job and pay, a bank account, a good and lovely wife, two beautiful children and a neat little home at the verge of a wood, near a brook. Sacco is a heart, a faith, a character, a man; a man lover of nature and of mankind. A man who gave all, who sacrifice all to the cause of Liberty and to his love for mankind; money, rest, mundain ambitions, his own wife, his children, himself and his own life. Sacco has never dreamt to steal, never to assassinate. He and I have never brought a morsel of bread to our mouths, from our childhood to to-day—which has not been gained by the sweat of our brows. Never. His people also are in good position and of good reputation.

Oh, yes, I may be more witfull, as some have put it, I am a better babbler than he is, but many, many times in hearing his heartful voice ringing a faith sublime, in considering his supreme sacrifice, remembering his heroism I felt small small at the presence of his greatness and found myself compelled to fight back from my eyes the tears, and quanch my heart trobling to my throat to not weep before him—this man called thief and assasin and doomed.   But Sacco's name will live in the hearts of the people and in their gratitude when Katzmann's and yours bones will be dispersed by time, when your name, his name, your laws, institutions, and your false god are but a *deem rememoring of a cursed past in which man was wolf to the man.* . . .

APPENDIX III

Vanzetti's Letter to Governor Fuller

Shortly before dictating the following letter to Governor Fuller, Vanzetti had been interviewed twice at the State Prison by the Governor. The first interview lasted almost two hours, and the second one, which took place at night after all the prisoners were in their cells, lasted over an hour. Vanzetti asked the Governor at the conclusion of the second interview whether he might write to him the many things which he had not covered in the interviews. The Governor gave him this permission, and in accordance with it, Mr. William G. Thompson, counsel for the two men, sent his secretary to the prison to take Vanzetti's dictation. The date of the letter, July 28, 1927, was six days before Governor Fuller issued his decision on the night of August 3, 1927.

July 28, 1927. Charlestown Prison

Hon. Alvan T. Fuller,
Governor of Massachusetts,
State House, Boston.

YOUR EXCELLENCY:

You told me Tuesday night that I might dictate to a stenographer the part of my statement which I wanted to make to you, but was prevented by lack of time from making. So I will say as follows:

1. I don't tell the truth to the police about my revolver, where I have been in West Bridgewater and on the night before, that they asked. I did all these things in order to avoid the arrest of my comrades, because I know that if the police would have been in the houses of my friends, they would have found Red literature, maybe a revolver, and that would have been enough to mean deportation, or even death to them. When I told these things I did not know that I was going to be indicted for the Bridgewater crime and South Braintree crime. After a while I understood, but I am not a man to put some other in trouble to go off myself from trouble. And my opinion was that even if the police would have found me a liar on such things as where I buy the revolver, they would not have been able to find me guilty on things that I have not done. And this is the real reason of what I told first to Katzmann and then to the others. For example, I told Katzmann that I was in a certain place the night before or two nights before, when he asked me where I have been.

When Katzmann did ask me where I was the day of the 24th December, 1919, and the 15th of April, 1920, I did not know that they were the day of any crimes. I remember the day of the 24th December because it was a very special day. I did not remember the 15th of April, which was more near, because it was an ordinary day, and I had nothing in particular to remember. I beg your Excellency to observe that the lies that I have said have no relation whatever with the crimes, or with concealing something related to the crimes. You can see it was only to spare a search of my friends' houses, arrest, and so on.

2. As I told you, we were warned a few days before that the Federal police were about to make other raids on the Radicals. For some months the papers had been full of talk about arrests of Radicals, and all Radicals of every kind were pretty thoroughly scared. I suppose you know that in Italy the common people has always been afraid of the police. It is hard to get over such ideas, especially when you know what they have done to our comrades in this country. They have murdered three or four or five men. I don't believe Salsedo committed suicide. I believe he was murdered by the Federal police in New York. If he committed suicide it was because they drove him to it.

3. Now about Boda. We were at the Johnson house, West Bridgewater, to take Boda's automobile together with Boda and Orciani. Your Excellency told me that there has been much suspicion of Boda in this case. I have known Boda for a long time. He was not a particular friend of mine but he was sympathetic with my ideas. There is nothing against Boda in this case. The last time I saw Boda's car before May 5th was at a picnic on the outside of Brockton, about a year before the Bridgewater crime, in the summer. Coming home from the picnic he gave me a ride in the car as far as Brockton. That is the last time I have seen his car. I don't know what kind of a car it was. I don't know anything about the different kinds of motor cars. When we spoke to Boda that night about the car he said, "Well, we'll go to see if it

is ready." Mr. Thompson has told me that Mr. Johnson said that Boda's car was out of repair for a long time before May 5, 1920. I don't know anything about it. Very soon before our arrest Chief Stewart spoke with Boda and did not arrest him, which meant that if Stewart had any suspicion of him it must have been very recent. He has, for what I know, a clean record. I knew that at one time Boda kept a cleansing store with his brother in Wellesley. After I came back from Mexico I saw him a few times. He told me that he was selling groceries and things like that. I don't know when Boda left the country, and he never told me why he left it. It isn't hard to imagine why he left. He knew he was with us on the night of May 5th. He saw that we were arrested and charged with a serious crime. He knew we were innocent, but still he saw that we were charged with these serious crimes. It isn't surprising that when he thought it over he made up his mind that he might get into the same trouble if he stayed around here. So I am told that he went directly to his native town, where they could have found him if they really wanted him. He knows he isn't guilty of any crime in this country. Mr. Thompson says he thinks he could get Boda back, but he is a fool if he came back in this country after he sees how two innocent men have been convicted of a crime we did not do.

The automobile at the garage was there from 1919 and could have no relation with the crime. He left Coacci's house because he remained alone—Mrs. Coacci go away, Coacci go away; he remain alone in that house; he had to leave.   I am told that Mr. Samuel Johnson was a neighbor of Boda's, and says that he remembered this time; he go many times, at every time of the day, by the Coacci house; saw many times the garage open; never saw any automobile in it, and never saw Boda to drive any automobile that winter and spring of 1920.

He knows there was never any Buick car in Coacci's shed.

Boda is a very small man.   He does not weigh over 120 pounds, something like that.   He had a very small moustache.   I don't think any witness described any such man at the Bridgewater crime, or neither at the South Braintree crime; and anyway, Mr. Katzmann and Mr. Williams said at the trial that they did not claim Boda was at the South Braintree crime.   I am told he is willing to come back here to face whatsoever, and if this is true, he is a fool, because with all the machinery of the state and the reactionary rabbles against us, nothing is more easy than another masterly and successful frame-up against him as it was against ourselves.   This is the man on whom you and they say to have plenty of suspicion, which cannot be but purely arbitrary.

4.   I want to ask your Excellency to remember that Mr. Stewart and the others seemed to have had at one time the same suspicion against Orciani that they had against Boda, and yet they let Orciani go, and he stayed around all during the trial, and they made no effort to show that he was guilty of anything.   I don't think that we ought to lose our lives because people have a suspicion which they cannot prove and which are not true against two of our friends.

They say that Orciani disappeared. I am told that Orciani often drove Mr. Moore's automobile during the trial, until the latter days of the trial. Orciani has a clean record, is an honest and steady worker, and has a good reputation; has a family and a job and good money. Nobody has ever suspected him. He was arrested the day after we were, and he proved his innocence of the Braintree crime by showing that on the day and on the hour of the crime he was working for a company in a foundry. On such proof they released him, not, I believe, because they could not have found perjurers to testify against him to put him on the Bridgewater crime, but because I have all the reason to believe that they saw on the same register of the same company that on the day of the Bridgewater crime he was equally working for the same company. The state could not get around such a record as that by any amount of perjury or identification. The most idiotic of men, seeing the mood, the nature, the character of the environment in which we were tried, the manner in which we were tried, could not help realizing how easy it is to be found guilty; and that Orciani, having been with us in West Bridgewater at Johnson's house, and having proved absolutely his innocence of both crimes, he could have equally been put under indictment as an accessory after the fact, I believe lawyers call it, and to be found guilty and yet be innocent, which was enough to ruin his life.

People don't seem to understand that Italians are

unpopular anyway, especially if they are poor and laboring people. Their habits are not the habits of ordinary Americans, and they are suspected. They don't get the same chance before an American jury that an American would get. The jury cannot help being prejudiced against them, and then if on top of that the Italians turn out to be Radicals, they have no show at all. One good looking American witness seems to outweigh a dozen Italian witnesses, even though we Italians know that the Italian witnesses are perfectly honest, truthful people. Before Americans will put an Italian on the same basis with themselves, and accept him as probably telling the truth, he has got to make money and own property.

Now you see, Governor, so far as Orciani and Boda are concerned, there is no reason whatever for going against us because of anything that they did or did not do.

5. Now, Governor Fuller, you have told me that almost all those who have seen me and say to have seen me have identified me. Now to show you that only such people as witnessed the crime or the passing of the bandits, or something relating to it, I will tell how Bowles did identify me. For three or four consecutive days he brought with company trucks gangs of people from Bridgewater to identify us at the Brockton Police station, hundreds and hundreds of people. You have no idea how many people were brought to identify us by Bowles and others. I remember in the crowd a Chinaman, Japanese, Salvation Army people, Negroes, and people of every kind and

class, even children.   Even suppose that only a third
of them came from Bridgewater.   You see that there
are a thousand or hundreds of people in a condition to
see the crime or the bandits, and out of these several
hundred only one or two persons said that they seen me
and all the others deny it squarely.   Now how can you
say to me that all the people who saw the crime identified me, or more than the smallest possible part, that
is, one or two people, or three, out of hundreds.   And
then you remember that these three all changed their
testimony between the time they talked to the detectives and the time they testified in court.   Out of the
five or six witnesses that perjured voluntarily against
me, only one or two have come to identify me when
they come together with these hundreds of people.

And one of these is Mrs. Georgina Brooks, and I
am told she is half blind.   I don't know this.   All this
time Mr. Bowles did not identify me.   Then they
brought me to the Plymouth jail.   When the preliminary hearing came in Brockton he was again
together with those that brought me from Plymouth to
Brockton.   After the first time that we were in Brockton we have to come back again on the second time,
and on the second time we met a funeral on the out-
skirts of Brockton, and have to stop the automobile,
which was driven by Chief Stewart.   Now when the
coffin went by before us we took our hats off, and in
that time Chief Stewart was sitting in front, and turned
to the side to talk to Bowles, and Stewart said, "Well,
what do you say, Bowles?" and Bowles said, "By gosh,
I think I know him, I think he is the man," but in a

very uncertain way.   Then at the hearing he went on the stand and he testified that I was the man, but that he cannot be positive, he was only pretty positive. Mr. Vahey at that time defended me, and Bowles left the stand red like a cooked lobster, all trembling, and accompanied by the smiles of the court.   And this is the way that he has had to identify me.   But the jury did not know that.   But I ask if a man that makes such identification can be believed.

I was really surprised, your Excellency, that you had not read the long letter that Mr. Thompson says he wrote you about these detectives' report, showing how Bowles, Harding, Cox changed their testimony from what they told the detectives right after the crime, and what they told on the witness stand several months later.   I don't see how I can get justice in this case unless you know that fact, and beside that, you can see even from the report of the preliminary hearing and the one of the trial that on these two times they are changed their testimony in order to describe the bandit looking as I am.   They can be American as they can be, but I am wronged if you want to believe them after all the proof you have that they have changed three times their testimony.

But not to make too long a story, I will also submit to you that these witnesses from Bridgewater came all together on the corridor at the trial, which was for them a real picnic.   They laugh and jeer at the Italians that were there, and myself, and there was a clique of them to create a hostile atmosphere in the court against the general sympathy that I have by all the people who know me.

Of course your Excellency cannot expect that any of the jury will admit to you that they made a mistake, or that any witnesses for the Government will now come forward and throw doubt on their own testimony. And you cannot expect that Mr. Vahey and Mr. Graham will admit anything which will show that they did not do their duty to me. The case has got to be decided on broader grounds than that. It is not on what the witnesses and the jury and the lawyers say now. It is on what they said and did at the trial of these two cases, and it is what the witnesses said before the trial, and it is their changes in testimony, and it is the methods that the police took to get them to identify me first, and then Sacco and me. Nothing that anybody can say now can change those facts or explain them away.

Just think of convicting a foreigner on the testimony of a boy who said he can tell a man is an Italian from the way he runs, or what nationality he is by the way he runs. Would that testimony convict an American before an American jury? He said that he identified me; he pointed to me and said, "The man in the booth," with all the despisement at his command, in order to impress the jury against me. If I am right he said at the trial that the bandit wore a light cap, and on the day of the crime he told the police or the detectives that the bandit wore a felt hat which fell on the ground.

Harding (this is the man that described me more

particularly, and my head as a funny bullet-shaped head) on the day of the crime, and also a few days later, said that the automobile was a Hudson, and he apologized to the detectives to be unable to testify against the bandit with the shotgun because all that he saw of the bandit was an overcoat, and not his face at all. Save mistake, he said at the trial that the bandit was bare-headed. He must have said so, for otherwise he could not have seen and studied his bullet-shaped head. So that till now we have a bandit who at one time wore a cap, a hat, and is bare-headed—all at one time; one witness says one thing, and another says another.

If your Honor knew the pitiable state of Georgina Brooks when she start to take the stand, you would realize that that woman was for an unknown reason compelled to do it against her own conscience, and I beg your Honor to look at her story and judge for yourself if it is possible to believe it—a woman that goes to see her parents for the Christmas vacation, with a valise in one hand and her children by the other hand, tried to cross the street, and was afraid of the automobile because the engine was going, and instead of passing back of the automobile she passed in front of the automobile. If she was afraid she would have passed in back, but she said she passed in front and saw the bandit. Then she looked at that man three or four times; went to the depot, and going on with these children and the valise she turned around three or four times, I don't know how many times, to look at these men. Later she said that she suspected that man. Why didn't she tell it to the police? She stayed about twenty or twenty-five minutes in the station waiting for the train. Why didn't she telephone the police? Now that I know the attitude of the Americans, that they telephone to the police whenever they see something suspicious, I believe that you could never believe such a thing, that she has had any suspicion. It looked to me that she rather is very suspicious herself.

6. Now, when Chief Stewart came to my home to take my clothes, he didn't take my two maroon sweaters that I have worn all winter long, and I just left them before to go to New York. They were both in my closet in my own room. He didn't take that because being a sweater with a high collar, it would be against the witnesses, that say I have a certain kind of a shirt, because with that sweater you could see nothing. Beside this, he didn't find no cap in my closet and he go around in the kitchen and in the other places in Mrs. Fortini's house looking for a cap. This is what he did. And he took that cap, that by chance was mine, from a nail inside by the cellar ladder leading from the kitchen. It hung on a nail there; and I think that is enough to show that he was ready to do anything.

7. Now on Mrs. Johnson. Of all the witnesses against us, the only one that said something true was Mr. and Mrs. Johnson, as in fact we were to their house. Yet they did all they could to induce the jury to believe that we act suspiciously at their house, in order to get the conviction and get the $200 reward

that they were promised. In fact, this woman described certain little things on the face of Sacco, and the color of the face of Sacco, that no person could have seen on a country road in a dark night as dark as it was when we were over there. After having described Sacco particularly she made a great mistake; she said that I have an overcoat and Sacco was in his coat. The things were just the reverse. When we were found guilty she went to the company in Brockton to get her $200 reward, and the company said that they would not pay until my sentence, and she made much noise and insisted for the $200 right away, so that it was reported by the Brockton press, and finally she was paid the $200 by the White company's lawyer. Don't forget that Mrs. Johnson has done all what she can to influence the jury against us in order to get the conviction in order to get this $200. Also her brother-in-law, Samuel Johnson, told the Advisory Committee that she had been paid that sum. I am told there was $1000 paid; the Johnsons got part and the policemen got another part.

8. Now about Capt. Proctor at the Plymouth trial. My cartridges were taken by me from Sacco's house on the day of the arrest, before going to West Bridgewater to get the automobile, with the intention to give them to one of my friends in Plymouth, who would give me 50c for the cause. I so told Rosie Sacco and Sacco. I suppose the cartridges weren't worth 50c, but he would give me 50c as a contribution to the cause, and I would have given him the cartridges. Rosie Sacco and Sacco were most willing to come to Ply-

mouth and testify that I have taken the cartridges from their house, but Mr. Vahey opposed absolutely their testimony on the ground that it would hurt Sacco. I never knew what was in the cartridges, and I never owned a shotgun since I have been in this country.

Do you think, Governor, that if I had been guilty of either one of these crimes, I would have been found on a street car carrying four buckshot cartridges in my pocket, and a revolver that was stolen from a murdered man? I think if I had committed a murder I should have been careful not to have any cartridges in my pocket, and certainly not to have a revolver that had belonged to a murdered man in my pocket. And when you think that the day I was arrested, May 5th, was five months after the Bridgewater crime and three weeks after the South Braintree crime, I don't think you would believe that anybody could possibly have been such a fool as they tried to make me out, to keep carrying on my person the evidences of guilt. You cannot have it both ways. If we are clever bandits, then we don't do such things as that. If we do such things as that, we are not bandits. Bandits try to put away the evidence of crime, not to carry it around with them.

9. Now, Governor, I have told you that Beltrando Brini has told the truth, and also the other seventeen or more witnesses. The only way to find us guilty is to make up your mind not to believe our witnesses, and not to want to believe our witnesses. To believe that a boy of twelve years, as I have told you, can resist for three or four hours of cross-examination of

Katzmann if the boy were telling a false story, is simply absurd; and to believe or to want to believe people that have changed three or four times their testimony at Bridgewater, is certainly not logic. If you do not want to believe Beltrando, you do not want to believe all the other of my witnesses. If such is the case, your Honor should indict all the Plymouth defence witnesses as perjurers. By deadly and personal experience with the Massachusetts judges, low and high, I really believe it easy to find a Thayer who would succeed to send them to prison as perjurers for having told the truths in the cause of Vanzetti. Then, having sent me to the chair for a crime I have not committed, give a medal and rewards to the Bridgewater state witnesses which changed their false testimony three times to doom an innocent man and help to doom another one.

10. When I was arrested I do not know that I could have refused to speak with the policemen. And beside that, they questioned us with a big stick at their side, one by one; and we know of the third degree, have heard of it in several cities of this country. If it had not been for that, I would not have told a lie. I would have waited for a lawyer, and I would have told my affairs to a lawyer, and I would have no reason to tell the lie, because I only told the lie because I believe that I must answer to them, and that if I did not lie they would go to my friend's houses; and that is what has compelled me to tell the lies when I told them to the police. Katzmann told me if I don't want, I can refuse to speak with him; but it seems that he was the only human being that I saw from my arrest, when he came to speak with us, and I told him more or less what I had told the police. I didn't know the difference at that time between the Federal police and the state police, and I think that everybody can arrest the Radicals. Chief Stewart said in court that he told me that I needn't answer his questions; but I never got that idea from him; I didn't understand it at the time.

I see I have spent a great deal of time talking about the different points in these two cases; but what is the use talking about all these points when the case comes down to a very simple point. I am an Italian, a stranger in a foreign country, and my witnesses are the same kind of people. I am accused and convicted on the testimony of mostly American witnesses. Everything is against me—my race, my opinions, and my humble occupation. I did not commit either of these crimes, and yet how am I ever going to show it if I and all my witnesses are not believed, merely because the police want to convict somebody, and get respectable Americans to testify against us? I suppose a great many Americans think that it is all right to stretch the truth a little to convict an anarchist; but I don't think they would think so if they were in my place. And if any of them were accused of crime in Italy, and tried before an Italian jury at a time when Americans were not very popular in Italy, I think they would realize the truth of what I have been trying to say.

I don't understand what your Excellency meant by telling me what the Fortini's said to you. Mrs. Fortini certainly saw me early in the morning of December 24th in her house and called me down-stairs, as she testified.   None of the other Fortinis testified at Plymouth.   Mrs. Fortini's testimony was true.   The same was true at Dedham.   Mrs. Fortini testified that I was in Plymouth selling fish.   The only man member of the Fortini family that has any brains is Tony Fortini, the nephew, who now lives with James Caldera in Plymouth.   He saw me on December 24, 1919, and I think he saw on me April 15th in Plymouth.   The youngest Fortini boy is simple-minded.   The father is alcoholic.   The oldest Fortini boy is a domestic tyrant, and I have told him many times that if I were his brother I would throw him out of the window for the way he treated his mother.   The other boy is a good boy, but not very intelligent.   The father and three sons usually left the house before seven o'clock in the morning to work, and I should be surprised if they saw me on April 15th; but I think that some of them must have seen me, as the mother did, on the early morning of December 24th.

> Respectfully yours,
>
> (Signed) BARTOLOMEO VANZETTI

APPENDIX IV

Vanzetti's Last Statement

A RECORD BY W. G. THOMPSON

This record was written by Mr. Thompson from notes he set down after his talk with Vanzetti on Monday, August 22, 1927, a few hours before the execution. He went directly from the death house of the Charlestown State Prison to his office and there transferred the experience to paper, while it was vivid in his mind. This record appeared in *The Atlantic Monthly* for February, 1928, and subsequently was reprinted in *The New Republic*.

Sacco and Vanzetti were in the Death House in the State Prison at Charlestown. They fully understood that they were to die immediately after midnight. Mr. Ehrmann and I, having on their behalf exhausted every legal remedy which seemed to us available, had retired from the active conduct of the case, holding ourselves in readiness, however, to help their new counsel in any way we could.

I was in New Hampshire, where a message reached me from Vanzetti that he wanted to see me once more before he died. I immediately started for Boston with my son, reached the prison in the late afternoon or early evening, and was at once taken by the Warden to Vanzetti. He was in one of the three cells in a narrow room opening immediately to the chair. In the cell nearest the chair was Madeiros, in the middle one Sacco, and in the third I found Vanzetti. There was a small table in his cell, and when I entered the room he seemed to be writing. The iron bars on the front of the cell were so arranged as to leave at one place a wider space, through which what he needed could be handed to him. Vanzetti seemed to be expecting me; and when I entered he rose from his table, and with his characteristic smile reached through the space between the bars and grasped me warmly by the hand. It was intimated to me that I might sit in a chair in front of the cell, but not nearer the bars than a straight mark painted on the floor. This I did.

I had heard that the Governor had said that if Vanzetti would release his counsel in the Bridgewater case from their obligation not to disclose what he had said to them the public would be satisfied that he was guilty of that crime, and also of the South Braintree crime. I therefore began the interview by asking one of the two prison guards who sat at the other end of the room, about fifteen feet from where we were, to come to the front of the cell and listen to the questions I was about to ask Vanzetti and to his replies. I then asked Vanzetti if he had at any time said anything to Mr. Vahey or Mr. Graham which would warrant the inference that he was guilty of either crime. With great emphasis and obvious sincerity he answered "no." He then said, what he had often said to me before, that Messrs. Vahey and Graham were not his personal choice, but became his lawyers at the urgent request of friends, who raised the money to pay them. He then told me certain things about their relations to him and about their conduct of the Bridgewater case, and what he had in fact told them. This on the next day I recorded, but will not here repeat.

I asked Vanzetti whether he would authorize me to waive on his behalf his privilege so far as Vahey and Graham were concerned. He readily assented to this, but imposed the condition that they should make whatever statement they saw fit to make in the presence of myself or some other friend, giving his reasons for this condition, which I also recorded.

The guard then returned to his seat.

I told Vanzetti that although my belief in his innocence had all the time been strengthened, both by my study of the evidence and by my increasing knowledge of his personality, yet there was a chance, however remote, that I might be mistaken; and that I thought he ought for my sake, in this closing hour of his life when nothing could save him, to give me his most solemn reassurance, both with respect to himself and with respect to Sacco. Vanzetti then told me quietly and calmly, and with a sincerity which I could not doubt, that I need have no anxiety about this matter; that both he and Sacco were absolutely innocent of the South Braintree crime, and that he (Vanzetti) was equally innocent of the Bridgewater crime; that while, looking back, he now realized more clearly than he ever had the grounds of the suspicion against him and Sacco, he felt that no allowance had been made for his ignorance of American points of view and habits of thought, or for his fear as a radical and almost as an outlaw, and that in reality he was convicted on evidence which would not have convicted him had he not been an anarchist, so that he was in a very real sense dying for his cause. He said it was a cause for which he was prepared to die. He said it was the cause of the upward progress of humanity, and the elimination of force from the world. He spoke with calmness, knowledge, and deep feeling. He said he was grateful to me for what I had done for him. He asked to be remembered to my wife and son. He spoke with emotion of his sister and of his family. He asked me to do what I could to clear his name, using the words "clear my name."

I asked him if he thought it would do any good for me or any friend to see Boda. He said he thought it would. He said he did not know Boda very well, but believed him to be an honest man, and thought possibly he might be able to give some evidence which would help to prove their innocence.

I then told Vanzetti that I hoped he would issue a public statement advising his friends against retaliating by violence and reprisal. I told him that, as I read history, the truth had little chance of prevailing when violence was followed by counter-violence. I said that as he well knew, I could not subscribe to his views or to his philosophy of life; but that, on the other hand, I could not but respect any man who consistently lived up to altruistic principles, and was willing to give his life for them. I said that if I were mistaken, and if his views were true, nothing could retard their acceptance by the world more than the hate and fear that would be stirred up by violent reprisal. Vanzetti replied that, as I must well know, he desired no personal revenge for the cruelties inflicted upon him; but he said that, as he read history, every great cause for the benefit of humanity had had to fight for its existence against entrenched power and wrong, and that for this reason he could not give his friends such sweeping advice as I had urged. He added that in such struggles he was strongly opposed to any injury to women and children. He asked me to remember the cruelty of seven years of imprisonment, with alternating hopes and fears. He reminded me of the remarks attributed to Judge Thayer by certain witnesses, especially by Professor Richardson, and asked me what state of mind I thought such remarks indicated. He asked me how any candid man could believe that a judge capable of referring to men accused before him as "anarchistic bastards" could be impartial, and whether I thought that such refinement of cruelty as had been practised upon him and upon Sacco ought to go unpunished.

I replied that he well knew my own opinion of these matters, but that his arguments seemed to me not to meet the point I had raised, which was whether he did not prefer the prevalence of his opinions to the infliction of punishment upon persons, however richly he might think they deserved it. This led to a pause in the conversation.

Without directly replying to my question, Vanzetti then began to speak of the origin, early struggles, and progress of other great movements for human betterment. He said that all great altruistic movements originated in the brain of some man of genius, but later became misunderstood and perverted, both by popular ignorance and by sinister self-interest. He said that all great movements which struck at conservative standards, received opinions, established institutions, and human selfishness were at first met with violence and persecution. He referred to Socrates, Galileo, Giordano Bruno, and others whose names I do not now remember, some Italian and some Russian. He then referred to Christianity, and said that it began in simplicity and sincerity, which were met with persecution and oppression, but that it later passed quietly into ecclesiasticism and tyranny. I said I did not think that the progress of Christianity had been altogether checked by convention and ecclesiasticism, but that on the contrary it still made an appeal to thousands of simple people, and that the essence of the appeal was the supreme confidence shown by Jesus in the truth of His own views by forgiving, even when on the Cross, His enemies, persecutors, and slanderers.

Now, for the first and only time in the conversation, Vanzetti showed a feeling of personal resentment against his enemies. He spoke with eloquence of his sufferings, and asked me whether I thought it possible that he could forgive those who had persecuted and tortured him through seven years of inexpressible misery. I told him he knew how deeply I sympathized with him, and that I had asked him to reflect upon the career of One infinitely superior to myself and to him, and upon a force infinitely greater than the force of hate and revenge. I said that in the long run the force to which the world would respond was the force of love and not of hate, and that I was suggesting to him to forgive his enemies, not for their sakes, but for his own peace of mind, and also because an example of such forgiveness would in the end be more powerful to win adherence to his cause or to a belief in his innocence than anything else that could be done.

There was another pause in the conversation. I arose and we stood gazing at each other for a minute or two in silence. Vanzetti finally said that he would think of what I had said.[1]

I then made a reference to the possibility of personal immortality, and said that, although I thought I understood the difficulties of a belief in immortality, yet I felt sure that if there was a personal immortality he might hope to share it. This remark he received in silence.

He then returned to his discussion of the evil of the present organization of society, saying that the essence of the wrong was the opportunity it afforded persons who were powerful because of ability or strategic economic position to oppress the simple-minded and idealistic among their fellow men, and that he feared that nothing but violent resistance could ever overcome the selfishness which was the basis of the present organization of society and made the few willing to perpetuate a system which enabled them to exploit the many.

[1] It is credibly reported that when, a few hours later, Vanzetti was about to step in the chair, he paused, shook hands with the Warden and Deputy Warden and the guards, thanked them for their kindness to him, and, turning to the spectators, asked them to remember that he forgave some of his enemies.

I have given only the substance of this conversation, but I think I have covered every point that was talked about and have presented a true picture of the general tenor of Vanzetti's remarks. Throughout the conversation, with the few exceptions I have mentioned, the thought that was uppermost in his mind was the truth of the ideas in which he believed for the betterment of humanity, and the chance they had of prevailing. I was impressed by the strength of Vanzetti's mind, and by the extent of his reading and knowledge. He did not talk like a fanatic. Although intensely convinced of the truth of his own views, he was still able to listen with calmness and with understanding to the expression of views with which he did not agree. In this closing scene the impression of him which had been gaining ground in my mind for three years was deepened and confirmed—that he was a man of powerful mind, and unselfish disposition, of seasoned character, and of devotion to high ideals. There was no sign of breaking down or of terror at approaching death. At parting he gave me a firm clasp of the hand and a steady glance, which revealed unmistakably the depth of his feeling and the firmness of his self-control.

I then turned to Sacco, who lay upon a cot bed in the adjoining cell and could easily have heard and undoubtedly did hear my conversation with Vanzetti. My conversation with Sacco was very brief. He rose from his cot, referred feelingly though in a general way to some points of disagreement between us in the past, said he hoped that our differences of opinion had not affected our personal relations, thanked me for what I had done for him, showed no sign of fear, shook hands with me firmly, and bade me good-bye. His manner also was one of absolute sincerity. It was magnanimous in him not to refer more specifically to our previous differences of opinion, because at the root of it all lay his conviction, often expressed to me, that all efforts on his behalf, either in court or with public authorities, would be useless, because no capitalistic society could afford to accord him justice. I had taken the contrary view; but at this last meeting he did not suggest that the result seemed to justify his view and not mine.[1]

---

[1] I afterward talked with the prison guard to whom I have referred in this paper. He told me that after he returned to his seat he heard all that was said by Vanzetti and myself. The room was quiet and no other persons were talking. I showed the guard my complete notes of the interview, including what Vanzetti had told me about Messrs. Vahey and Graham. He read the notes carefully and said that they corresponded entirely with his memory except that I had omitted a remark made by Vanzetti about women and children. I then remembered the remark and added it to my memorandum.

INDEX

INDEX